An Ordered Society

Mary Ann Glendon

An Ordered Society

Gender and Class
in Early Modern England

Susan Dwyer Amussen

COLUMBIA UNIVERSITY PRESS
NEW YORK

Columbia University Press Morningside Edition
Columbia University Press
New York   Oxford

Library of Congress Cataloging-in-Publication Data

Amussen, Susan Dwyer.
    An ordered society : gender and class in early modern England /
Susan Dwyer Amussen.
        p.   cm.
    Originally published: Oxford, UK ; New York, NY, USA : B.
Blackwell, 1988, in series: Family, sexuality, and social relations
in past times.
    Includes bibliographical references and index.
    ISBN 0-231-09979-7 (pbk.)
    1. Family—England—History.   2. Women—England—History.
3. Villages—England—History.   4. England—Rural conditions.
I. Title.
HQ615.A78   1993
306.85'0942—dc20   93-38125
                                                            CIP

∞

Casebound editions of Columbia University Press books are
Smyth-sewn and printed on permanent and durable acid-free paper.

Printed in the United States of America

c 10 9 8 7 6 5 4 3 2 1
p 10 9 8 7 6 5 4 3 2 1

Contents

To the memory of
Ada, Alice and Lorna
and to
Dolores, Diane and Gretchen
whose stories taught me to hear
the experience of women

Preface

This book is about social relationships and social hierarchies. It began as a thesis prospectus more than eight years ago, and while some of the central questions have remained the same – What is the relationship between class and gender? How was that relationship affected by the emergence of English rural capitalism in the seventeenth century? – the overall framework has changed radically. This change was due in no small part to the difficulty I had in answering the questions as I had originally intended; I was forced to look to the ideological world to explain some of the connections and patterns I was seeing. Over the years, too, I have been forced to see the historical relevance, at least for the early modern historian, of the feminist slogan that 'the personal is political'. In any assessment of social relationships in the past, there is no substitute for masses of detail, and for the many stories from which the historian reconstructs the past. Only after this reconstruction can we proceed to theoretical statements or generalizations. I am first of all grateful to the people of seventeenth-century Norfolk for being as willing as they were to go to court.

The debts accumulated in the process of working on a project like this are enormous, if their acknowledgment seems platitudinous. First and foremost, I am grateful to the staff of the Norfolk Record Office, who were unfailingly kind and helpful in my visits there. I am especially grateful to Miss Susan Maddock, who not only guided me through the King's Lynn Borough archives, but also helped with obtaining permission to microfilm parish registers. The Parochial Church Council of Stow Bardolph graciously allowed me to microfilm their first register, and the Wimbotsham Parochial Church Council, especially Mrs J. R. Forgan, hospitably fed me while I checked their register. Mrs Janet Hammond of

Sedgeford generously allowed me to use the papers of George Sawer which are in her possession.

My research in Norfolk benefited enormously from conversations with Tim Wales, whose familiarity with the Norfolk sources – and whose similar interests – provided stimulation and challenge as we worked through many of the same sources. The historians at the Centre for East Anglian Studies at the University of East Anglia, particularly Hassell Smith, Victor Morgan and Nesta Evans, were generous with both time and information for an American struggling to get to know the county. Mr J.C. Barringer, the Cambridge University Extra-mural tutor in Norfolk, directed me to villages with good estate records and maps; his guidance when I arrived in Norwich saved me several months of digging. He also took me on field trips and shared some of his maps of Cawston with me. Together with the Parsons and Homberger families who housed me on return visits to Norwich, these people made research in Norwich a delightful experience.

My dissertation was directed by David Underdown, and throughout the process it has benefited from his wisdom, criticism and encouragement. As teacher, colleague, friend and sometime intellectual opponent he has forced me to clarify my thinking, define my arguments and refine my writing (which still isn't as good as C.V. Wedgwood's). Burr Litchfield introduced me to the literature of family history and forced me to develop a conceptual framework to understand the issues I was discussing. He also helped with the statistical analysis of the wills in chapter 3, and kindly allowed me to use his data-input program. Over the past few years, encouraging criticism has come from Judith Bennett, David Cressy, Christopher Hill, Clive Holmes and Randolph Trumbach. Keith Wrightson read and commented helpfully on the entire manuscript.

This book is rooted in women's history as well as early modern English history. Joan Scott's own work, and her comments on my thesis, have provided intellectual guidance; so has the work of Natalie Davis. Nancy Grey Osterud has helped me conceptually numerous times. Miranda Chaytor has provided a special companionship with our shared interest in peasant women: she will undoubtedly be dissatisfied with the result, but without her questioning this book would have been far less focused.

Parts of the book were given as papers at the University of Sussex Renaissance Club, the Berkshire Conference of Women's History

(1984), The American Historical Association (1983) and the Cambridge Seminar on Early Modern History conference on the 'Public and the Private Interest', and I greatly benefited from the criticism and comments I received at those times.

My students at Connecticut College have forced me to clarify the connections I was positing between the good stories I told about village life and the political events recounted in their textbooks and later lectures: they have been patient and critical listeners to my attempts to construct a more inclusive narrative of early modern English history. The conclusion especially owes a great deal to their questions.

Like all authors, I have undoubtedly talked too much and listened too little; I have certainly not done everything my critics and friends suggested. But the questions they asked have make this a far better book, though I am, of course, responsible for its failings.

The research and writing of the thesis was done with the assistance of a Beneficial Foundation Travel Grant from Brown University, the Wellesley College Alice Freeman Palmer Fellowship and a Woodrow Wilson Foundation Dissertation Research Fellowship in Women's Studies. Further work was completed while on a Mellon Postdoctoral Teaching Fellowship at Cornell University; funds for research were also provided by the Connecticut College Faculty Travel, Study, and Research Fund and History Department Gift Fund.

Parts of several chapters have appeared in my essay 'Gender, Family and the Social Order, 1560–1725' in *Order and Disorder in Early Modern England*. I am grateful to the editors, Anthony Fletcher and John Stevenson, and to Cambridge University Press for permission to reprint this material.

Finally, I was blessed by having a father who encouraged my early love of stories and language, as well as a mother who thought getting lost in a book was normal and who encouraged me throughout the process of research and writing. My family and friends have put up with an occasionally impossible, obsessed and cantankerous person with remarkable patience.

Throughout the book, spelling has been modernized, and punctuation inserted when it clarified the meaning of obscure passages. The year has been taken to begin on 1 January.

Susan Dwyer Amussen

List of Abbreviations

ANW   Archdeaconry of Norwich
ANF   Archdeaconry of Norfolk
BL   British Library
CSPD   *Calendar of State Papers, Domestic*
DNB   *Dictionary of National Biography*
KL   King's Lynn Borough Archives, King's Lynn
NCC   Norwich Consistory Court
PCC   Prerogative Record of Canterbury
PRO   Public Record Office
TRHS   *Transactions of the Royal Historical Society*

Unless otherwise noted, all documents are in the Norfolk Record Office, Norwich

1

Introduction

It is nearly seventy years since Alice Clark wrote her classic study of the *Working Life of Women in the Seventeenth Century*.[1] The seventeenth century, she argued, constituted a turning point in the history of women because production moved from household to capitalist enterprises – in larger farms and workshops – which employed individuals, not families. Her central insight was that a society in which production took place in households embodied fundamentally different relationships both within and outside families from one where individual employees worked for individual employers. This still deserves attention, though other aspects of the argument are problematic. Medieval and early modern historians are now (rightly) sceptical of the rosy hues in which Clark painted pre-industrial society, but no one would dispute that vast changes came with industrialization. Clark's mistaken placement of the change from household to capitalist production in the seventeenth century – at least a century before it actually took place – makes it incumbent on students of early modern England to continue to study the family as the fundamental economic unit of society in that period.

The family was not only the fundamental economic unit of society; it also provided the basis for political and social order. It is well-known that in this period the family served as a metaphor for the state; in conventional political thought the king was a father to his people, the father king in his household. The idea is a

---

[1] Alice Clark, *Working Life of Women in the Seventeenth Century* (London, 1919; reprinted with an introduction by Miranda Chaytor and Jane Lewis, 1982); the introduction to the 1982 edition raises many of these points more fully.

commonplace, endlessly repeated but rarely questioned.[2] And yet the conceptual and interpretive implications of this idea are far reaching. The analogy implies that the family and the state were inextricably intertwined in the minds of English women and men of the sixteenth and seventeenth centuries, and that we cannot understand politics (as conventionally defined) without understanding the politics of the family. Or, to put it another way, the ordering of households provided a model for ordering villages, counties, church and state. At the very least, the analogy means that it is inappropriate to dismiss what happened in the family as 'private'; the dichotomy so familiar to us today between private and public is necessarily false when applied to the experience of early modern England.

Both economic realities and political and social thought, then, draw us to the family as a central institution in English society. But they do so not by separating the family from other subjects of study, but by weaving the family into other aspects of early modern English history. If the family is the central institution – as both economy and ideology suggest – we must shift our focus; both women and men must be placed in the households which shaped their experience, and the different levels of social organization – from family, to village, county, church and state – must be analysed to understand the models they offered each other. Such an analysis needs to be undertaken on a number of levels – economic and ideological, inside the family and inside the village, county or nation. Such an approach makes possible a broad re-interpretation of the experience of early modern England.

This book offers a beginning of that re-interpretation through a study of English villagers between 1560 and 1725. It will examine the internal dynamics of families and villages in order to unravel the popular uses of the analogy between family and state. It will analyse the structure and exercise of authority and the maintenance of order, as well as threats to authority and disruptions of order. Such an examination of the distribution and use of power is

---

[2] G.J. Schochet, *Patriarchalism in Political Thought: the authoritarian family and political speculation and attitudes especially in seventeenth century England* (New York, 1975) provides the standard account of these ideas; see also the discussions in C. Hill, *Society and Puritanism in Pre-Revolutionary England* (New York, 1964), chapter 13, and Michael Walzer, *The Revolution of the Saints* (Cambridge, Massachusetts, reprinted New York, 1976), pp. 183–98.

political in the broadest sense. It assumes that though members of families and inhabitants of villages shared common goals and assumptions, they might have different interpretations of those goals, contending ambitions and conflicting interests. The simultaneous investigation of relations within families and villages opens up the question of how English women and men lived with the concept – as commonplace to them as it is to us – of a parallel between different social institutions. Because the village was the most local level of political organization, it was in villages that the political nature of familial authority and the familial nature of political authority was most evident and immediate.

Examination of the internal relations of family and village requires an analysis of two separate systems of social hierarchy: those of rank or class, and gender. Both systems provided power to superiors at the same time as they demanded obedience of inferiors. Ideally at least these were reciprocal relationships, in which obedience was given in return for care and protection. The hierarchies of class and gender were similar in many ways, and were assumed to be in harmony with each other; in fact, they often came into conflict. The class hierarchy is the more familiar: property and its extent determined the relationships among its possessors and was also thought to reflect their moral worth. English society was finely graded, and villagers lived with a far more intricately ranked society than most historians have acknowledged. The gender hierarchy was superficially much simpler than that of class: as wives were subject to their husbands, so women were subject to men, whose authority was sustained informally through culture, custom and differences in education, and more formally through the law. Yet the relationship between husband and wife was not an appropriate model for *all* relations between women and men. As parents, mistresses and even as wealthy neighbours women might have authority over men – a contradiction which made gender a problem in the class system, just as class became a problem in the gender system.[3]

[3] Natalie Z. Davis, 'Women's history in transition: the European case', *Feminist Studies*, 3 (1976), pp. 83–103; Joan Kelly-Gadol, 'The social relations of the sexes: methodological implications of women's history', *Signs*, 1 (1976), pp. 809–24; Joan W. Scott, 'Gender: a useful category of historical analysis', *American Historical Review*, 91 (1986), pp. 1053–75; the class hierarchy of English society is described in Keith Wrightson, *English Society, 1580–1680* (London, 1982) chapters 1–2.

This analysis of gender and class assumes that both systems are socially constructed and historically conditioned. While we are familiar with changes in class relations, we are less so with changes in those of gender. Class, as the term will be used in this study, refers to the socio-economic hierarchy and the social relations imposed by it. Gender is the process by which meaning is given to the perceived biological differences between women and men, a process which turns biological facts into social relationships. The character of these perceptions, and the consequent relationships, have changed over time. Neither gender nor class are autonomous systems, but are shaped by each other and by other aspects of social identity – political, cultural and economic.[4]

Any investigation of gender and class must be grounded in the economic as well as the ideological world of English villagers; this one will be based on the experience of villagers in Norfolk. Norfolk was 'a large shire and great', with a long coastline dotted with harbours, numerous rivers to bring the products of the land to the coast, towns and cities with long traditions of continental trade, good corn and pasture lands and a successful woollen industry.[5] It was a densely populated county which saw the early development of both capitalist agriculture and manufacturing. General prosperity coexisted with poverty that was even more widespread then elsewhere in England. The county had a cloth industry specializing in the 'new draperies', but it also had a stocking-knitting industry, as well as a variety of agricultural economies. At the end of the seventeenth century 'Norfolk husbandry' – the complex system of new crop rotations involving (among other things) the cultivation of clover and turnips – became a by-word for agricultural innovation; its practice required heavy capital investment and encouraged the expansion of farms in the arable region of the county. The county town, Norwich, was the second or third largest city in the country throughout this period, and served as an economic, social and administrative centre. Because of its position outside the main axes of travel in seventeenth-century England, people were in Norfolk only if they wished to be there; vagrants and beggars in Norfolk were less

---

[4] Scott, 'Gender'; Kelly-Gadol, 'Social relations of the sexes'; Gayle Rubin, 'The traffic in women: notes toward a political economy of sex', in *Toward an Anthropology of Women*, ed. Rayna R. Reiter (New York and London, 1975), pp. 157–210.

[5] Christobel M. Hood, ed., *The Chorography of Norfolk* (Norwich, 1938), p. 67.

common – and from a more local area – than in the rest of the country. Finally, both because of its geographical and political position, Norfolk was relatively untouched by armies during the Civil War, so that its social experience was more continuous than that of other counties.[6]

Since the mid-1960s, historians have become ever more aware of the diversity of English society, and so have turned increasingly to the local or regional study. This form narrows the focus and allows greater precision in analysis.[7] To a certain extent I have followed the model provided by these local studies, and they provide a necessary background for my research. The nature of social relations and social meanings cannot, however, be examined wholly from the perspective of one village, group of villages, or even county: for some purposes I have therefore drawn evidence from Norfolk and when appropriate, Suffolk, but some issues require a more national focus. The sources available to us, especially court records, allow us to go further than earlier historians have done in examining how people interpreted their lives. This cannot be done as systematically as we might wish, or as

[6] Susan Dwyer Amussen, 'Governors and governed: class and gender relations in English villages, 1590–1750', Brown University Ph.D. Thesis, 1982, pp. 28–39 passim; for the Norfolk economy see Walter Rye, ed., *State Papers Relating to Musters, Beacons, Shipmoney, etc. in Norfolk* (Norwich, 1907), pp. 180–1; Hood, ed., *The Chorography of Norfolk*; A. Hassell Smith and D.A. MacCullough, 'The authorship of the chorographies of Norfolk and Suffolk', *Norfolk Archeology*, 36 (1977), pp. 327–41; K.J. Allison, 'The Norfolk worsted industry in the sixteenth and seventeenth centuries', *Yorkshire Bulletin of Economic and Social Research*, 12 (1960), pp. 73–83; Paul Slack, 'Vagrants and vagrancy in England, 1598–1664', *Economic History Review*, second series, 27 (1974), pp. 360–79; K.J. Allison, 'The sheep–corn husbandry of Norfolk in the sixteenth and seventeenth centuries', *Agricultural History Review*, 5 (1957), pp. 12–30; Joan Thirsk, 'The farming regions of England and Wales' in *The Agrarian History of England and Wales*, ed. H.P.R. Finberg (Cambridge, 1967), vol. IV: *1500–1640*, ed. Joan Thirsk, pp. 1–112; Naomi Riches, *The Agricultural Revolution in Norfolk* (Chapel Hill, North Carolina, 1935); for the civil war in Norfolk, R.W. Ketton-Cremer, *Norfolk in the Civil War* (Hamden, Connecticut, 1970); Clive Holmes, *The Eastern Association in the Civil War* (Cambridge, 1974); for an example of the effects of the war in other areas, see David Underdown, *Revel, Riot, and Rebellion: popular politics and culture in England, 1603–1660* (Oxford, 1985), esp. chapters 6–9.

[7] W.G. Hoskins, *The Midland Peasant* (London, 1957); Margaret Spufford, *Constrasting Communities: English villagers in the sixteenth and seventeenth centuries* (Cambridge, 1974); David Hey, *An English Rural Community: Myddle under the Tudors and Stuarts* (Leicester, 1974); J.R. Ravensdale, *Liable to Floods: village landscape on the edge of the fens, AD 450–1850* (London, 1974); Thirsk, 'Farming regions' provides a useful introduction to the agricultural regions that are discussed in these studies; Keith Wrightson and David Levine, *Poverty and Piety in an English Village: Terling, 1525–1700* (New York and London, 1979) begins to move toward some of the questions I am asking.

thoroughly as the records of a police state would allow, but it is possible.

The examination of social meanings requires us to ask questions that the evidence is rarely designed to answer. It also rarely provides clear-cut patterns or changes. It is not easy to investigate changes in the family relationships of the elite; it is even more difficult at the popular level, where those on whom we have detailed evidence – local troublemakers, criminals and even diary keepers – are almost certainly atypical.[8] These problems can be partially avoided by examining not the specific content of relationships, but the underlying assumptions about how they ought to work and how people ought to act. Once these assumptions have been unravelled, the factors which aided or hindered the translation of assumptions – the ideal – into action begin to emerge. The focus of this book will therefore be less on what people in families and villages thought of each other, but on what they expected of each other, and why those expectations might be disappointed. The exigencies of the sources make it virtually impossible to find out how things worked when they went right.

The examination of the hierarchies of class and gender through the internal dynamics of families and villages must take place on several levels. First, it must be securely rooted in the material world of early modern villagers, in a study of the economy, population and the distribution of wealth and power. Villages in the different agricultural regions of Norfolk have therefore been studied to provide access to both the material context and some of the measurable aspects of family and village relations. Without such a grounding, social relations are incomprehensible. But the material world does not shape social relationships in a vacuum, for material experience is always interpreted through the concepts and ideas of a particular society. A second level of analysis must therefore engage with the ideological construction of hierarchy –

---

[8] For the difficulties of working with elite families, see Lawrence Stone, *The Family, Sex, and Marriage in England, 1500–1800* (New York, 1977); for the perils of work on non-elite families, see G.R. Quaife, *Wanton Wenches and Wayward Wives* (New Brunswick, New Jersey, 1979); Amussen, 'Governors and governed', pp. 9–18; one approach to the problem of change is to suggest there is none: Wrightson, *English Society*, chapter 4; Alan Macfarlane, *Marriage and Love in England: modes of reproduction, 1300–1840* (Oxford and New York, 1986).

using sermons and advice manuals, works of social description and political theory. These provide the commonplaces of English thought, conveyed through catechisms and homilies to the humblest villagers. It cannot be assumed, of course, that people acted just as the theoretical writers would have wished, but the didactic literature provides at least a framework for their behaviour. The gaps between ideal and practice direct us to some of the problems and concerns of early modern society. When the material and ideological contexts have been set out, we can turn to the relationships themselves. Some family relationships will be examined through the analysis of inheritance and marriage patterns. Other more qualitative aspects of both family and village relations will then be explored through court records.

Social relationships are neither perduring nor ahistorical. Any society has shared assumptions about relationships, derived from a social and economic system that both justifies and is justified by those relationships. Everyone in early modern England believed that all relationships were hierarchical; the superior in one relationship was the inferior in another. By examining both the economic and ideological background of social relations, we can better understand the process of change in those relationships – both the nature of the change and the reasons for it. At the same time, we can appreciate more clearly that the social experience of early modern villagers was grounded in a series of hierarchical relationships.

There were some experiences that no village in early modern England could completely escape. The most important was rapid demographic growth. Between 1500 and 1655 the population of England and Wales more than doubled, from about 2.5 million to nearly 5.3 million people. After 1658 the population declined until about 1690, and then grew slowly until the 1740s. Although towns and cities (especially London) absorbed a disproportionate share of the increasing population, most villages grew rapidly as well. The less regulated and originally more sparsely settled pastoral parishes of the forests and fens were particularly likely to be affected by rapid growth. In these parishes the growing population could more easily be supported by marginal economies of crafts, fishing and poaching. Even the archetypal stable arable village felt the effects, however, whether in the form of vagrants wandering through, or in the increased demand (and consequently higher prices) for the corn it grew, a demand which often stimulated changes in land use, agricultural methods and even land distribution.[9]

The other factor which affected all villages in England in the sixteenth century was inflation. Between 1500 and 1620 the real income of English wage labourers was cut at least in half, as prices multiplied sixfold and wages merely tripled. It does not require an examination of hundreds of account books for us to realize that such a situation benefited those who held land securely at low rents or fixed entry fines (especially if they produced a surplus for the market), and that landowners whose lands were let in that way, as well as wage labourers, would suffer. What is not so clear is the way in which these two factors – the growth of population and inflation – worked together, and how each region, and indeed each village, responded to its experiences in what would be, no matter what, a difficult time.[10]

The growing population of England had to be fed, housed, clothed and employed, which undoubtedly contributed to both the rise in the cost of food and the decline in real wages. But the impact of these changes depended on regional economies and, particularly, the resources available – common land, woodland, minerals, fishing or industrial employment. Villages with large areas of common land, particularly in the fens and forests, grew rapidly because new inhabitants could piece together a living; in arable farming areas, the increased demand for corn encouraged agricultural innovation and more intensive exploitation of the land. In all areas, the increase in population was disproportionately distributed, increasing both the relative and real numbers of the poor.

These trends are national ones, but because this study will move between the national and the local, it is useful to make these

---

[9] E.A. Wrigley and R.S. Schofield, *The Population History of England, 1541–1871* (Cambridge, Massachusetts, 1981) p. 528; E.A. Wrigley, 'A simple model of London's importance in changing English society and economy, 1650–1750', *Past and Present*, 37 (1967), pp. 44–70; V.H.T. Skipp, *Crisis and Development: an ecological case study of the Forest of Arden, 1570–1674* (Cambridge, 1978).

[10] Peter Bowden, 'Agricultural prices, farm profits, and rent', in *Agrarian History IV*, ed. Thirsk, pp. 598–601 and 608–9 for the relative position of labourers and p. 865 (in Bowden's 'Statistical appendix') for the index of the standard of living; this partially revises E.H. Phelps Brown and Sheila V. Hoskins, 'Seven centuries of the prices of consumables, compared with builders' wage rates', *Economica*, 22 (1955), pp. 195–206 and 23 (1956), pp. 296–314. Both sets of figures may exaggerate the decline somewhat, as they exclude payment in kind.

generalizations concrete through local examples. Five Norfolk parishes will be used throughout as particular case studies. Norfolk contained three major agricultural regions (see map 1): the sheep–corn area which stretched in a wide arc from the south-west corner of the county along the north coast almost to Great Yarmouth; the wood–pasture area, inside that arc along the Suffolk border; and the fens in the west and the broads in the east of the county, with a mixed arable and pastoral economy. Our villages represent these three regions.[11]

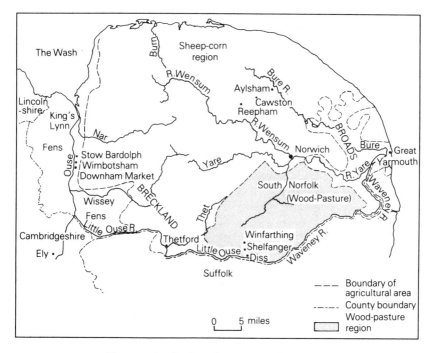

Map 1 Agricultural regions of Norfolk

The village of Cawston (see map 2) lies in the sheep–corn region some twelve miles to the north of Norwich. Although it had a weekly market and annual fair, these were insignificant when compared to those in the adjoining towns of Reepham and

---

[11] For a fuller discussion of developments in these villages, see Amussen, 'Governors and governed', chapters II–IV.

Aylsham. Cawston was primarily an agricultural village, but like many in north-east Norfolk, it had a weaving industry, and in the seventeenth century, stocking knitting.[12] The large heath provided pasture for sheep and cattle, as well as fuel for the poor.

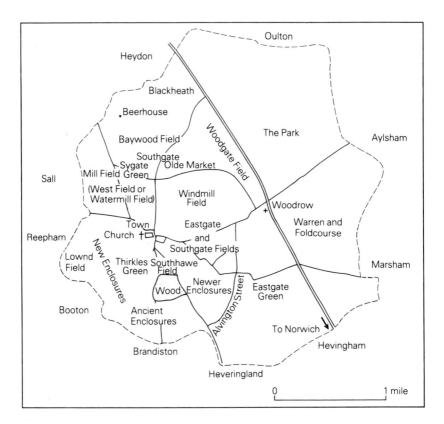

Map 2   Cawston, based on early seventeenth-century maps

The most important characteristic of Cawston's agriculture – as in much of north Norfolk – was the fold-course, which shaped the use of the fields after the harvest. At that time the lord's flock of sheep, which had pastured on the common throughout the summer along with sheep belonging to tenants, was 'folded'

[12] Thirsk, 'Farming regions', pp. 42–6; Allison, 'The sheep–corn husbandry of Norfolk'; Walter Rye, *An Account of the Church and Parish of Cawston in the County of Norfolk* (Norwich, 1898); Allison, 'Norfolk worsted industry', p. 73.

through the town fields sequentially. The sheep ate the stubble in the fields and simultaneously fertilized the land. This arrangement set up a symbiotic relationship between the lord of the manor and village landholders, as the lord profited from the flock, and the tenants from both the right to pasture some sheep, and from the application of fertilizer to their lands. The grain and the wool produced by this system contributed to the prosperity of those who could take advantage of it. But the fold-course system represented a delicate balance between landlords and tenants which could easily be disturbed. That balance was disturbed in the early seventeenth century by more intensive exploitation of both land and of the fold-course. The profits available from the production of corn for the market steadily undermined communal agriculture in Cawston.[13]

Winfarthing and Shelfanger are neighbouring villages in the wood–pasture region of Norfolk, next to the market town of Diss and some seventeen miles south of Norwich (see map 3). They were closely connected by ties of marriage and landholding.[14] The wood–pasture area of Norfolk and Suffolk was characterized by an emphasis on cheese production for the market, though the region was also usually self-sufficient in grain. Much of the region had long been enclosed, though as late as 1720 the Shelfanger town meadow was still farmed in strips. As in much of the Waveney valley, hemp was grown and linen woven in the villages.[15]

There was little common land in either village; instead, cattle were kept in closes of pasture, so there were few resources for

[13] This description of the fold-course is based on the information in PRO E. 134 43/44 Elizabeth Mich. 7.

[14] Amussen, 'Governors and governed', pp. 83–5: twenty-two inhabitants of both villages specified land in more than one village in their wills, and of those fourteen held land in both villages; wills also demonstrate kinship links, e.g. ANF Wills 1637 OW 108, George Pulham; NCC 1627 OW 385, Faith Roper, wid., and ANF Wills 1641 98, Richard Roper.

[15] Arundel Castle Archives P5/36 (1720); DEP/52 (1689) Francis Leach con Obadiah Browne, Cler., testimony of William Banes of Gissing; the assessment of agricultural production is based on inventories from Winfarthing and Shelfanger filed in the Consistory Court of Norwich; Nesta Evans, 'The community of the South Elmhams (Suffolk) in the sixteenth and seventeenth centuries', University of East Anglia M.Phil. thesis, 1978; Thirsk, 'Farming regions', pp. 46–9; Eric Kerridge, The Agricultural Revolution (London, 1967), pp. 83–7; Hood, ed., The Chorography of Norfolk, pp. 67–8; Nesta Evans, The East Anglian Linen Industry: rural industry and the local economy, Pasold Studies in Textile History, 5 (Aldershot, Hants, 1985), esp. map 3; Evans demonstrates the regional character of the industry.

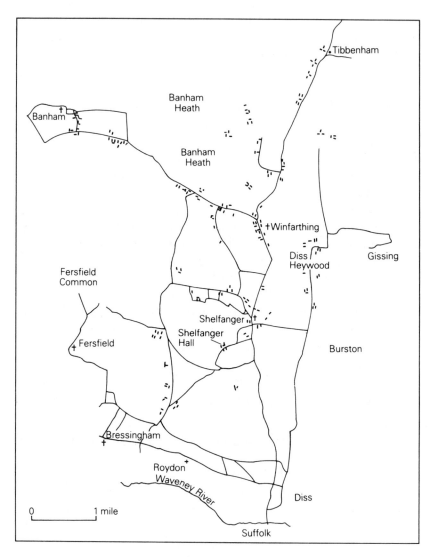

Map 3 Winfarthing and Shelfanger

those without land. Even linen weaving appears to have been an adjunct to prosperous farming, not an activity for the poor.[16] The yeomen of Winfarthing and Shelfanger – even with estates of only fifty acres – were increasingly prosperous in the seventeenth century. This reflects, however, diversification as a form of agricultural innovation, not specialization. Yeomen and farmers were increasingly involved in the debt economy and practised convertible husbandry: the land in the villages was suited for both arable and pastoral farming. Not only wheat, oats and barley, but also turnips appear with some prominence in post-Restoration inventories.[17]

Norfolk lies on the broad flat plain that stretches east from the Midlands into the North Sea; the rivers which drained this area, though critical to trade, were often prone to flooding. Large areas of west Norfolk, and the adjoining areas of the Isle of Ely, Lincolnshire and Huntingdonshire, were dominated by the fens, marshy areas which flooded in winter but were used for summer cattle pasture. They also contained peat for use as fuel. The villages of Stow Bardolph and Wimbotsham are on the eastern edge of the fens (see map 4); they are on the east side of the River Ouse some ten miles south of King's Lynn, but on the west side of the river a large area of fenland served as common land for the villages and the adjoining town of Downham Market. As in Cawston, the fen was the subject of competition, and changes in access to it were crucial to the agricultural development of the villages. In such competition, the fortunes of the villagers of Stow Bardolph and Wimbotsham were dominated by the activities of the Hare family, important west Norfolk gentry who made their home at Stow Hall in Stow Bardolph, and who were lords of the manors of Stow, Wimbotsham and Downham Market.

---

[16] Seventeen inventories from the villages show evidence of involvement in linen, although only one inventory is of a 'linen-weaver'; most of the inventories record small amounts of hemp or flax, or seed; some have spinning wheels. In all cases, however, this is in addition to other activities, and none of the inventories list looms. Ten of the inventories are valued at over £100, and even Thomas Alden, Sr, linen-weaver, possessed yarn and linens worth less than his cattle (valued at £27) and only a small fraction of his wealth, which amounted to £220: NCC INV 50B/105; cf. Evans, *Linen Industry*, pp. 69–73.

[17] This analysis is based on inventories from the villages in the Consistory Court of Norwich; for a fuller discussion, see Amussen, 'Governors and governed', pp. 88–90; the inventories are not an ideal source (they are heavily biased toward the more prosperous farmers, and the crops listed depend very much on the time of year they were made; furthermore, there are only eighteen from before 1642, and eighteen between 1660–1725.) NCC INV 74A/123 (Thomas Browne of Shelfanger).

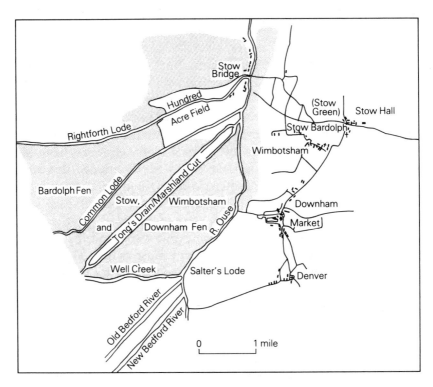

Map 4   Stow Bardolph and Wimbotsham

The economy of the fen-edge village was a dual one. The drier land on the east side of the Ouse supported a conventional sheep–corn economy like that of Cawston. On the west side of the Ouse the fen – which contained more than 3700 acres – supported cattle, brick-makers, reed-cutters and fishermen. The fen made settlement in the area attractive: one could survive with little, or even no, land. The use of the fen was theoretically attached to particular pieces of property, 'ancient commonable messuages', but the Court of Salter's Lode, which administered the fen, made little attempt to limit its use. Between 1611 and 1635, the court repeated its regulations about pasturing, but the fine of 2s. was low enough to serve more as a fee for use than a deterrent. The regulation of peat-cutting was stricter, but the court still allowed the cutting of more peat in the early seventeenth century than was good for the fen.[18] It was not until the 1660s that drainage and enclosure transformed the fen economy.

The population history of all three areas of the country mirrored the national pattern of growth in the early seventeenth century, although the evidence for Norfolk's population is scantier than one might wish.[19] The population of Cawston was between 530 and 630 in the early seventeenth century; by the 1670s it had grown 25 to 50 per cent, to between 830 and 930 – though probably closer to the lower figure. Later evidence is more ambiguous, but suggests a decline of about 25 per cent to about 650 in 1709.[20] In 1603, the population of Shelfanger was 142, that of Winfarthing 189; by the 1670s, the population of Shelfanger had grown to at least 153, and that of Winfarthing to 271; and in 1736, the Norfolk historian Francis Blomefield (who lived in the neighbouring village of Fersfield) gave figures of 200 for Shelfanger and 260 for Winfarthing. If the villages are considered together, their population grew by about 30 per cent from 1603 to 1676, and then remained stable for

[18] The Court Books for Salter's Lode are found in Hare 29–31; unfortunately, they only exist for the period 1611–35; for fen regulation see especially Hare 29, 24 October 12 James I and Hare 31, n.d. f. 1, and 8 July 1635.

[19] Amussen, 'Governors and governed', pp. 45–7, 75, 85–7, 116–18; this analysis is made more difficult by the absence of Protestation returns for the county. Wrigley and Schofield, *Population History*, pp. 528–9, 531–4. The decline in the villages may be explained by urban growth at a time when the overall population was stagnant: Wrigley, 'London's importance'.

[20] B.L. Harleian Ms. 595, f. 122v; two copies of 'The number of inhabitants as well persons of ability as others' survive, one in NRS 2604 and the other in the possession of Mrs Janet Hammond (the latter list has one extra name on it); see Tim Wales, 'Poverty, poor relief, and the life-cycle; some evidence from seventeenth century Norfolk', in *Land, Kinship, and Life-cycle*, ed. Richard Smith (London, 1984), pp. 351–404, esp. pp. 369–75, 389–94; another undated list in NRS Accn. 1.8.63 P186D gives a total of 138 households: forty-five contribute, thirty do not contribute, forty-nine are poor labourers and widows (with 138 people) and fourteen (with thirty-nine people) were relieved weekly. This would suggest just over 500 inhabitants. For population estimates, see Peter Laslett, 'Mean household size in England since the sixteenth century', in Peter Laslett, ed., with Richard Wall, *Household and Family in Past Time* (Cambridge, 1972), p. 133. Compton Census xerox in NRS Ms. 21489 P137C. The hearth tax returns for Norfolk are badly damaged, but J.H.C. Patten has extrapolated a figure of 173 households from the list: John H.C. Patten, 'The urban structure of East Anglia in the sixteenth and seventeenth centuries', Cambridge University Ph.D. 1972, Appendix A, South Erpingham Hundred; the exemption certificates list more than 120 exempt households: PRO E. 179/336, 337, 338. The original of the 1709 list is in MSC/10, a typescript in PD 193/110; the 1693 survey is NRS 25690.

the rest of the period.[21] The evidence of population growth in early seventeenth-century Stow Bardolph and Wimbotsham comes from the number of inmates and newly built cottages recorded in the court books. By the 1670s, Stow Bardolph had a population between 290 and 360, while Wimbotsham had one of between 160 and 195. The inmates' numbers must have been made up by migrants, however, because baptisms exceeded burials for only three decades between 1580 and 1680. The population of Stow Bardolph and Wimbotsham declined slightly in the later seventeenth century, more rapidly after 1720.[22]

The different regional economies, combined with population growth and inflation, distributed people differently through the social hierarchy, although all villages were marked by an increasing number of poor people, and a greater polarization of rich and poor. The process of polarization, however, and its extent, varied among the villages. In Cawston, a small group of wealthy farmers were clearly distinguished from their neighbours; in Winfarthing and Shelfanger a larger group of yeomen dominated the villages, and there was somewhat less poverty than in Cawston; and in Stow Bardolph and Wimbotsham the wealth of the Hares dwarfed everyone else's, and by their allocation of land they could somewhat limit the number of poor. The polarization of wealth in Cawston took place largely between 1574 and 1617; in Winfarthing and Shelfanger between 1610 and 1635; and in Stow Bardolph and Wimbotsham not until the 1660s.[23]

The social distribution of population can be seen best in Cawston. On a number of occasions between 1596 and 1601, George Sawer of Cawston, who frequently served as churchwarden and overseer of the poor, made up lists of the

[21] Amussen, 'Governors and governed', pp. 85–6: I take the figures on communicants given by Francis Blomefield and Charles Parkyn, *An Essay Towards a Topographical History of the County of Norfolk* (11 vols, London, 1805–10), I, pp. 116, 190 as those of total population because otherwise there would have been a drop by the time of the Compton Census (NRO Ms. 21489); the hearth tax figures (PRO E. 179 154/697) give a 1674 figure of 180 in Shelfanger, 308 in Winfarthing. These figures are all sufficiently problematic to serve only as a guide to the local population.

[22] Above, n. 18; PD 305/1 and L.R. Turner deposit 1.8.79 Q187D, Wimbotsham Register transcript; NRS 21489 (Compton Census xerox in NRO); Patten, 'Urban structure', Appendix A; Hare 3527b(16) 1709; Thirsk, 'Farming regions', pp. 38–40, 109–10 for migration to fens and forests; J.D. Chambers, *Population, Economy and Society* (London, 1972), p. 98; Amussen, 'Governors and governed', pp. 116–18.

[23] Amussen, 'Governors and governed', pp. 52–4, 93–9, 132–40.

population to aid him in his work. In 1601, for example, he divided Cawston into four groups: sixty-eight households paid local rates, twenty households (with fifty-six members) did not contribute to local rates but had either a house or a cow, fifty-seven households (with 179 members) had neither a house nor a cow and twenty-two households, with seventy-two members, received parochial relief. The central division was based on the payment of rates, but Sawer made important distinctions among those who did not contribute to those rates. There were also differences among those who did contribute, as Sawer noted that only fourteen landholders had more than forty acres of land. This group remained constant: a 1693 survey still reported only fourteen landholders with more than forty acres. However, while less than one-third of the tenants of the manor had less than five acres in 1617, more than half did in 1693. In the 1672 hearth tax, more than two-thirds of the population of Cawston were excused from payment on the grounds of poverty. The fourteen landholders with more than forty acres found an increasingly large group of poor in need of their assistance, with a shrinking middle group to assist them in their support of the poor.[24]

The wood–pasture area of the county was less divided than the sheep–corn area. Throughout the region it took relatively less land to achieve prosperity, so there was a large proportion of yeomen. In 1589, twelve copyhold tenants of Shelfanger held less than ten acres; by 1660 the number had risen to twenty-eight, and by 1719, dropped again to twenty-two. Throughout the period, four landholders held more than fifty acres of copyhold land from the manor, but in 1660 and 1719, no one held between thirty and fifty acres. Polarization, though clearly present, was somewhat less marked than in Cawston: in the hearth tax, approximately 40 per cent of the households paid, and half of those paid on more than four hearths. At the same time, no one paid on more than eight hearths, so the top group in the villages was both diffuse and

---

[24] NRS 2604; for an analysis based on another of Sawer's lists, see Wales, 'Poverty, poor relief and the life-cycle', pp. 369–75, 389–94; NRS 25690: unfortunately it is not altogether clear what is included in this survey – it lists fewer houses than households, so it may not include the entire town. Patten, 'Urban structure', Appendix A and PRO E. 179 154/697 (County roll) and E. 179/337, 338 (exemption certificates); T.C. Wales, 'Poverty and parish relief', unpublished paper; cf. Wrightson and Levine, *Poverty and Piety*, pp. 35–6 and Spufford, *Constrasting Communities*, pp. 36–45.

relatively level.[25]

There was no question that the Hare family dominated Stow Bardolph and Wimbotsham; outside of the commons and fens, they controlled more than two-thirds of the land in the two villages. An inventory of Stow Hall in the time of Sir John Hare (1623–37) – including furniture, plate, cattle and horses – was valued at over £4000, more than ten times the highest inventory value in the village before the eighteenth century; the landed income of the estate in 1663 was £4433. In 1625, Stow Bardolph was the more prosperous village: more of its residents held more than fifty acres, and fewer held less than four acres than in Wimbotsham. Smallholders could flourish because the fen provided livings for those without much land. Although none of the later evidence for the villages is directly comparable, it suggests that the proportion of poor in Wimbotsham stayed about the same, while the proportion of poor in Stow Bardolph grew. The group that disappeared in Stow, however, was not the richest group, but that in the middle.[26]

In both Cawston and Stow Bardolph and Wimbotsham, social structure was simultaneously shaped by, and shaped access to, the crucial resources provided by common land; and in both, that access changed during the seventeenth century. In Cawston the

[25] I am grateful to Mrs Nesta Evans for information about the distribution of yeoman wills from the Consistory Court of Norwich; the use of copyholds is problematic, because they were frequently held in conjunction with freeholds and leaseholds – especially by wealthier tenants; Amussen, 'Governors and governed', pp. 91–5; the Shelfanger Court Books on which this analysis is based are Warnes 19.12.68 R192D–E, and the survey PRO KR 46, ff. 46 ff, transcribed by Rev. W.R. Harrison in PD 80/90. Between 1600 and 1635 six of thirty-five mortgages were forfeited, between 1636 and 1672 eight of fifty-six, and between 1676 and 1719 only three of sixty-three; similarly, the decade 1610–19 saw twenty sales, and the following decade twenty-seven, though in no other decade in the period were more than fifteen land sales recorded; cf. Spufford, *Contrasting Communities*, pp. 83, 100, and 41 for the difficulties of the hearth tax; PRO E. 179/336 and E. 179 154/697; Patten, 'Urban structure', Appendix A; Amussen, 'Governors and governed', pp. 97–9. The figures for both Cawston and Winfarthing and Shelfanger are higher than those for the hundreds of South Erpingham (Cawston) – 57.3 per cent exempt – and Diss (Winfarthing and Shelfanger) – 47 per cent exempt – which had exceptionally high levels of poverty: Wales, 'Poverty and parish relief'. Four hearths reflects a fairly substantial house; unfortunately, the Norfolk Hearth Tax roll is badly damaged, and the number of hearths in the Cawston return is largely illegible, while the section covering Stow Bardolph and Wimbotsham is in worse condition than that covering Cawston.

[26] Hare 3351 232X, surveys of Stow and Wimbotsham; Hare 3527b (10); Hare 5460 222x5; Hare 5536 223x6 (Hare inventory, n.d.); NCC INV 49/22, Henry Harwicke, yeo., 1650 was valued at £341 19s. 2d. Amussen, 'Governors and governed', pp. 136–7.

issues are spelled out in a pair of lawsuits in 1601; in Stow Bardolph and Wimbotsham they are articulated during the draining of the fen and its enclosure in the 1660s and in consequent social developments.

The reciprocal lawsuits in Cawston were brought between Thomas Hyrne, Gent., who farmed the warren and foldcourse of Cawston, and George Sawer, current overseer of the poor, Edward Hammond, the rector of Cawston and a large landholder in his own right and William Batch and Robert Eston, churchwardens in the previous year, as well as other unnamed inhabitants of Cawston. Hyrne complained that villages were illegally grazing sheep on the heath, that they had wrongly enclosed lands in the fields, that Hammond had encouraged tenants to kill rabbits on the warren and that other tenants had trespassed on the heath. The villagers rejected the accusation of trespass by claiming pasture rights on all the commons; they also complained of Hyrne's enclosures on the adjoining (and shared) common of Heverland, and asserted that Hyrne had violated tradition by increasing both the number of sheep in the fold-course and rabbits in the warren, leaving fewer resources for the tenants.[27]

In the lawsuit, the villagers alleged that although Cawston had 'been a town of trade . . . at this present [it] is grown into great poverty'.[28] They sought to blame the poverty on Hyrne's activities, but both Thomas Hyrne and the large tenants of the manor were trying to extend their rights at the expense of others. Both sides were enclosing lands at the same time that they sought to prevent others from doing so. The resources fought over were varied: land for growing corn, pasturing sheep and cattle and raising rabbits both for fur and for meat. Because the tenants of Cawston could, for the annual payment of a penny, collect unlimited amounts of fuel from the heath, fuel resources were also at stake. Many of the poor in Cawston supported themselves by gathering fuel, and village notables feared that the more intensive exploitation of the heath by Hyrne would undermine such activities. The lawsuit defended access to the heath for the

---

[27] The main information on the lawsuit is PRO E. 134 43/44 Elizabeth I Mich. 7; additional information is contained in notes made by George Sawer in the Norfolk Record Office, esp. NRS 24831 135x1.

[28] PRO E. 134 43/44 Elizabeth I Mich. 7.

poor, but in so doing it also defended the enclosures of the larger landholders, and served to protect them from additional burdens of poor relief.[29]

Although Cawston's fields were ostensibly open, the communal farming this implies was undermined by agricultural improvement. The dispute with Hyrne was not over whether the lands of the village should be more efficiently exploited, but by whom. This becomes more evident later in the century, with the increasing importance of turnip cultivation. Turnips were grown during the winter months when the village sheep customarily grazed the fields; those who grew turnips therefore compensated the owner of the fold-course, but other tenants who lost access to grazing received nothing. Communal agriculture no longer existed in Cawston.[30]

In Stow Bardolph and Wimbotsham, the crucial resource was the fen. In some aspects of fen regulation, villagers had divided loyalties. When the fen suffered from overuse in the early seventeenth century, those who might have tried to control excessive pasturing and peat-digging would also have had to pay higher poor rates and perhaps lose tenants had they imposed restrictions which were too rigid. The regulation of fen use was therefore necessarily weak.[31] In other areas there was more unanimity. The Hares, for example, helped ensure that drainage costs in the village were kept down. The drains which kept Bardolph Fen relatively dry were maintained by the villages of Upwell and Outwell, just to the west of the fen. The sluices, however, which could be closed when the drains were full (thus flooding fields in Upwell and Outwell) were controlled by the Hares. When the protection of the beasts of one village might mean

[29] PRO E 134 43/44 Elizabeth I Mich. 7, testimony of Henry Yonge; this is not merely magnanimity; as the tenants paid poor rates – which could be a considerable burden – self-interest was also involved.

[30] NRS 27237 and NRS 24902 135x5 for payments; cf. E.P. Thompson, 'The grid of inheritance: a comment', in *Family and Inheritance: rural society in Western Europe, 1200–1800*, ed. Jack Goody, Joan Thirsk and E.P. Thompson (Cambridge, 1976), pp. 328–60. It is possible that the establishment of a stint for tenants in Cawston at the time of the 1601 lawsuit benefited the wealthier villagers directly: Amussen, 'Governors and governed', pp. 50, 64.

[31] Hare 29–31; for other fen occupations and economies, see Joan Thirsk, *Fenland Farming in the Sixteenth Century*, Department of English Local History, University College of Leicester, Occasional Papers no. 3 (Leicester, 1953); Spufford, *Contrasting Communities*, chapter 5; Ravensdale, *Liable to Floods*; Thirsk, 'Farming regions', pp. 38–40.

the destruction of the fields of another, political power was a necessity; and although in 1629 the villagers of Upwell and Outwell broke down the sluice doors to protect their lands, they lost the ensuing suit in Star Chamber.[32]

The influence of the Hares did not always command full support. The drainage of the fens was a pet project of early Stuart governments, chiefly because of the profits it promised, both for the Crown and the projectors. Plans for drainage were fought every step of the way by the fenmen, who believed – rightly – that drainage and enclosure would dramatically disrupt their lives.[33] The fens near Stow Bardolph and Wimbotsham were drained in the 1650s, and conclusively divided by the Commissioners for Draining the Great Level in 1665. Initially Sir Ralph Hare sought to enclose 2489 acres of fen for his own use; not surprisingly, his tenants found this excessive, and argued that he deserved only one-seventh of the land available. In the end, Sir Ralph received 1000 acres, while each commonable messuage was assigned between twenty and twenty-five acres. Sir Ralph's share – more than one-quarter of the land available – was undoubtedly a tribute to his position.[34]

The draining and enclosure of the fen was a turning point in the agricultural and social history of Stow Bardolph and Wimbotsham. Though it made the cultivation of the fen possible, it effectively eliminated marginal economies and made the position of the poor more precarious. Agriculture became more specialized, with an emphasis on dairying and stock-rearing; grain was grown almost exclusively for domestic consumption. Most crops were used to

[32] Notes on laws of Sewers between 7 James I and 12 Charles I in Hare 5091, 5128, 5121, 5106, 5124 and 5126; Sir John Hare's complaint to Star Chamber is recorded in Hare 5139, and the English text of the decree is found in Hare 5165; the conflict continued after the Restoration: PRO E. 112 486/375, E. 134 32 Chas. II Mich. 34 and E. 126 vol. 13, f. 295d (6 June 33 Chas. II).

[33] For fen disturbances, see Keith Lindley, *Fenland Riots and the English Revolution* (London, 1982); Clive Holmes, 'Drainers and fenmen: the problem of popular political consciousness in the seventeenth century', in *Order and Disorder in Early Modern England*, ed. Anthony Fletcher and John Stevenson, (Cambridge, 1985) pp. 166–95; H.C. Darby, *The Draining of the Fens*, 2nd edn (Cambridge, 1956), chapter II; Mark E. Kennedy, 'Charles I and local government: the draining of the east and west fens', *Albion*, 15 (1983), pp. 19–31.

[34] This conflict is described in Hare 3488 and 3357; the division recorded in Hare 5166 and 5167; Hare 5145 (1665), Commissioners for Draining the Great Level, summons.

feed the cattle which were the principal sources of wealth.[35] As we shall see, it also shaped the process of inheritance. Social structure in the villages had shaped access to the fen, but that in turn reshaped social structure.

The experience of these Norfolk villages suggests the range of experience available even within one county, and the types of patterns – of agricultural change, social structure and conflict over resources – which might exist. It also makes the abstractions with which we are familiar concrete: agricultural improvement means enclosing land or pasturing more sheep; polarization means that the poor lost access to the fens; and feeding the growing population required transformations of agricultural practice, and consequently, social structure. This material background is one of the contexts in which social relations in the period must be examined.

General economic developments define only one part of the experience of English villages and families in the early modern period; religion and the developing impact of the Reformation define another. Changes in doctrine, especially the doctrine of the priesthood, had a gradual but profound impact in villages. Many parishes had no experience of committed Protestant ministers until late in Elizabeth I's reign; after that time, however, there were enough university-trained ministers to have a wider influence. Although not all of these newcomers were 'Puritan', most were Calvinist. Puritanism too often seems to be a vague notion which serves as an explanation for any change the historian observes in early modern society; but it did exist and flourished particularly in the towns and cities. It is best defined loosely as particularly zealous Protestantism. During Elizabeth's reign Puritans repeatedly sought to change the religious settlement in Parliament; the failure of the Presbyterian programme in the 1580s, and the Star Chamber and High Commission trials of the early 1590s, led to a new focus on personal piety and discipline, and on the moral reformation of society. It is this later type of Puritanism – within the Church – that I will be referring to in the

---

[35] Amussen, 'Governors and governed', pp. 126–30; NCC Inventories from Stow Bardolph and Wimbotsham.

remainder of this book.[36]

Religion was often a divisive issue in early modern England, and different religious perspectives fostered different attitudes toward social roles and relations. Such conflicts can be seen in both Cawston and Winfarthing. In Cawston, Edward Hammond, the rector between 1573 and 1621, illustrates some of the conflicts. Hammond was a wealthy man: his spiritual living alone made him one of the two wealthiest landholders in the village, but he also had an extensive personal estate. Hammond had a more worldly view of his role than did some of his parishioners. In 1605 he was presented for his failure to live in the parsonage, which he had allowed to fall into decay, and he had also ploughed up the parsonage garden; he was also 20s. in arrears for his 1602 poor rates. The previous year he had failed to read the injunctions and to catechize the youth of the parish. In 1581, Hammond had even been accused of simony, and a conflict with George Sawer is suggestive: before 1590 Hammond had had Sawer presented to the Archdeacon for failure to receive Communion; Sawer was, according to Hammond, 'very precise and made some doubt of certain points of divinity touching the Lord's supper' – in other words, a Puritan. Hammond died in 1621 after forty-eight years as rector, but he left nothing to the Church or poor of Cawston; they would remember him instead because he asked to be buried in the

---

[36] A.G. Dickens, *The English Reformation* (London, 1964); J.J. Scarisbrick, *The Reformation and the English People* (Oxford, 1984); Patrick Collinson, *The Elizabethan Puritan Movement* (Berkeley and Los Angeles, 1967); Walzer, *Revolution of the Saints*; Hill, *Society and Puritanism*; Spufford, *Contrasting Communities*, part III, esp. chapter 10; Wrightson and Levine, *Poverty and Piety*, chapter 6; Patrick Collinson, *The Religion of Protestants: the Church in English society, 1559–1625* (Oxford, 1982); Nicholas Tyacke, 'Puritanism, Arminianism and counter-revolution', in *The Origins of the English Civil War*, ed. Conrad Russell (London, 1973), pp. 119–43. Margaret Spufford, 'Puritanism and social control?' in *Order and Disorder*, ed. Fletcher and Stevenson, pp. 41–57, uses the behaviour of early fourteenth-century parish elites as a comparison to argue that the interest in disciplining others evinced by Puritan parish elites was based on their social position, not their religion. I do not see that the observation that parish elites are behaving as they had 300 years earlier is incompatible with a recognition that in the seventeenth century discipline was effected by Puritans who justified that discipline through their faith. Puritanism is not unique as a religious position which could justify such a crackdown on disorder, but in the seventeenth century it was used far more than either mainstream Anglicanism or Arminianism: see also Keith Wrightson, 'Two concepts of order: justices, constables, and jurymen in seventeenth century England' in *An Ungovernable People*, ed. John Brewer and John Styles (New Brunswick, New Jersey, 1980), pp. 21–46; also Paul S. Seaver, *Wallington's World: a Puritan artisan in seventeenth-century London* (Stanford, 1985).

chancel of the church, with his grave raised one yard above the ground with mason's work. His cooperation with his neighbours in the lawsuit against Thomas Hyrne reflected common secular interests, to which he paid assiduous attention; but he did not – as some of his parishioners wished – seek to build a godly commonwealth in Cawston.[37]

Religion entailed not just different views of the role of the rector, but also of social and political struggles, both local and national. This was evident in the conflict which rocked the elite of Winfarthing in the early 1690s. The ostensible cause was the question of who should have keys to the chest where the parish records were kept. Henry Chamberlain, churchwarden when the keys to the chest were lost in 1690, suggested that only three new keys be made – one for each churchwarden and one for the rector. But Winfarthing had an endowment of lands for the upkeep of both the church and the poor, and several of the feofees who managed this endowment, as well as other 'ancient inhabitants', argued that such an arrangement violated precedent: only the feofees had access to the box in which the 'town evidences' were kept, and that box was in the parish chest. The town lands were important, as they often obviated the need for rates. Control of the deeds provided power.[38]

The argument was not just about keys, but also about social status. There is evidence elsewhere of a decline in the social status of churchwardens in the late seventeenth century. While the feofees of the town lands – a nominated and self-perpetuating body – included men from families long resident in the village, Chamberlain was a newcomer who was not even a landholder, but 'only a farmer there', according to George Pulham, a former churchwarden who had never had a key to the box. Pulham's

[37] Wrightson and Levine, *Poverty and Piety*, pp. 124, 135–9; Wrightson, 'Two concepts of order', pp. 41–4; these conflicts can be traced in DEP/30, Book 32, Funston con Sawer (1598), testimony of Edward Hammond; notes about his arrears in NRS 2604 12B2; 1604 and 1605 draft presentments in NRS 2604; DEP/18, Hugh Robinson, Cler., con Edward Hammond, ff. 152–64v, 190v–91; exceptions in DEP/19, ff. 164–9v; his will in NCC Wills 1621 Hudd 44. The simony case may have interrupted Hammond's tenure as rector in 1580: Rye, *Cawston*, p. 46.

[38] The conflict is recorded in C/S1/10, Norwich Sessions of October 1689, January, April and July 1691; C/S3/58A 2Wm. & Mary; also DEP/52, Henry Chamberlain con William Chapman, 9 June 1619 and Henry Chamberlain con John Middleditch, Henry Chamberlain con Thomas Barron, 10 June 1691; the income of the town lands is recorded in PD 78/47: in some years the income from the town lands reached £30, but these were exceptional.

father had brought him to the church when he was fourteen to hear the evidences read. For Pulham, the feofees were respected neighbours. He saw no reason to trust a newcomer – and possible transient – with critical evidence about the income of the town.[39]

Chamberlain's position as a farmer and relative newcomer suggests social tensions, but there were also religious divisions in Winfarthing. In a defamation suit at the time of the conflict over the town chest, Chamberlain complained that Richard Chapman had called him 'as rank a papist as any is in England, [who] was concerned in the late conspiracy or Popish Plot'. On the face of it, the accusation is absurd. Insofar as it existed, the Popish Plot of 1678 hardly involved an obscure Norfolk farmer. But the accusation does direct us to religious and political questions. There is considerable circumstantial evidence that the feofees for the town lands included non-conformists, their kin or their sympathizers. The Compton Census indicated that 12 per cent of the adults in Winfarthing were dissenters; one of Chamberlain's few allies in the whole dispute was the rector.[40] Evidence of political affiliation is more elusive than that of religion, so it is impossible to be certain of the political dimensions. However, the insult to Chamberlain demonstrates that what appears initially as a trivial parochial dispute in the politically and religiously divided atmosphere of 1690 set old inhabitants against newcomers, dissenters against the Establishment and perhaps even Whig against Tory.

Puritanism encouraged in its adherents a sense of being set apart as the elect. In the countryside, it has been argued, it appealed particularly to the gentry and more substantial yeomen, whose social and material experience already set them apart from their neighbours. Their sense of separateness shaped their response to the problems, especially poverty and disorder, brought on by demographic growth and inflation. Poverty was not a creation of the sixteenth century, but the scale of the problem intensified dramatically during the period. The drastic decline in real wages

[39] See esp. DEP/52, Henry Chamberlain con Thomas Barron, evidence of George Pulham and Robert Valliant; cf. Wrightson and Levine, *Poverty and Piety*, p. 104.

[40] DEP/52, Henry Chamberlain con William Chapman, 9 June 1691; the evidence on religious affiliation is circumstantial but compelling: C.B. Jewson, 'Return of conventicles, 1669', *Norfolk Archeology*, 33, p. 25; the kin links can be traced in NCC Wills OW 1661 23, and NCC Wills OW 1663 19 and 105; for a fuller discussion of these issues see Amussen, 'Governors and governed', pp. 105–9; although the political affiliations are nowhere specified, they are strongly suggested by the use of the Popish Plot accusation.

was not reversed until after 1660, and even then the improvement was slow and slight. At the same time, as we have seen, small landholders were being pushed off the land, and land was concentrated in fewer and fewer hands. Thus an increasing proportion of a growing population depended on wages for its livelihood; labourers' incomes were often inadequate to maintain a family, even if wives also worked for wages. The response of government was twofold: it sought to limit the dependence of labourers on wages by requiring that all cottages have at least four acres of land, and in 1597 it extended earlier statutes to require a more systematic provision of poor relief: the responsibilities of parishes were now clear, and more adequate means of support for the indigent were made available.[41]

This legislation formed the basis for the activities of local government. The actions of local notables in governing their communities usually reflect common goals and assumptions. Even in Winfarthing, parish notables worked closely together on questions of settlement and parish relief.[42] Local notables united against others in defence of their rights or to reduce the number of the poor, even when divided among themselves about the basis for, and nature of, local power and authority. In Cawston we can see how a group of notables – yeomen and minor gentlemen – managed their affairs between 1595 and 1615. The records of this activity survive because of George Sawer, whose descriptive lists of Cawston's population have already been mentioned: he was a compulsive bureaucrat who kept all his papers. As one of those named in the lawsuits with Thomas Hyrne, he kept drafts of the complaints and notes on the points to be raised by particular witnesses. Sawer served as churchwarden or overseer at least seven times between 1601 and 1619, and his notes provide an unusually

---

[41] Spufford, *Contrasting Communities*, chapters 2–5; Clark, *Working Life*, chapter III; E.M. Leonard, *The Early History of English Poor Relief* (Cambridge, 1900), pp. 73, 133–5.

[42] An example of how this might work is the case of Elizabeth Rix of Winfarthing: PD 100/123, PD 78/48, 1712–13, and C/S2/6, July 1712; Amussen, 'Governors and governed', pp. 103–4 and 'Féminin/Masculin: le genre dans l'Angleterre de l'époque moderne', *Annales ESC*, 40:2 (1985), pp. 269–87, esp. p. 275.

full picture of early seventeenth-century local government.[43]

That picture begins with a crisis – the disastrous harvest of 1596. Sawer made two separate lists that year, one of those who were to be given special access to grain, and the other of those who were to bring grain to market weekly to sell to those in need. Each list reflects both intimate local knowledge and discrimination. Those with access to corn at the market – 103 households – were divided into four groups: the forty-five poorest households paid 6d. a peck for barley and peas, seven ½d. a peck for rye; those 'somewhat more able' paid a little more; twelve households with no corn growing could buy, but without a guaranteed price; finally, the fourteen households with some, but insufficient, corn for their needs could buy any grain that was left over. The parish officers were aware of the resentment that such arrangements might create, so they arranged that the sellers would serve the different groups in turn. The list of those assigned to bring corn to the market covers eight months, from January to August 1597. Fifty-three men were required to bring corn at least once, twenty-three of them only once; Edward Hammond was summoned twenty-three times, while only two others brought grain more than ten times. Most brought one combe (four bushels) of grain each time they appeared in the market, but some brought only two bushels, and George Peter, who was only summoned twice, brought six combes on one day. Cawston, following the Book of Orders, had mounted a major – and successful – relief campaign; because of another poor harvest, a similar operation was undertaken the following year.[44]

George Sawer had a penchant for categorizing people; at least in his early years as a parish officer he regularly made a census of the town, dividing the poor into groups by various criteria – relative wealth, age or possessions. Such lists were presumably the basis for

---

[43] Sawer's papers are found in NRS 2604 12B2, NRS Accn. 1.8.63 P186D, in the possession of Mrs Janet Hammond (microfilms are in the Norfolk Record Office), and scattered through the Bulwer collection; it is not clear who kept these papers, and how they came to survive, as they almost certainly were out of the possession of the family members. Only one man served as an officeholder more often than Sawer, based on Sawer's notes and the parish register (PD 193/1): Amussen 'Governors and governed', pp. 66–7; Susan Dwyer Amussen, 'A Norfolk village: Cawston, 1595–1605', *History Today* 36 (April, 1986), pp. 15–20.

[44] The lists are found in NRS Accn. 1.8.63 P186D, and the list of those bringing corn to market in papers belonging to Mrs Janet Hammond; Paul Slack, 'Books of Orders: the making of English social policy, 1577–1631', *TRHS* 5th Ser., 30 (1980), pp. 1–22; PD 193/1 shows no increase in mortality for the crisis years.

both relief and parish rates. Sawer was also an avid valuer of lands. Some of his rating lists show the valuation, not the actual tax; such lists must always have existed and been regularly updated, though they rarely survived. Parish office thus represented a heavy responsibility in collecting and distributing funds: George Sawer did all this fairly and efficiently. A hint of partiality in an assessment would have undermined the collection of rates. Rates could be substantial: in 1597 Sawer was collecting at least 8s. 11d. weekly – and for three months in 1618–19 he collected double rates, 50s. 3d. each month. These activities were necessary to maintain the poor of Cawston.[45]

This description presents an altruistic image of parish government, but that is only a partial picture. Though not all were as diligent as Sawer, many others also took on the largely thankless burden of parochial office. Parochial office-holding was a recognition of status. In Cawston, officers can be identified for fifteen years between 1600 and 1620; during that time only nineteen men held office, ten of them more than once. These ten were the core of the local elite. In a draft seating plan of the women's side of Cawston church made in 1615–16, the wives of current officers were placed in the second seat, just behind the rector's wife and the wives of three gentlemen. Such a position symbolically affirmed social position and local leadership, which made church seating and its implicit hierarchy a frequent cause of conflict in early modern villages.[46]

Local leadership, especially in the absence of a resident lord of the manor, had more than symbolic importance. In 1601 George Sawer, then overseer of the poor, received £20 from Edward Hammond, William Batch and Robert Eston, to prosecute the suits between the villagers and Thomas Hyrne. Both the positions

---

[45] The 1618–19 rate is in NRS Accn. 1.8.63 P186D and the 1597 list in NRS 2604 12B2; valuations can be found in both bundles; for a discussion of some of these categories, see Wales, 'Poverty, poor relief, and the life-cycle'; Amussen, 'Governors and governed', pp. 55–9 analyses these lists more fully. Sawer may have been assisted in his work as a parish officer by experience as a surveyor: Peter Eden, 'Land surveyors in Norfolk, 1550–1850', *Norfolk Archeology*, 36 Pt. 2(1975), pp. 119–48, though there is no direct evidence linking the George Sawer who made a map of the Felbrigg estate (p. 142) in 1598 to the one who lived in Cawston.

[46] NRS Accn. 1.8.63 P186D, Churchwarden's Accounts, 1615–16; for the wealth of Cawston parish officers, see Amussen, 'Governors and governed', pp. 66–7 and cf. Wrightson and Levine, *Poverty and Piety*, pp. 104–5; for a fuller discussion of the implications of church seats, see below, chapter 6.

of those involved and the nature of the defence suggest that these lawsuits were undertaken in the name of the village, but none of those involved was disinterested. As relatively large landholders they would benefit from continued access to the common, even if a stint was set at two beasts per acre. It may also be significant that Sawer, Batch and Hammond were among those who had enclosed land in the fields. Parish leadership gave them the opportunity to define the interests of the village in a way that sustained their own.[47]

Cawston's government, with its clear organization of relief and shared action in defence of village rights, resulted from the absence of a resident lord who could dominate the village, and from the presence of a relatively small and clearly defined group of parish notables. The situation was dramatically different in Stow Bardolph and Wimbotsham, where the dominance of the Hares was unmistakable. This may explain why a number of seventeenth-century inhabitants of Stow Bardolph distinguished between parts of the village – Stow Green, with Stow Hall and the church, and Stow Bridge, a mile closer to the river – when making bequests to the poor. Stow Bridge was less closely governed than was Stow Green, and somewhat more independent. The same was true of Wimbotsham. Many inhabitants of Stow Bardolph – including inmates in the Stow almshouses – were buried in Wimbotsham. In Wimbotsham it was possible to be buried in a place of greater honour than in Stow Bardolph: the seventeenth-century memorials inside Stow Church are all of the Hares or their servants.[48]

We have already seen how the Hares defended their rights to the fen – and indeed often tried to enlarge them – not only against the inhabitants of Upwell and Outwell, but also against their own

---

[47] The agreement to prosecute the suit is in NRS 2604 12B2, as are some of the church rates; others are in NRS 1.8.63 P186D; enclosures are marked on NRO map 4521 E; it is possible that Sawer was paid because the lawyer in London was his son Edmund: cf. Spufford, *Constrasting Communities*, pp. 97–8 for the role of a lawyer son in another such dispute.

[48] Blomefield and Parkyn, *History of Norfolk*, VII, pp. 443–6 for monuments in Stow Church. At least 125 residents of Stow Bardolph (whether Stow Green or Stow Bridge is usually unspecified) were buried in Wimbotsham between 1634 and 1721: see the Wimbotsham parish register transcript, L.W. Turner Deposit 1.8.79, Q187D, Box 3; such burial is explicitly requested in ANF Wills 1590 Bk. 30 447, Thomas Lassell, husbandman; ANF Wills 1630 6, Thomas Goose, husbandman; and ANF Wills 81 1661 139, John Shering, thatcher. Sixteen will makers throughout the period described themselves as inhabitants of Stow Bridge, Brink or Ward, and it was specified in bequests by William Jarvis (ANF Wills Book 37 (1608) 147) and Robert Asshely, (ANF Wills Book 33 (1597) 94), among others.

tenants.[49] But they did not only use their position for material gain; they also used it in defence of their tenants. Theories of obligation were reciprocal: deference was owed in return for protection and good rule. The Hares provided good rule. Litigation from Stow Bardolph and Wimbotsham reflects not personal feuds but petty crime: personal feuds appear to have been arbitrated within the villages. And the Hares never tried to obtain perfection; disorder was merely kept at a distance. There are seventeen surviving alehouse licences or cases of unlicenced alehousekeeping in the villages, all but three in Stow Bridge (out of the sight of the Hares) or Wimbotsham. Most of the brawls in Stow also took place at Stow Bridge.[50] Resistance to the Hares was not overt, but subtle: drinking in Stow Bridge away from their vigilance, requesting burial in Wimbotsham Church or even leaving bequests to the poor of Stow Bridge, rather than to the almshouses at Stow Green. The geographical boundaries of disorder reinforced the social distance between the Hares and everyone else.

The villages lacked an organized voice, even in their opposition to fen drainage and enclosure. This may account for the patchy survival of parochial records. The only records of churchwardens or overseers which have survived are those scribbled in his almanac by Walter Drury, rector of Wimbotsham and vicar of Stow Bardolph from 1674 to 1722. Both livings were in the gift of the Hares, and Drury also worked on estate business. His almanacs have survived because of the tithe suit in the Court of Exchequer in the 1740s, when they were entered into evidence by the Hares. Stow Bardolph and Wimbotsham were governed villages, not self-governing ones.[51]

---

[49] In addition to the disputes over fen drainage, see PRO REQ 2 297/2.

[50] C/S3/11,12A, 13, 17, 18, 26, 29A, 37, 39, 40 for alehouse licences and prosecutions: this is the minimum, because Stow Bridge may not always have been designated, as it had no legal existence. Four defamation cases appear from Stow and Wimbotsham in the NCC, but they arose out of only two incidents: DEP/30, Bk. 32, White con Thompson, Cler., and Edmund Cooper con Thompson, Cler., ff. 296–8, 202–3; and DEP/31, Welles con Langman and Welles con Chaunter, ff. 239v–40v, 357–8; the latest of these incidents is in 1601 – after that the closest one comes to a personal feud in the villages comes when Joan Reeve was accused of theft and countered with an accusation of attempted rape against one of the witnesses: C/S3/51, 26 Charles II, Informations to Edward Barber, Esq., 25 and 28 May 1674.

[51] Drury's almanacs are in the Hare Collection, Hare 3527a and b, and Hare 5672; the court case is PRO E. 134 13 Geo.II Easter 6; opposition to enclosure is described in Hare 5166 232X; for bequests see above, n. 48. There is, of course, a certain amount of luck in the survival of documents.

The 1596 crisis which prompted the relief effort in Cawston was part of a series of poor harvests which caused hardship and even sometimes starvation in many areas of England. Several years of poor harvests drove small landholders into debt, and ultimately forced many to sell their land; vagrancy appeared to have grown alarmingly. Even those who were in normal times well able to maintain their families with corn suffered. But the system of poor relief developed at this time was controlled by parishes, which supported only those officially settled in them: vagrants, it was thought, were dangerous, especially in times of dearth. Dearth often led not only to an increase in vagrancy and a consequent increase in crime, but also to local discontent and to grain riots. Grain rioters sought both to lower the price of available grain and to prevent the export of grain when supplies were scarce; while usually limited in scope and action, riots still threatened the control of local governers. Vagrancy was even worse: away from home, seeking both food and employment, vagrants were outside all the usual local structures used to impose order. For this reason, dearth was one of the major social problems faced by English governments, and remained so until after the Restoration.[52]

Poverty was associated with disorder not only in times of dearth, but also in times of prosperity. Both village notables and gentry feared the disorders of the poor. The late sixteenth century saw an increase in prosecutions for all forms of disorderliness, including vagrancy, witchcraft and many other crimes, prosecutions directed at those whose behaviour disrupted both families and villages. Parish officers were responsible for local discipline, which like the Cawston lawsuit, gave concrete social meaning to their position. The churchwardens' presentments might be an opportunity to prosecute a private feud, or to impose one's own standards of behaviour upon one's neighbours. In many parts of England during this period churchwardens' presentments reveal a

[52] Leonard, *Early History of English Poor Relief*, pp. 73, 133–5; Keith Wrightson and John Walter, 'Dearth and the social order in early modern England', *Past and Present*, 71 (1976), pp. 22–42; J. Walter, 'Grain riots and popular attitudes to the law: Maldon and the crisis of 1629', in *An Ungovernable People*, ed. Brewer and Styles, pp. 47–84; Andrew Appleby, *Famine in Tudor and Stuart England* (Stanford, 1978).

sustained attack on the culture of the poor.[53] Those from Cawston certainly show that those who did not pay rates were somewhat more likely to feel the heavy hand of ecclesiastical discipline than their more prosperous neighbours. On the other hand, ten of the twelve Cawston inhabitants who repeatedly appeared before the eccelesiastical courts did pay rates; they were presumably less vulnerable to pressure from parish officers.[54] It was the responsibility of the rector and parish officers – chosen from among the wealthiest and most respected in the community – to ensure order. In Stow Bardolph and Wimbotsham the task was apparently taken on by the Hares and their officials; in Cawston in the early seventeenth century it was effectively carried out by a relatively small group of villagers.

We do not know whether the increase in prosecutions in the early seventeenth century reflects more crime and disorder or the more frequent failure of informal methods of dealing with it. Both possibilities, however, suggest not only the insecurity of local notables, but also an increasing gulf between rich and poor in early seventeenth-century villages. Local notables appear to have been

---

[53] Wrightson and Levine, *Poverty and Piety*; Wrightson, 'Two concepts of order'; Alan Macfarlane, 'Witchcraft in Tudor and Stuart Essex', pp. 72–89 and J.S. Cockburn, 'The nature and incidence of crime in England, 1559–1625: a preliminary survey', in *Crime in England, 1550–1800*, ed. J.S. Cockburn (Princeton, 1977), pp. 49–71; J.A. Sharpe, *Crime in Early Modern England, 1550–1750* (London, 1984) is the most recent survey of the subject; Hoskins, *Midland Peasant*, pp. 141–7; Wrightson, *English Society*, chapter 6; David Underdown, 'The taming of the scold: the enforcement of patriarchal authority in early modern England', in *Order and Disorder*, ed. Fletcher and Stevenson, pp.116–36; Cynthia B. Herrup, 'The common peace: legal structure and legal substance in East Sussex, 1594–1640', Northwestern University Ph.D. 1982, for a study of the workings of the legal system in one county.

[54] Presentments are found in ANW 6/4, 5, 6 and ANW 2/42; for problems with churchwardens in Cawston, see the dispute about the two cows given to the church by Ann Gurney, wid. in 1595: ANW Wills 1595 225 Holmes; in a draft presentment Sawer noted that the cows – or their price – had not turned up in 1604 and 1605: NRS 2604; the two churchwardens involved – William Batch and Robert Eston – presented Robert Money, for alleging that they were making a profit on their jobs: ANW 2/42 28 March 1601; for distrust of parish officers in general, see e.g. C/S3/17, 9 James I, Petition vs. Edward Durrant, and C/S3/20, 13 James I, Petition vs. Edmund Waskott of Enmeth; cf. Wrightson and Levine, *Poverty and Piety*, chapter 5; Wrightson, 'Two concepts of order'; idem, 'The Puritan reformation of manners with special reference to the counties of Lancashire and Essex, 1640–60', Cambridge University Ph.D. 1973, esp. chapters 2–6; Underdown, *Revel, Riot and Rebellion*, chapter 3; Amussen, 'Governors and governed', pp. 66–71: between 1601 and 1605 46.3 per cent of those brought before the church courts were rated, while in a 1604 list of households, 54.8 per cent were rated – a relatively slight difference. Unfortunately, comparable data for the other villages do not survive.

more secure after 1660; certainly anxiety about disorder, especially in families, was less marked in the more stable conditions of the Restoration. This security, both economic and social, of local notables in the Restoration shaped not just relations in villages, where prosecutions declined, but also in families.[55]

The factors we have been discussing – population growth, inflation, Puritanism, the polarization of wealth and the increase in poverty, and the fear of disorder – were common to all England; throughout the kingdom those in authority had to resolve as many local conflicts as possible, feed the poor and maintain order as best they could. As their governors struggled with these problems, villagers in early modern England were made constantly aware of the social implications of an analogy between family and political order. In the first half of the seventeenth century, rapid social change led to an increased concern for the maintenance of order – not just in villages, but also in families. The relationships of power within families were never explicitly challenged; those in villages were. Order in families was therefore easier to enforce than order in villages. After the Restoration, with the slight decrease in population, rising real wages and a less active land market, there was a marked decrease in the use of the courts to enforce order, both inside and outside families. It was just at this time – when the family was no longer as necessary to maintain social order – that the first attempts to separate the family from politics in theory took place. Village notables were able to abandon the earlier ideological formula when the social situation changed, but so too were political and social theorists. It is to this process of ideological change that we now turn.

---

[55] Susan D. Amussen, 'Gender, family and the social order, 1560–1725', in *Order and Disorder*, ed. Fletcher and Stevenson, pp. 196–217 for an analysis of the causes of the decline of prosecutions for disorder; see also below, chapter 5 and 6.

2

Political Households and Domestic Politics: Family and Society in Early Modern Thought

The economic developments we have been discussing did not operate on social relations in a vacuum. Changes in the material circumstances of villagers were interpreted through existing ideological constructs. The way in which relationships developed depended to a great extent on how those involved perceived the world and the language they used to express those perceptions: How was it ordered? How ought it to be ordered? How were the various communities which made up English society connected to each other? What images could be used to explain these ideas? The answers to these questions are not found in sources indigenous to Norfolk, but in works on political, social and familial order written in the sixteenth and seventeenth centuries. The problem of order was of consuming interest in this period, both for writers of theoretical treatises and manuals, and for those whose responsibility was to govern communities. This cannot be an exhaustive survey of the literature on the subject; instead it will focus on manuals for householders, and on the use of familial metaphors in discussions of political and social order.[1]

[1] For the crisis of order, see Wrightson, *English Society*, chapter 6; Underdown, *Revel, Riot and Rebellion*, chapter 2; Wrightson, 'Two concepts of order'; W.H. Hunt, *The Puritan Moment: the coming of revolution in an English county* (Cambridge, Massachusetts, 1983); for the family, see Susan Cahn, 'Changing conceptions of women in sixteenth and seventeenth century England', University of Michigan Ph.D. Thesis, 1981; Chilton Latham Powell, *English Domestic Relations, 1487–1653: a study of matrimony and family life in theory and practice as revealed by the literature, law, and history of the period* (New York, 1917); for familial language in political thought, see Schochet, *Patriarchalism*; Mary Shanley, 'Marriage contract and social contract in seventeenth century English political thought', *Western Political Quarterly*, 32 (1979), pp. 79–91.

Both household manuals and political treatises were part of a national culture. If English men and women of the early modern period were concerned primarily with issues in their own localities, there were also many institutions and ideas which encouraged common approaches to and assumptions about these local issues. This national culture affected not just the gentry, but at least in some ways, almost the entire population. The national culture was generated not only by the universities and the Inns of Court, or attendance at quarter sessions and assizes, although these were significant for the gentry, and in the latter cases, yeomen.[2] It was also, far more universally, rooted in the Church of England. Though attendance at church services probably never attained the ideal, until the Civil War most English women and men – especially when they were young – attended Anglican services, and more importantly, were catechized. The catechism provided the most accessible statement of the commonplace ideas we will examine, and though there might be other more thorough statements of these ideas, the fundamental assumptions of all of them – Puritan and Arminian, royalist and parliamentarian – were virtually the same.

The Canons of 1604 required that 'the youth and ignorant persons' of every parish be catechized by the rector, vicar or curate for half an hour before evening prayer *every* Sunday. Failure to do this – as well as the failure of parents or masters to send children or servants to be catechized – was presented in archdiaconal visitations.[3] In addition to its doctrinal instruction, the catechism taught young people how to be good subjects. In doing so, it asserted that the family was the fundamental social institution, and that order in families was both necessary for, and parallel to, order in the state. In the catechism, this idea is developed in the

---

[2] Wrightson and Levine, *Poverty and Piety*, esp. chapter 1, makes this evident; Clive Holmes, 'The county community in Stuart historiography', *Journal of British Studies*, 19 (1980), pp. 54–73.

[3] Canon LIX, 'Constitutions and canons ecclesiastical, 1604', in *Synodalia: a collection of articles of religion, canons, and proceedings of Convocation in the province of Canterbury from the year 1547 to the year 1717*, ed. E. Cardwell (2 vols, Oxford, 1842, reprinted Farnborough, Hants, 1966), I pp. 280–1; PD 62/33, Bacton, Visitation Articles, 1631; DEP/28, William Ellyet, Cler., John Toolye and Thomas Bygott con Silvester Oldman, Gent., ff. 444–5v; also 'Interrogatories, July 1560' and 'Interrogatories for the diocese of Norwich, 1561', in *Visitation Articles and Injunctions of the Period of the Reformation*, ed. W.H. Frere, Alcuin Club Collections XIV–XVI (3 vols, London, 1910), vol. III, pp. 87–93, 101–7.

discussion of the Fifth Commandment, to 'honour thy father and mother'. The 1559 Prayer Book's catechism treated each of the two tables of the Ten Commandments (duty to God and to neighbour) as entities, rather than dealing with each commandment separately, and summarized their implications:

> My duty towards my neighbour is to love him as myself, and to do to all men as I would they should do unto me: to love, honour, and succour my father and mother: to honour and obey the King and all that are put in authority under him: to submit myself to all my governors, teachers, spiritual pastors and masters: to order myself lowly and reverently to all my betters: . . . to learn and labour truly to get mine own living, and to do my duty in that state of life unto which it shall please God to call me.[4]

The brevity of the Prayer Book catechism encouraged many ministers to write expanded versions, but all accepted this interpretation of the Fifth Commandment. As a result of these catechisms – as well as homilies and other exhortations – everyone understood that what happened in their families was related to what happened in the state. The family was a social, public institution, not a private one that could be left to its own devices. On that everyone was in agreement.

Everyone also agreed that the model for relations in the family and the state was the relationship between God and man.[5] This model provided a reference point, and all writers – on family, society or politics – who attempted to explain the nature of power began with God. The model had four components: God's creation of the world and commandments to it established God's power; human failure to observe God's commandments then emphasized God's mercy in sending Jesus to redeem sinful humans. The combination of supreme power (creation and the ability to condemn us to damnation) and unmerited mercy (the salvation of

---

[4] Quoted in Schochet, *Patriarchalism*, p. 78; for alternative versions, see Andrew Sharp, ed., *Political Ideas of the English Civil Wars, 1641–9* (London, 1983), pp. 27–9.

[5] See John Dod, *A Plaine and Familiar Exposition on the Lords Prayer* (London, 1635), pp. 25–7; Matthew Griffith, *Bethel: or a forme for families, in which all sorts, of both Sexes, are so squared, and framed by the Word of God, as they may best serve in their severall places, for usefull pieces in God's Building* (London, 1633), p. 45.

at least a few) was a powerful tool in the rhetoric of power relations. There was only one divisive question: Who was God's representative on earth? God apparently no longer revealed himself to individuals, and so there had to be some substitute. Writers chose the individual most suited to their own arguments – for political writers usually the King, for writers of household manuals the father or head of the household.

The analogy between the household and the state was available to all those interested in authority and the enforcement of order in early modern England. It must be understood as an analogy, however, not an equation. As an analogy it could be used in many different ways. Those who employed the analogy were not all in agreement on the fundamental nature of faith, the family or the state, and few of them (except during the political pamphlet wars of the 1640s and 1650s) actually dealt with the assumptions that others made. These differences will become clear as we examine the various uses of the analogy.

There be two things which a *Christian* should especially *desire*, and *endeavor* to approve himself; namely, both a good *servant* to *God*, and a good *Subject* to the *King*: and my scope in this *Manual*, is to teach both.[6]

A family is . . . a little Commonwealth . . . a school wherein the first principles and grounds of government and subjection are learned . . . So we may say of inferiors that cannot be subject in a family; they will hardly be brought to yield such subjection as they ought in Church or Commonwealth.[7]

As every man's house is his Castle, so is his family a private Commonwealth, wherein if due government be not observed, nothing but confusion is to be expected.[8]

It is impossible for a man to understand how to govern the common-wealth, that doth not know to rule his own house,

---

[6] Griffith, *Bethel*, f. A6.

[7] William Gouge, *Of Domesticall Duties: Eight Treatises*, 3rd edn (London, 1634), p. 17.

[8] Richard Brathwait, Esq., *The English Gentleman: containing sundry excellent rules, or exquisite observations* (London, 1630), p. 155.

or order his own person; so that he that knoweth not to govern, deserveth not to reign.[9]

These statements represent the consensus of those who wrote manuals for householders in the late sixteenth and early seventeenth centuries. The family was central to social order; disciplined families were therefore a prerequisite of that order. Household manuals affirmed the public importance of familial relations that was implicit in the catechisms. They shared a common form and common ideals, though some were more concerned with practical problems, others with biblical precedent.[10] All the manuals analysed families on the basis of scripture, and as much as possible buttressed their arguments and prescriptions with scriptural example. William Gouge's *Of Domesticall Duties*, one of the most clearly organized manuals, is divided into eight treatises. The first analyses the scriptural passage chosen to structure the book, Ephesians 5:22–6:9. The second defines marriage and the mutual duties of husband and wife; the remainder of the book follows Ephesians: first the duties of wives to husbands, followed by those of husbands to wives; next, the duties of children to parents, followed by those of parents to children; finally, the duties of servants to masters are followed by those of masters to servants. The three sections on husbands and wives dominate the book; the sections on children and servants seem repetitive and perfunctory in comparison.

The very structure of Gouge's book and of the other household manuals made two points. First, relationships within the household were reciprocal; the obedience owed a husband, father or master was due in return for the performance of certain duties on his part. Second, the relationships in the household were all different: according to Robert Clever, 'all in the family are not to be governed alike. There is one rule to govern the wife by, another for children, another for servants'.[11] If family relations are mirrored in other hierarchies, there are a multiplicity of models to be drawn upon. If it is indeed different to be governed

[9] John Dod and Robert Clever, *A Godly Forme of Household Government: for the ordering of private families, according to the direction of God's Word* (London, 1612), f. A8v.

[10] Powell, *English Domestic Relations*, esp. pp. 128–9, 137–8.

[11] Dod and Clever, *Godly Forme*, f. A8v.

as a wife than as a child, there could be no single conception of authority. If the family was a little commonwealth, is the governor of the larger one a father, husband or master?

It is intuitively obvious to us that the relationship of a man to another adult, his wife, must be different from that of a man to his children, and that that relationship in turn would differ from that of a man to his servants. Children, after all, were the parents' permanent responsibility; servants, in spite of the rhetoric, served on a contractual basis for a set period of time. All, however, were in the family, and all owed obedience to the head of the household. The necessity of obedience is repeatedly stressed in all the manuals. This obedience was expected in the context of a loving and caring family life.

Happiness was the result of care in the selection of a spouse, careful rearing of children and the careful choice and government of servants. The relationship between husband and wife was critical. Edmund Tilney suggested that a husband should be kind and gentle to his wife, to gradually 'steal away her private will, and appetite, so that of two bodies there may be made only one heart'. Marriage for Tilney was based on 'true, and perfect love'.[12] William Gouge saw the sexual relationship of husband and wife as indispensable to marriage, so he would allow divorce in cases of impotence but not barrenness: those who were barren could still yield 'due benevolence' to their spouse.[13] The character and behaviour of the head of the household were, after the relationship between husband and wife, most important in setting the tone of family life. Matthew Griffith stressed his obligations: he should direct daily worship, make sure that the household attended church on Sundays, exercise discipline and provide 'competent bodily provisions, that so they may live a peaceable and comfortable life under their roof'.[14] The power of the head was extensive, but it was not tyrannical, and all the manuals insisted that love of each other and of God held the family together. The model was of benevolent patriarchy, not authoritarian government.

---

[12] Edmund Tilney, *A Brief and Pleasant Discourse of Duties in Marriage, Called the Flower of Friendshippe* (London, 1571), ff. Biiibv-Biiic, Biiia.

[13] Gouge, *Domesticall Duties*, pp. 182–3; for the long-term contradictions posed by these ideas, and their effect on gender ideology in the eighteenth century, see Edmund Leites, *The Puritan Conscience and Modern Sexuality* (New Haven, Connecticut, 1986).

[14] Griffith, *Bethel*, pp. 393–409 passim, esp. p. 405.

Of the relationships in the family, the simplest were those of parents and children, and masters and servants. The authority of parents and masters and mistresses was extensive. Servants and children owed honour, reverence and obedience. For servants the stress was on obedience: they were to help maintain their masters' goods, do the work they were set and not corrupt children or other servants. For children, the emphasis was on honour and reverence, with obedience as a corollary. Children were expected to pray for their parents, and to help maintain their parents if ever they should become poor and sick.[15] Servants' duties were more limited in time and degree than those of children, but both children and servants were expected to be obedient and accepting of correction.

The responsibilities of masters and mistresses to their servants were parallel to those of parents to children. Both servants and children should have a moral and practical education. Dorothy Leigh insisted that her sons teach all their servants to read, while others stressed the importance of teaching servants occupations and trades. Mistresses and masters were to keep servants from idleness, teach them good manners, make sure they attended church and correct their faults, firmly but gently – according to Clever and Dod, as a parent would![16] Parents' responsibilities were similar, though extended in time: mothers were to breast feed their children, and all children were to be taught to read, especially the Bible. Parents were also to teach their children 'good manners' (reverence to their superiors and respect one to another), to hate vice and love virtue and to ensure they knew a trade or profession. These goals were reached through early and moderate correction of children, as well as the careful choice of masters and dames when children were apprenticed or sent into service. Parents were to aid their children in the choice of a spouse, though the extent of parents' authority over their children's marriages was a subject of debate.[17] The termination of relationships with both servants (when they left service) or

---

[15] E.g., Dod and Clever, *Godly Forme*, ff. Aa4v, X1.

[16] Dod and Clever, *Godly Forme*, ff. B2-D6v, Z6; Dorothy Leigh, *The Mother's Blessing. Or the godly counsaile of a Gentlewoman not long since deceased, left behind for her Children. Containing many good exhortations and godly admonitions, profitable for all Parents to leave as a legacy to their Children, but especially for those who by reason of their young yeares stand most in need of Instruction* (London, 1616), pp. 58–9.

[17] For nursing see Dod and Clever, *Godly Forme*, ff. P3v-P5, and Gouge, *Domesticall Duties*, pp. 515–26, esp. p. 522; for education, Leigh, *Mother's Blessing*, pp. 24–5, 47; Gouge, *Domesticall Duties*, p. 538; and Dod and Clever, *Godly Forme*, ff. Q1–R7 passim.

children (at death) required further action by masters and mistresses and parents. While masters should pay servants regularly and adequately, at their departure there should be a parting gift based on the duration and quality of a servant's service. And as death approached, parents, especially fathers, should make wills to provide for their children and avoid strife and contention. Masters and mistresses as well as parents provided guidance, education and discipline from the beginning to the end of the relationship, and that guidance was deemed a benefit to the recipient.[18]

The relationship between masters and mistresses and servants and that between parents and children was straightforward. As in other deferential hierarchies, respect and obedience were owed in return for care, protection and guidance. The relationship between husbands and wives was more complicated, although writers sought to bring it into conformity with other relationships. The complications arose from the role of wives in the household: according to Clever and Dod, 'the Governors of families . . . are first the *chief governor*, which is the *Husband*, secondly, a *fellow-helper*, which is the Wife'.[19] Or, in Dorothy Leigh's formulation, 'If she be thy wife, she is always too good to be thy servant, and worthy to be thy fellow.'[20] Wives were joined with their husbands in the management and supervision of the household. The household manuals expected women to make an important economic contribution to the household: they emphasized the wife's role in provisioning the household, and the importance of her thrift; Fitzherbert declared that when either husband or wife went to market, they should return with an accounting for the other. Gouge made the husband and wife jointly responsible for the wealth and prosperity of the family.[21]

---

[18] Gouge, *Domesticall Duties*, pp. 579–83; John Dod and Robert Clever, *A Treatise or Exposition upon the Ten Commandments, Grounded upon the Scriptures Canonicall* (London, 1603), pp. 9–11, 15v–19v. Cf. Lewis Bayley, *The Practise of Piety* 3rd edn, (London, 1613), pp. 809–12.

[19] Dod and Clever, *Godly Forme*, f. B2.

[20] Leigh, *Mother's Blessing*, p. 55; Gouge, *Domesticall Duties*, p. 361: 'The Husband must account his wife a yoke fellow, and companion'; cf. Leites, *Puritan Conscience*, chapter 4 passim.

[21] [John] Fitzherbert, *Booke of Husbandrie. Devided Into foure severall Bookes, very necessary and profitable for all sorts of people. And now newly corrected, amended, and reduced, into a more pleasing forme of English then before* (London, 1598), pp. 177–8; Gouge, *Domesticall Duties*, pp. 255–6; cf. also Dod and Clever, *Godly Forme*, f. L4.

In spite of the obvious importance of the wife in running the household, her subjection to her husband, as well as her love and respect for him, were crucial to maintaining a godly, orderly household. In this she often fell short; Gouge complained that of all those 'of whom the Holy Ghost requireth subjection, wives for the most part are most backward in yielding subjection to their husbands'.[22] The results were disastrous: according to Thomas Gataker, 'where the wife maketh head against the husband; there is nothing but doing and undoing, and so all things go backward, and the whole house runneth to ruin'.[23] Not surprisingly, this double message caused some complications. Dod and Clever argued that a wife's subjection to her husband did not mean that she ceased to think, merely that she did so in the context of her duty toward him. Furthermore, 'she may in modest sort shew her mind; and a wise husband will not disdain to hear her advice, and follow it also, if it be good'.[24] Such vague formulations were troubling in a society which valued clear lines of authority.

This discomfort is evident in discussions of the extent of a husband's authority over his wife, and especially his ability to 'correct' her faults. All commentators were agreed that a husband should admonish his wife for her faults, but they did not agree on how far that discipline might extend. Some, like Clever and Dod, were ambiguous: a husband is 'never to lay violent hands upon' his wife, but is to correct her gently, with 'testimony of goodwill'; he should never be 'bitter, fierce, or cruel unto his wife', but should be her 'defender, instructor, teacher, and comfort'.[25] In the seventeenth-century context, 'correction' probably included physical punishment, but Dod and Clever are not explicit. William Whately argued at great length (and with great discomfort) that although a husband probably ought not beat his wife 'because it seemeth too imperious in him to do it, and too servile in her to suffer it', he might do so if 'she give just cause, after much bearing and forebearing, and trying all other ways, in case of utmost necessity, so that he exceed not measure'; she should not, however, be beaten for 'those weaknesses which are incident even

---

[22] Gouge, *Domesticall Duties*, p. 24.

[23] Thomas Gataker, *Marriage Duties Briefely couched togither* (London, 1620), p. 10; cf. Dod and Clever, *Godly Forme*, f. F3v.

[24] Dod and Clever, *Godly Forme* ff. F3v, O7.

[25] Dod and Clever, *Godly Forme*, ff. K8v, L3v, L4v, N4v–5.

to virtuous women'.[26] William Gouge, on the other hand, was firmly opposed to any physical punishment of a wife by a husband: they were so close that in beating his wife he would be beating himself. If a wife did need to be beaten, 'it is fitter for an husband to refer the matter to a public magistrate . . . and not to do it with his own hands'.[27] After this high-minded discussion, Gouge added that beating was also one of the less effective forms of correction available to husbands.

Most writers of domestic conduct books seem to have hoped that the difficulties would disappear with the definition of complementary relationships between husband and wife, based on conventional attributes of women and men. Edmund Tilney gave the husband absolute authority over the wife,

> The man being as he is, most apt for the sovereignty being in government, not only skill and experience to be required, but also capacity to comprehend, wisdom to understand, strength to execute, solicitude to prosecute, patience to suffer, means to sustain, and above all, a great courage to accomplish, all which are commonly in a man, but in a woman very rare.[28]

The acceptance of these conventional characteristics supported a sexual division of labour which (by and large) made the woman responsible for the internal affairs of the household, the man for the external. Tilney stressed the complementarity of these tasks:

> The office of the husband is to bring in necessaries: of the wife, well to keep them. The office of the husband is, to go abroad in matters of profit: of the wife, to tarry at home, and see all be well there. The office of the husband is, to provide money, of the wife, not wastefully to spend it. The office of the husband is, to deal, and bargain with all men, of the wife, to meddle or make with no man . . . The office of the husband is, to be Lord of all, of the wife, to give account

---

[26] William Whately, *A Bride-bush; or A Direction for Married Persons Plainely describing the duties common to both, and peculiar to each of them* (London, 1623), pp. 106–7.

[27] Gouge, *Domesticall Duties*, pp. 395–7.

[28] Tilney, *Flower of Friendshippe*, f. Ei.

of all, and finally I say, that the office of the husband is to maintain well his livelihood, and the office of the woman is, to govern well the household.[29]

The responsibilities of the husband (and his authority over his wife) were based on 'natural' differences between them; his duty to 'provide' for his wife and children was equally natural. This theory of complementary abilities and duties helped many writers of household manuals gloss over the contradictions between a wife's responsibility for the household and her subordination to her husband, but it did not completely resolve it.

The contradictory impulses are best seen by following the discussion of a wife's subordination through one work. William Gouge was the Puritan rector of Blackfriars in London. His popular household manual was the one chosen by Nehemiah Wallington when he sought guidance on running his household. He had delivered his *Of Domesticall Duties* as a series of sermons before their publication, and he dedicated the book to his parishioners; his discussion of the wife's position begins in the dedication. He remarks that 'when these Domestical Duties were first uttered out of the pulpit, much exception was taken against the application of a wives subjection to the restraining of her from disposing of the common goods of the family without, or against, her husband's consent'. He repeated the exceptions he had made to the restriction, but still felt obliged to explain and justify his position. Later in the dedication he commented,

When I came to deliver the husband duties, I showed, that he ought not to exact whatsoever his wife was bound unto (in case it were exacted by him) but that he ought to make her a joint governor of the family with himself, and refer the ordering of many things to her discretion, and with all honourable and kind respect to carry himself towards her . . . That which maketh a wives yoke heavy and hard, is an husband's abuse of his authority: and more pressing his wife's duty, than performing his own, which is directly contrary to the Apostle's rule . . . I so set down an husband's duties, as if he be wise and conscionable in observing them, his wife can

[29] Tilney, *Flower of Friendshippe*, f. Ciiiib (v); cf. Dod and Clever, *Godly Forme*, f. L4.

have no just cause to complain of her subjection . . . . This just Apology I have been forced to make, that I might not ever be judged (as some have censured me) *an hater of women*.[30]

Gouge's sermons had apparently occasioned a great deal of discussion about the subjection of women and the authority of men, and he found it necessary to defend his position.

The tension Gouge raised in the dedication recurs throughout the book. While the husband 'is as a king in his own house . . . the wife also ought to be able to be an help to him therein'. The respect a wife owed her husband was based on fear, but 'it is no slavish fear of her husband which ought to possess the heart of a wife'.[31] Gouge explains with care the criteria for selecting a spouse, and insists that spouses should be equal in 'Age, Estate, Condition, Piety'; age, however, was the least necessary, 'because he is an head, a governor, a protector of his wife'. On the other hand, 'if a man of great wealth be married to a poor woman, he will think to make her as his maid-servant, and expect that she should carry her self towards him as beseemeth not a yoke-fellow, and bed-fellow'.[32] Husbands ought to respect their wives, to appreciate their wives' talents and 'not to exact of their wives, whatsoever wives ought to yield unto if it be exacted'. Instead, they must think of what is most 'convenient, expedient, fit for their wives to do, yea, and what they are most willing to do before they be too peremptory in exacting it'.[33] These limits were necessary because 'the wife is by God's providence appointed a joint governor with the husband of the Family'.[34]

---

[30] Gouge, *Domesticall Duties*, pp. 3v, 4. Gouge may have been particularly sensitive on this point because of the contemporary debate on the nature of women: see Underdown, 'The taming of the scold', pp. 118–19 and Katherine Usher Henderson and Barbara F. McManus, *Half-humankind: contexts and texts of the controversy about women in England, 1540–1640* (Urbana and Chicago, Illinois, 1985); Seaver, *Wallington's World*, p. 79; the reaction of women is appropriate, as the household code in Ephesians was part of an attempt to control egalitarian impulses in early Christianity: Elisabeth Schüssler Fiorenza, *Bread Not Stone: the challenge of feminist biblical interpretation* (Boston, Massachusetts, 1984), pp. 70–9 passim.

[31] Gouge, *Domesticall Duties*, pp. 260, 270–1, 276–7.

[32] Gouge, *Domesticall Duties*, pp. 188–9.

[33] Gouge, *Domesticall Duties*, pp. 366–9, 370; this is the material Gouge referred to in his dedication.

[34] Gouge, *Domesticall Duties*, pp. 255–6.

Gouge recognized that his description of the position of the wife was unappealing, so he answered the hypothetical objection that, 'if the case be such betwixt man and wife, it is not good to marry'. His answer sustains his earlier ambivalence:

> This is no good inference; for all the seeming hardness of a wife's case is the lewdness of an husband, who abuseth his place and power: and not in that subjection which is required by God. For if an husband carry himself to his wife as God requireth, she will find her yoke to be easy, and her subjection a great benefit even unto herself.[35]

The idea that subjection, however limited, is a benefit to women assumes women's inferiority: life is easier when the husband rules. Neither wealth nor intelligence changed the expectations; since 'most women' were inferior, all were subject. One could not have too much uncertainty.[36]

Gouge's ambivalence reflects the difficulty of defining the rules of an unequal partnership. Other models of authority – parental and royal – downplayed the elements of partnership and gave clear dominance to the parent/king. Most of the writers of household manuals knew that something was different between husband and wife. There was a further problem: the household manual was by and large a 'Puritan' genre, and for Puritans the only absolute authority was God: before God all men – and women – were equal.[37] Within the household they were trying to define an unequal partnership between spiritual equals: in all relationships one had to be superior. Thomas Gataker put it thus:

> For the first, there can be no ordinary intercourse and commerce or conversing between person and person, but there must be a precedency on the one part, and a yielding of it on the other. Now where they be equal, there may be some question, some difficulty, whither shall have priority, and

[35] Gouge, *Domesticall Duties*, p. 343.

[36] Gouge, *Domesticall Duties*, p. 190; cf. Gataker, *Marriage Duties*, pp. 10–11.

[37] Powell, *English Domestic Relations*, p. 123; Keith Thomas, 'Women in the Civil War sects', in *Crisis in Europe, 1560–1660*, ed. Trevor Aston (London, 1965), pp. 317–40.

they take it commonly, as it falleth out or by turns. But where there is an apparent inequality, there is without question that the inferior is to yield to the superior . . . so we may well say here, that a man-kind woman or a masterly wife is even a monster in nature.[38]

The husband had to be the head, but to recognize the practical and spiritual importance of the wife; he could not have too much power.

The message of the household manuals on the surface supported public order. In practice it was not so simple. When the household is a godly commonwealth, then relations between households become the equivalent of foreign relations. The godly household could (and did) separate itself from other households to maintain its purity.[39] Clever and Dod insisted that 'the husband without any exception, is master over all the house, and hath more to do in his house with his own domestical affairs, than the magistrate'.[40] Household manuals assumed no conflict between their goals (and those of their readers) and those of the state. Yet the structure, definitions and ambiguities of household manuals meant that when conflicts emerged, especially in the 1640s, they could sustain various interpretations of the duties of subjects, wives and children. The link between household manuals and the political debate is found in the images of English society presented in works of social description, which purported to explain not how things ought to be in household or state, but how things were.

Works of social description take us from a world defined by scripture to one defined by law and custom. In doing so, they make explicit the transition from the family to the state, and form a bridge between household manuals and political controversy. Three of them, each selected from the large corpus of such works

---

[38] Gataker, *Marriage Duties*, pp. 8, 9–10; John Stuart Mill confronts this same problem in *The Subjection of Women*, and uses Gataker's argument to argue for equality: J.S. Mill and Harriet Taylor Mill, *Essays on Sex Equality*, ed. Alice Rossi (Chicago and London, 1970), pp. 168–9.

[39] See e.g. Wrightson and Levine, *Poverty and Piety*, pp. 154–66; Hill, *Society and Puritanism*, pp. 454–8, 465–70, 479–81.

[40] Dod and Clever, *Godly Forme*, f. L6v–L7.

to provide a different perspective, show how English life and society were perceived and understood. Sir Thomas Smith was an Elizabethan lawyer and diplomat, who wrote his *De Republica Anglorum* in the late 1570s; his perspective was chiefly legal and formal, but he also included observations on social practice. Thomas Platter was a German who travelled in England in 1599; he was chiefly interested in such things as the sights to be seen and the state of the roads, but he also recorded the habits and manners that struck him as odd. Finally, the Restoration courtier Edward Chamberlayne wrote *Angliae Notitia* in 1669, describing English society and recent changes in it.

None of these sources is without difficulty, and the relationship between what they say and the experience of English women and men in the sixteenth centuries is problematic. For instance, both Platter and Chamberlayne record the same proverb about England (England is a woman's paradise, a servant's prison, because their masters and mistresses are very severe, and a horse's hell or purgatory); Chamberlayne adds that servants' position had improved through the years. The proverbial status of the saying may diminish its usefulness as an indicator of conditions in the country.[41] Chamberlayne gives little evidence to support his contention that the condition of servants had improved in England, and Platter gives little to support his assertion of severity on the part of masters and mistresses. Chamberlayne explained that hirings were by the year, and that masters and mistresses had the duty to 'correct' their servants. Smith, while not citing the proverb, described the legal framework which may have given the impression of severity: by law all those between the ages of fifteen and forty-five who were unmarried and without estates of their own were required to be in service; such people could be forced into service, sent to gaol or punished as vagabonds. The law was enforced only sporadically, but it may have been used more often to compel unwilling young people to

[41] *Thomas Platter's Travels in England, 1599*, tr. Clare Williams (London, 1937), pp. 181–2; Edward Chamberlayne, *Angliae Notitia; or The Present State of England: Together with Divers Reflections upon the Antient State thereof*, 2nd edn (London, 1669), p. 461.

enter service.[42] Similarly, little is said about the condition of children in England, beyond Chamberlayne's remark that the complete testamentary freedom of fathers increased their authority over children.[43] Insofar as they discuss the discipline of children and servants, then, these works of social description confirm the broad authority of parents and mistresses and masters, but they fail to provide concrete descriptions of its use.

All three works offer a relatively full discussion of the position of women, particularly wives, in England. Sir Thomas Smith noted that while by law women were completely subject to their husbands,

> yet they be not kept so strait as in mew and with a guard as they be in Italy and Spain, but have almost as much liberty as in France, and they have for the most part all the charge of the house and household ... which is in deed the natural occupation, exercise, office, and part of a wife.[44]

Thomas Platter went even further in his assessment of the freedom of English women, who 'have far more liberty than in other lands, and know just how to make good use of it, for they often stroll out or drive by coach in very gorgeous clothes, and the men must put up with such ways, and may not punish them for it'.[45] The problem of independent wives was so great, according to Platter, that women often beat their husbands, and he described the ritual 'rough music' customarily provoked by such incidents. The situation does not appear to have changed after the Restoration; according to Chamberlayne, by law women did not even own their clothes, their husbands were responsible for their crimes and they

---

[42] Chamberlayne, *Angliae Notitia*, pp. 462–3; Thomas Smith, *De Republica Anglorum: a discourse on the commonwealth of England*, ed. L. Alston (Cambridge, 1906), pp. 138–9; C/S3/58A, 2 Wm. and Mary, Indictment of Robert and Thomas Spirling, Thomas, Mary and Hannah Wright of Winfarthing; PRO ASSI 16/18/4, Indictment of Elizabeth Wilder, Alice and Dorothy Woodcock, Elizabeth Moy, Anna Heylock, Margaret Jarey, Elizabeth Jenkinson and Cicely Bridges, spinsters of Cawston; Christopher Hill, *The World Turned Upside Down: radical ideas during the English Revolution* (New York, 1972), chapter 3 discusses the problem of masterless men; the statutory basis for the regulations is 5 Eliz. I cap. 4: Leonard, *Early History of English Poor Relief*, pp. 140–1, 178–9n.

[43] Chamberlayne, *Angliae Notitia*, pp. 458–9.

[44] Smith, *De Republica Anglorum*, pp. 126–7.

[45] *Thomas Platter's Travels in England*, pp. 181–2.

had no legal existence. But if their legal position was especially bad, 'their condition de facto is the best in the world'. Their husbands gave them precedence, and put upon their wives 'no drudgery or hardship'.[46] One need not take such allegations at face value to see that the dilemma about the extent of husbands' authority had been decided on some level in favour of women. The authority of husbands over their wives was not exercised as openly or as repressively as it apparently was elsewhere. At least in their public appearances, English women hardly appeared to be a 'subject race'.

When Thomas Platter decribed the rough music directed at families where the woman beat her husband, he noted that 'the nearest neighbour is placed on a cart and paraded through the whole town as a laughing-stock for the victim, as a punishment – he is informed – for not having come to his neighbour's assistance when his wife was beating him'.[47] Villages were, according to the Attorney General in 1608, 'the first societies after [the] propagation of families wherein people are united . . . in . . . the mutual comforts of neighbourhood and intercourse one with another'.[48] Sir Thomas Smith agreed that the village was the natural outgrowth of the family: grown children began separate households, building first a street, then a village, a city, a borough.[49] It is appropriate then, that the shaming of a disorderly family involved mocking not only that family, but the neighbours who suffered the disorder to occur. If families were not orderly, neighbours – an 'extended family' – were to impose order. Order was sustained in both local and national communities by the social hierarchies which were superimposed on the network of families. These social hierarchies are predictable: Chamberlayne and Smith both began their description of the social hierarchy with the nobility, followed by the different ranks of gentlemen, then yeomen and tradesmen, followed at the end by 'the feet of the body politic' or 'men which do not rule' – cottagers and day-labourers.[50]

[46] Chamberlayne, *Angliae Notitia*, pp. 449–53, esp. 452–3; *Thomas Platter's Travels in England*, p. 182.

[47] *Thomas Platter's Travels in England*, p. 182.

[48] Quoted in Clive Holmes, *Seventeenth-century Lincolnshire*, vol. VII of *History of Lincolnshire*, ed. Maurice Barley, (Lincoln, 1980), p. 29.

[49] Smith, *De Republica Anglorum*, pp. 23–4.

[50] Smith, *De Republica Anglorum*, pp. 31–47 passim, esp. 46–7; Chamberlayne, *Angliae Notitia*, chapters XVIII and XIX passim, esp. p. 445; husbandmen fell between the two lower categories – if they held local office, it was one of the least important ones.

For our purposes, the most important are the yeomen and tradesmen. They did the routine work of local government, and were thus both agents and helpers of the gentry. They staffed (along with the minor gentry) the grand juries which made indictments at quarter sessions and assizes, they formed the hundred juries which listed local grievances and they (or their social inferiors) acted as constables in running down local offenders and bringing them before the justices of the peace. As churchwardens and overseers of the poor they not only controlled parish relief, but often oversaw property belonging to a village or town. Although low on the lists made by Smith and Chamberlayne – and most historians have followed them in dividing the upper ranks of English society more finely than the lower – the yeomen were important and respected members of their communities, necessary adjuncts to the gentry in the maintenance of order.[51]

There are two characteristics of yeomen that deserve comment. First, at least in the late sixteenth century it was assumed that yeomen not only had sufficient estates, but that they were married and had children: this gave the yeoman, according to Smith, 'some authority among his neighbours'.[52] The link between family position and social position was thus explicit. Second, the position of yeomen was ambiguous. Yeomen were theoretically inferior to the nobility and gentry, but both Smith and Chamberlayne stress that the authority of the latter was weaker in practice than in theory. Rather like wives, yeomen were too important to local order to be treated roughly. For example, Smith acknowledged that the legal process of 'attainting' a jury (when one party thought the jury verdict unfair) was rarely used. The attaint involved a jury of twenty-four gentlemen hearing evidence against the judges and the original jury of twelve yeomen. However, 'the gentlemen will not meet to slander and deface the honest yeomen their neighbours: so that of a long time, they had rather pay a mean fine than to appear and make the inquest. And in the mean time they will

[51] Smith, De Republica Anglorum, pp. 42–5; Chamberlayne, Angliae Notitia, p. 442.

[52] Smith, De Republica Anglorum, p. 45; cf. Thomas Fuller, The Holy State and the Profane State, ed. Maximilian Graff Walter (2 vols, New York, 1938), vol. II, p. 212: 'married men, especially if having posterity, are the deeper sharers in that state wherein they live, which engageth their affections to greater loyalty.'

intreat so much as in them lyeth the parties to come to some composition and agreement'.[53]

For Smith, the reluctance of the gentry to criticize their yeomen neighbours had a constructive ending: the mediation of a dispute by the local gentry. In his view, government placed responsibilities on the governors as much as on the governed. His awareness of the dependence of the gentry on yeomen, and of the links between them, was not unusual. During his time and into the early Stuart period, many of those concerned with order acknowledged this dependence, and even worried that the gentry were not doing their part. In the early seventeenth century there was a heated pamphlet debate about styles of gentility: in one pamphlet, a dialogue between 'Cloth-breeches' and 'Velvet-breeches', Cloth-breeches successfully defended his way of life, especially his familiarity with local yeomen and tradesmen, against Velvet-breeches' wealth, court connections and fine clothes. A relationship with local yeomen was one of the political and social obligations of the gentry – to the extent that on a number of occasions James I ordered all gentry to leave London and return to their estates, there to keep hospitality for their neighbours.[54]

Chamberlayne, not surprisingly for one with his court connections, took the position of Velvet-breeches in the pamphlet. In 1599 Thomas Platter had been impressed by the prosperity of the English, but sixty years later Chamberlayne argued that this prosperity had dire consequences:

The *Nobility* and chief Gentry of England have been even by Strangers compared to the finest Flower, but the lower sort of common People to the coarsest bran; the innate good nature, joined with the liberal education and converse with Strangers in foreign Countries, render those exceeding civil; whereas the wealth, insolence, and pride of these, and the rare

---

[53] Smith, *De Republica Anglorum*, p. 111.

[54] Felicity Heal, 'The idea of hospitality in early modern England', in *Past and Present*, 102 (1984), pp. 66–93; Karl Westhauser, 'The English gentleman: changing definitions and perceptions, 1560–1630', Cornell University Independent Study, 1983: I am grateful to Mr Westhauser for drawing my attention to these debates; *Stuart Royal Proclamations*, vol. I: *Royal Proclamations of King James I, 1603–25*, ed. James F. Larkin and Paul L. Hughes (Oxford, 1973), Proclamations 143 (1614) and 235 (1622); Robert Greene, *A Quip for an upstart courtier: Or A Quaint Dispute betweene Velvet-breeches and Cloth-breeches. Wherein is plainely set downe the disorders in all Estates and Trades* (London, 1635).

converse with Strangers, have rendered them so distasteful, not only to the few Strangers who frequent England, but even to their own Gentry, that they could sometimes wish that either the Country were less plentiful, or that the Impositions were heavier; for by reason of the great abundance of Flesh and Fish, Corn, Leather, wool, &c, which the Soils of its own bounty, with little labour doth produce, the *Yeomanry* at their ease and almost forgetting labour, grow rich, and thereby so proud, insolent and careless, that they neither give that humble respect and awful reverence which in other kingdoms is usually given to *Nobility, Gentry*, and *Clergy*, nor are they so *industrious* or so skillful in Manufactures as some of our Neighbour Nations.[55]

Chamberlayne has turned the pre-occupation with the obligations of the gentry to the people into criticism of the people for not honouring the gentry sufficiently; he has rejected the reciprocity of the relationship. He sees the importance of the yeomen, and condemns it; his vision of authority as providing power without any limitations was a problematic one in seventeenth-century England, as the Civil War and Revolution demonstrated. More importantly, Chamberlayne appears to be aware that the model he would prefer does not exist in England. Thus, though he rejects a reciprocal relationship in theory, in the course of doing so he has confirmed its dominance in seventeenth-century English society. Reciprocity was so embedded in society that Chamberlayne had to wish the country less wealthy or more taxed in order to get rid of it!

Smith, Platter and Chamberlayne help us to place the family into society. The autonomy of individual families was limited by social obligation and the power of law. Families were not all equal, and the emphasis of the household manuals on reverence for superiors was carried out of the household and applied to social as well as domestic superiors; so was the insistence on the reciprocal duties of superiors to those they governed. Just as hierarchy disciplined families, so the social hierarchy maintained order in village, county

---

[55] Chamberlayne, *Angliae Notitia*, pp. 60–1; *Thomas Platter's Travels in England*, p. 184; cf. John Swan, *Redde Debitum, or, a Discourse in defense of three chiefe Fatherhoods* (London, 1640), pp. 32–3.

and nation. But as in the family, the lines of authority were never as clearly drawn as commentators would have wished. The same problem emerged in the state as well.

> So when the common wealth is evil governed by an evil ruler and unjust . . . if the laws be made, as most like they be always to maintain that estate: the question remaineth whether the obedience of them be just, and the disobedience wrong: the profit and conservation of that estate right and justice, or the dissolution: and whether a good and upright man, and lover of his country ought to maintain and obey them or seek by all means to abolish them?[56]

Sir Thomas Smith raised the question which lay at the centre of political debate in seventeenth-century England: what remedy, if any, had the citizen against an evil and immoral government? For Smith the question was academic, but fifty years later it was not. The political debate turned on conceptions of authority, which frequently depended on relations within the family. This is not surprising: in insisting that God was our only true Father, Matthew Griffith suggested that 'all others are our Fathers but as they represent unto us the image of God's *paternity*'. The others were, of course, parents, magistrates, ministers and old men.[57]

It is fortunately not necessary for our purposes to survey the entire history of political thought in this period.[58] Instead, we will examine the use of familial images in discussions of political authority. The family was central to one of the major strands of political thought in the period, patriarchalism. But familial language was not only used by believers in the patriarchally based theory of divine-right monarchy. Richard Hooker, who held a consensual theory of the origin of the state, used paternal authority

---

[56] Smith, *De Republica Anglorum*, p. 13.

[57] Griffith, *Bethel*, p. 45.

[58] Useful surveys include Schochet, *Patriarchalism*; J.P. Somerville, *Politics and Ideology in England, 1603–1640* (London, 1986); J.W. Allen, *English Political Thought 1603–1660*, vol. I: *1603–44* (London, 1938); Perez Zagorin, *A History of Political Thought in the English Revolution* (London, 1954); J.G.A. Pocock, *The Ancient Constitution and the Feudal Law: a study in English historical thought in the seventeenth century* (Cambridge, 1957) and *The Machiavellian Moment: Florentine political thought and the Atlantic Republican tradition* (Princeton, New Jersey, 1975), esp. part III; and Quentin Skinner, *The Foundations of Modern Political Thought*, vol. II (Cambridge, 1978).

to explain why consent was necessary: although fathers had supreme power within their own families, there was no one who naturally had that kind of power over all the fathers of families, 'but by consent of men, or immediate appointment of God'. Furthermore, the resemblance of a king's power to that of a father provided the basis for calling kings 'fathers' of their people.[59] The familial image even came into the Putney Debates in 1647: when Henry Ireton invoked the Fifth Commandment to oppose the extension of the franchise, Colonel Rainborough responded that 'the great dispute is, who is a right father and a right mother?'[60] Whatever their vision of the origin or nature of government, the analogy between family and state remained a basic tool for most writers of political theory in the seventeenth century. John Locke would not have worked so hard to undermine it had it not been so important.

The most extended use of the family in political thought was that employed by the patriarchal thinkers. Patriarchal political theory had a long history, and as it developed in the seventeenth century into a justification of divine-right absolutism, its assumptions about the family fitted well with the prescriptions of the writers of household manuals. Two examples of the genre will suffice.[61] In 1615, James I was so impressed by Richard Mocket's *God and the King*, that he ordered it purchased by every householder, and studied in all schools and universities. Mocket began with the justification of royal authority by means of the Fifth Commandment arguing, 'that there is a stronger and higher bond of Duty between Children and the Father of their Country, than the Fathers of Private Families'.[62] He went on, at great length, to show that the King received his authority from God, was answerable to no one but God and that the bond of obedience could not be broken. The proof of these assertions came from Biblical and (where possible) historical example. The only comfort Mocket offered readers was that if the King sought to destroy the Church,

---

[59] Richard Hooker, *Of the Laws of Ecclesiastical Polity*, ed. Christopher Morris, MA (2 vols, London, 1907), vol. I, p. 191 (Book I, x(4)).

[60] *Puritanism and Liberty, Being the Army Debates (1647–9) from the Clarke Manuscripts*, ed. A.S.P. Woodhouse (London, 1951), pp. 60–1.

[61] See Schochet, *Patriarchalism*, for a fuller discussion.

[62] [Richard Mocket], *God and the King: or A Dialogue shewing that our soveraign Lord King Iames, being immediate under God within his DOMINIONS, Doth rightfully claime whatsoever is required by the Oath of Allegiance* (London, 1615), pp. 1–2.

God would not let him succeed, and he would be suitably punished in heaven. A similar comfort was offered to those suffering under tyrants. In either case, the people must repent of the sins that brought their church or their country into such danger. Mocket assumed that there was no such thing as individual freedom: just as all are born subject to parents, all are born into subjection to God and the King.[63]

Mocket directed his proof of the impossibility of rebellion at Catholics; in the 1630s and 1640s, opposition to royal policies came from Protestant gentry. It was in this context, some time before 1642, that Sir Robert Filmer wrote his defence of royal power, *Patriarcha, or the Natural Power of Kings*, in which he set out to deny the premise that 'Mankind is naturally endowed and born with freedom from all subjection, and at liberty to choose what form of government it please'.[64] To do this, Filmer, like Mocket, used the 'natural' subjection of children to parents. He also argued that the power of the King was directly derived from the power of Adam over his descendants. Just as we cannot choose our fathers, so we cannot choose our kings; just as children have no remedy against their parents, so subjects have none against the King. No human law can limit the power of a king, and because he is created by God, no prior contract can limit his power. Law exists not to control the King, but to control the people. Kingly power accrues not only to those who inherit a throne; but also to those who obtain it through election or usurpation: God's support, shown by success, gives a king the power of a father. Finally, Filmer showed that Parliament was created to give advice to the King, that it existed at the pleasure of the King and that laws were made by the King at the request of Parliament, not by Parliament itself. Parliament was nothing without the King.

Filmer's history, at least as regards the power of Parliament, is certainly more 'accurate' than that of parliamentarian controversialists. His image of familial relations is less realistic, however, and it certainly does not represent the only use of familial images in the political controversy of the 1640s.

---

[63] [Mocket], *God and the King*, p. 81.
[64] Robert Filmer, *Patriarcha and Other Political Works*, ed. Peter Laslett (Oxford, 1949), p. 53, and for date, p. 3; James Daly, *Sir Robert Filmer and English Political Thought* (Toronto, 1979), esp. chapter 6, has stressed the ways in which Filmer's equation of royal and paternal authority diverged from other royalists (p. 71n.) and carried implications which they rejected; J.P. Somerville has suggested that many of Filmer's ideas derive from the earlier anti-Catholic controversy: 'From Suarez to Filmer: a Reappraisal', *Historical Journal*, 25:3 (1982), pp. 525–40.

Mocket and Filmer had taken the easy way out. The authority of the father over his children was clear to all, and if few would have agreed with Filmer that it extended into adulthood, the image had its power. However, the use of the relationship between husband and wife in discussions of authority could present royalists with greater problems. The pamphlet debates of the 1640s raised many questions about marriage: What was the nature of marriage? Was it ever terminable? Under what conditions? By whom? What rights had a wife in marriage? and many others. If the royalists had the best of the argument when dealing with the history of Parliament, the parliamentarians were on firmer ground when dealing with familial relations.[65]

This political discussion must be placed in the context of family law. Divorce was not permitted by the Church of England. An annulment was available in cases of impotence or other impediments (like a prior marriage), but in ordinary cases of marital breakdown – marked by adultery, violence or desertion – the church courts offered only a separation *a menso et thoro*. Though re-marriage after a separation was officially impossible, the only ecclesiastical penalty was the forfeit of a bond, which became a fine on those who offended; in 1604 bigamy became a felony in the criminal law. In theory, both parties had equal rights to separation; in practice, men obtained separations from their wives on more limited grounds that women obtained them from their husbands. Attempts to legalize divorce in the mid-sixteenth century had ended with the defeat of the general reform of the canon law then proposed.[66]

The relationship between husband and wife was most commonly used in discussions of contract theories of the state. Contract theory was congenial to those with the legal training of the English gentry, royalist and parliamentarian alike; it also had

---

[65] Earlier in the seventeenth century, marriage had also been used as a model in 'designation theory' to confirm royal power: a husband, it was argued, was chosen by the wife but derived his authority not from her consent to it, but from his status as a husband: Somerville, *Politics and Ideology*, p. 25.

[66] George Elliot Howard, *A History of Matrimonial Institutions, Chiefly in England and the United States* (3 vols, Chicago and London, 1904), vol. II, pp. 47–92 passim, esp. pp. 77–9; Parliament tried to clarify the position in 'An Acte to restrayne all persons from Marriage until their former Wyves and former Husbandes be deade', 1 James I cap. 11, which made bigamy a felony; for the Reformation debate on divorce, see Powell, *English Domestic Relations*, chapter III.

definite advantages over patriarchal theory for parliamentarians. Marriage was an accessible model for contract theorists. The political questions were obvious, if problematic: If there was an original contract between King and people, what were its terms? Under what conditions could it be broken, and by whom? The parliamentarian Henry Parker reminded his readers that in cases of marital breakdown the ecclesiastical courts protected both partners, and argued that the wife could be almost equal to her husband. He continued, 'And if men, for whose sake women were created, shall not lay hold upon the divine right of wedlock, to the disadvantage of women: much less shall Princes, who were created for the people's sake, challenge any thing, from the sanctity of their offices, that may derogate from the people?'[67] Parker stressed the lack of arbitrary or unlimited power in marriage, and by implication, the state. Parker also gave more independence to children than did royalist writers: the Fifth Commandment, he argued, did not give parents the right to order their children's marriages, or to discipline them after they were married; children grew up to become independent adults. His vision was transferred to government: 'And who now hath any competent share of reason, can suppose, that if God and nature have been so careful to provide for liberty in Families, and in particulars; that Man would introduce, or ought to endure slavery, when it is introduced upon whole States and Generalities?'[68] Parker assumed that princes had not existed from creation, but had been chosen by the people; the prince owed service to the people more than the people owed obedience to the prince.

There were two arguments that could be used against Parker. First, because monarchy was instituted by God, princes were owed unlimited allegiance, and second, the freedom Parker found in the family did not exist. Thus John Swan, in his pamphlet *Redde Debitum, or a Discourse in defense of three chief Fatherhoods . . . written chiefly in confutation of all disobedient and factious kind of People, who are enemies both to the Church, and State*, used the Fifth Commandment parallels to establish both civil and ecclesiastical hierarchy. The King, as God's anointed, could only be

---

[67] Henry Parker, *Jus Populi, Or a Discourse wherein clear satisfaction is given, as well concerning the Right of Subjects, as the Right of Princes. Shewing how both are consistent, and where they border one upon the other* (London, 1644) TT E.12 (25), pp. 4–5, 32.

[68] Parker, *Jus Populi*, pp. 32, 42; this image of the family is far closer to that of the household manuals than that of royalist thinkers.

questioned by God: like Mocket, Swan believed that the only remedy for those troubled by an unjust king was prayer. Swan was not really interested in the family, and he used the familial metaphor in a very different way from Parker: the inclusion of the mother as an object of honour and blessing with the father meant 'that not the meanest officer, which the King . . . shall constitute, may be cursed or despised'.[69] For Swan, the power of the father was unchallengeable; he is remarkable only because, unlike Filmer, he admitted that the mother was mentioned in the Fifth Commandment, and integrated her presence into his argument.

The images used in the pamphlet war became confused; royalist writers in particular used both paternal and spousal images to defend their argument, assuming that paternal and husbandly authority was the same. In Dudley Digges' *The Unlawfulnesse of Subjects taking up Armes against their Soveraigne*, the first image used was that of the father:

> For the King is *Pater Patria*, a common Father to all without a metaphor: what ever power Fathers have *over* and consequently whatsoever honour as an effect of this power, was due to them *from* their children, he hath right to challenge the same of all . . . . We can no more lawfully disrespect, give law to, resist upon hard usage, or say he is less honourable than all we, then children by agreement may dispense with their duty to their parents.[70]

Digges then merged the images:

> If a Father promise any thing to his children, they have a full right to his performance; but in case he prove dishonest, he doth not thereby lose his right to govern them, nor are they excused from their duty of honour and obedience: So there is a contract between Husband and Wife, the violation of which on the man's part doth not bereave him of his dominion over the woman. . . . Fathers must not provoke their children to

[69] Swan, *Redde Debitum*, pp. 13, 20–7 passim: Swan discusses the family for only eight pages in his 240-page book.
[70] Dudley Digges, *The Unlawfulnesse of Subjects taking up Armes against their Soveraigne, in what case soever, Together with an Answer to all Objections scattered in their severall Books* (Oxford, 1643), TT E. 29(1), p. 61.

wrath: but bring them up in the nurture and admonition of the Lord (Ephes. 6:4). Husbands should give honour to their wives as unto the weaker vessels (1 Peter 3:7). Suppose some fathers prove forward, some husbands unkind, yet cannot their faults dispense with the duty of children and wives. The king . . . is both husband and father.[71]

He finally turned to marriage alone:

The consent of the woman makes such a man her husband, so the consent of the people is now necessary to the making of Kings (for conquest is but a kind of ravishing, which many times prepares the way to a wedding . . .) . . . As in marriage so: in monarchy there are two parties in the contract; though without the mutual agreement there could be no covenant, yet after it is once made the dissent of the inferior party, let it be not upon fancied, but real discontents, cannot dissolve the compact. Consent therefore joined man and wife, King and people, but divine ordinance continues this union; marriages and government both are ratified in heaven . . . . It is very observable though it was permitted to the man in some cases, to give a bill of divorce, yet this license was never allowed to women; so fathers might abdicate their children, not they their fathers, women cannot unmarry, nor the people unsubject themselves.[72]

The family supported Digges' image of monarchy, but the family he described represents theory untroubled by experience. All wives had some rights against their husbands; women of the aristocracy in particular were increasingly protected by settlements defended in Chancery.[73] As we have seen, wives and children had different rights and responsibilities within the family. Their independence may have been limited, but they were not slaves.

[71] Digges, *Unlawfulnesse*, pp. 112–13.

[72] Digges, *Unlawfulnesse*, pp. 113–14.

[73] Given his assumptions, it is not surprising that Digges was unmarried. See below, chapter 3; Stone, *Family, Sex and Marriage*, pp. 330–1, though requirements for the purchase of land may not have been as common as he suggests: Randolph Trumbach, *The Rise of the Egalitarian Family: aristocratic kinship and domestic relations in eighteenth century England* (New York, 1978), pp. 81–3, and Lloyd Bonfield, *Marriage Settlements 1601–1740: the adoption of the strict settlement* (Cambridge, 1983), pp. 99–100; Eileen Spring, 'Law and the theory of the affective family', *Albion*, 16 (1984), pp. 1–20, esp. pp. 8–10.

The actual experience of women contradicted the assumptions of writers like Digges about their rights in marriage. Women did not lack protection: most petitions for separation came from wives; women could (and did) turn to neighbours for protection from violent husbands, and could also have their husbands bound to keep the peace against them. For the sake of their argument, royalist thinkers had to re-write the experience of women. They could then assert that as women had no right to divorce their husbands, subjects could not divorce their King.[74] It is in this political context that Milton defended divorce, picking up a line of argument that had not been addressed for a century. Milton's personal interest in divorce was linked to critical questions in the debates in which he was already engaged.[75] Politics made the nature of marriage a subject of controversy.

The discussions of the state and marriage in royalist and parliamentarian pamphlets had a broad social impact. These learned treatises, full as they were of scriptural and historical references, were not only part of a debate within the elite. During the Civil War many people of all classes became political actors. The breakdown of censorship allowed almost anyone to express their views on the subjects of the day. Literacy was sufficiently widespread to allow many people access to these views, especially as the shorter pamphlets could be read aloud. Once the war broke out, there was no way to keep the conflict within the elite.[76] But funny things happened to the metaphors and analogies of the elite on their way to the people, and some of the rhetoric received a rapid grounding in reality. This process, and the general acceptance of familial language to discuss politics, can be seen in the visions of Elizabeth Poole.

Elizabeth Poole was a widow who testified before the Council of the Army twice, in December 1648 and January 1649. Little is

[74] I.e. H[enry] Ferne, *Conscience Satisfied. That there is no warrant for the Armes now taken up by Subjects. By way of reply unto Severall Answers made to a Treatise formerly published for the Resolving of Conscience upon the Case* (Oxford, 1643), TT E. 97(7), p. 70. See below, chapter 4, for practice in domestic breakdown cases.

[75] Shanley, 'Marriage contract and social contract'; Powell, *English Domestic Relations*, pp. 92–100, appendix B; many Puritan writers of household manuals had a view of divorce more flexible than that of the church courts; Christopher Hill, *Milton and the English Revolution* (London and New York, 1978), pp. 121–35.

[76] Hill, *The World Turned Upside Down*, is the classic study of this involvement; David Cressy, *Literacy and the Social Order: reading and writing in Tudor and Stuart England* (Cambridge, 1980), pp. 1–19 passim, chapters 4–6; Underdown, *Revel, Riot and Rebellion*, looks at the roots of that involvement.

known about her; she had been part of a gathered church and thrown out, and she was dependent on regular work for her survival.[77] In her testimony she recounted a dream, the import of which was that the army ought *not* to behead the King. She acknowledged that the army held kingly power. However,

> the King is your Father and husband, which you were and are to obey in the Lord, and no other way, for when he forgot his subordination to divine Fatherhood and headship, thinking he had begotten you a generation to his own pleasure, and taking you a wife for his own lusts, thereby is the yoke taken from your necks . . . . You have all that you have and are, and although he would not be your father and husband, Subordinate, but Absolute, yet know that you are for the Lord's sake to honour his person . . . . And although this bond is broken on his part; You never heard that a wife might put away her husband, as he is the head of her body . . . And accordingly you may hold the hands of your husband, that he pierce not your bowels with a knife or sword to take your life. Neither may you take his . . .'[78]

Dudley Digges would have been horrified. Poole accepted the political implications of family relations, but gave them substance from her experience. She was more comfortable with images of marriage than of parenthood. And while she recognized the honour due a husband, it was limited: a wife did not give up all rights upon marriage. Poole accepted the ability of the Army to hold power, but within the context of the 'marriage' between King and state they could not execute him. Her language gives a hint of the way in which the political debate was heard by uneducated people. Familial language allowed them to use their own personal experience to define the proper relations between ruler and ruled. Their interpretations may have been less clear and were certainly less abstract than those of other theorists, but their very presence reveals the political significance of the familial analogies. They

[77] *Puritanism and Liberty*, ed. Woodhouse, pp. 469–71; Elizabeth Poole, *An Alarum of War, Given to the Army and to their High Court of Justice (so called) revealed by the will of God in a Vision to E. Poole* (London, 1649), TT E. 555(23), pp. 7–8: I am grateful to Rachel Weil for drawing my attention to this pamplet.
[78] Poole, *Alarum*, pp. 3, 4, 5–6.

offered meanings to authority which could be based as much on popular experience as theoretical descriptions, and thus provided an avenue by which everyone could understand politics.

Elizabeth Poole raised again that vexed question from the household manuals: What was the authority of a husband over his wife? The debate among the contract theorists gave the answer implications not just for 'private' familial relations, but also for political action. Relations between parents (especially fathers) and children also had political implications. The royalists may have overstated the extent of a wife's subordination to her husband, but the fuzziness of the household manuals on the subject offered little assistance. As long as the analogy between the family and the state was accepted, and as long as the family was seen as a natural institution, resistance to royal authority was difficult to justify. At the same time, familial language could never support unrestricted power as clearly as royalists would wish. The implications of familial language in political discourse in the long run suited neither side.

Criticism of the familial analogy had existed in the early seventeenth century, especially, though not exclusively, among Catholic thinkers. The impulse to escape the analogy, either because of its limits or because of its absolutist implications, gained momentum in the second half of the century. In the *Leviathan*, Thomas Hobbes argued that not only the power of the King, but also that of the father was based on contract, but that within the family the mother actually had more real power over children than did the father. Having recognized this problem, Hobbes never addressed the relation between husband and wife, but instead explained how men formed the commonwealth. He came close to saying that the family is not a natural institution. While he recognized and pointed out some of the problems arising from the use of familial language, in the end he failed to resolve them.[79]

Familial language remained an important part of political discourse after the Restoration. Charles II's government sought to turn the clock back when it ordered the re-publication of Mocket in 1662. Patriarchalism remained a commonplace, though theoretical

[79] For earlier arguments against familial analogies, see Somerville, *Politics and Ideology*, pp. 61–2; Thomas Hobbes, *Leviathan*, chapter 20 passim.

debate was muted until the Exclusion Crisis of 1679–81 opened deep divisions within the political nation. The Exclusion Crisis occasioned a heated debate about royal power, inheritance and the location of sovereignty. *Patriarcha* was first published in 1680, in a complete edition of Filmer's works, and three other editions were published by 1685. *Patriarcha*'s defence of unfettered sovereignty received attention from some of the most important supporters of Exclusion. James Tyrrell published an attack, *Patriarcha non Monarcha*, in 1681, and Algernon Sidney's *Discourses Concerning Government* (themselves evidence of treason, according to Judge Jeffreys at Sidney's trial) were a detailed refutation of Filmer. Sidney's trial gave *Patriarcha* the status of official doctrine on royal power, and Sidney apparently saw Filmer as representative of everything he disagreed with. In *The Very Copy of a Paper deliver'd to the Sheriffs, upon the Scaffold on Tower Hill*, Sidney claimed that he was being executed for his attack on Filmer, and he repeated the main points he had made in the (yet unpublished) *Discourses*.[80]

It was during this period of political ferment that John Locke wrote his *Two Treatises on Civil Government*, which sought to establish new ways of thinking about the state. The *First Treatise* was a direct attack on Filmer, and Locke gleefully criticized Filmer's arguments, using scripture, history and logic. He denied that history was a guide to what ought to be, and used a combination of wit and scholarship to undermine Filmer's assumptions. In the *Second Treatise*, he attacked the conventional assumptions of his day in two ways. He asserted that 'the power of a magistrate over a subject may be distinguished from that of a father over his children, a master over his servants, a husband over his wife, and a lord over his slave';[81] thus he denied the usefulness of the familial analogy for understanding the nature of political authority. For those who refused to abandon the familial analogy, Locke offered a radical re-definition of the nature and basis of

---

[80] In general, see Schochet, *Patriarchalism*, chapters X, XI; Shanley, 'Marriage contract and social contract', pp. 85–7; Filmer, *Patriarcha*, ed. Laslett, pp. 33–43 passim, pp. 47–8; Daly, *Sir Robert Filmer*, pp. 9–11; *CSPD 1661–2*, p. 583; Blair Worden, 'The Commonwealth kidney of Algernon Sidney', *Journal of British Studies*, 24 (1985), pp. 1–40.

[81] John Locke, *Two Treatises on Civil Government*, ed. Peter Laslett (Cambridge, 1960), Second Treatise, pp. 286, and for date, pp. 45–66; for the timing of publication, see Charles Tarlton, ' "The rulers now on earth": Locke's *Two Treatises* and the revolution of 1688', *Historical Journal*, 28 (1985), pp. 279–98.

familial authority: marriage was a voluntary contract, of which both the terms and the duration were negotiable as in any other contract; and *parental* power (*not* paternal) was absolute in infancy, and thereafter diminished as children gained independence; finally, the honour due to parents was based not on the role of the parents in begetting their children, but their role in nourishing and educating them: an implicit contract.[82] If one took Locke on his own terms, there would be no way that familial analogies could support divine-right absolutism.

While Locke's conception of the state was in some ways dominant in the eighteenth century, his conception of the family was less popular.[83] Tory writers like Bolingbroke continued to use the family as the first political society, and fathers as the first magistrates. But Bolingbroke did not return to Filmer's notion of 'royal fatherhood', and made it clear that when natural societies (families) joined together to form civil societies, the King whom they chose was *not* a father.[84]

In the eighteenth century, the family, and the nature of relationships within it, was no longer a central issue in political debate. This partly reflects the consensus in favour of 1688 which remained in spite of party and factional strife: the elite was now at least generally in accord about the nature and aims of government. The social position of the gentry was more secure as well. While hierarchy and obedience formed the basis of seventeenth-century political thought, law played a greater role in that of the eighteenth century. Hierarchy was assumed; law could take care of the rest.[85]

---

[82] Locke, *Two Treatises*, pp. 325–34 passim; Shanley, 'Marriage contract and social contract'; in spite of his attack on the family as a political institution, Locke had *men* joining together to form civil society.

[83] Hilda Smith, *Reason's Disciples: seventeenth century English feminists* (Urbana, Illinois, 1982) shows that feminists did not support Locke, whose individualism undermined the informal power that many upper-class women had.

[84] Isaac Kramnick, *Bolingbroke and His Circle: the politics of Nostalgia in the age of Walpole* (Cambridge, Massachusetts, 1968), pp. 90–100 passim; Henry St John, Viscount Bolingbroke, *Letters on the Spirit of Patriotism and on the Idea of a Patriot King*, ed. A. Hassall (Oxford, 1917): in *The Idea* he does refer to the King as a father, but without ever developing the analogy, and in his view a good king rules under law: see e.g. pp. 74, 92, 102, 106, 115.

[85] For law as ideology in eighteenth-century England see E.P. Thompson, *Whigs and Hunters: the origins of the Black Act* (New York, 1975), pp. 258–66; Douglas Hay, 'Property, authority, and the criminal law', *Albion's Fatal Tree: crime and society in eighteenth century England*, ed. Douglas Hay et al. (New York, 1975), pp. 17–63.

Writers of both household manuals and of political tracts were convinced that the family was an institution of public significance, the basis of order in church and state. But much of the writing on politics ignored the facts of which writers of household manuals were uncomfortably aware: there were a series of relationships in the family, in which authority was defined in different ways, and that authority was not always clear-cut. Political theorists believed they were dealing with natural and immutable relations; writers of household manuals knew they were dealing with social and mutable ones. The family failed to provide as secure a basis for the state as political theorists hoped, but it provided the appearance of one. Familial language did not merely, as the theorists had hoped, give the political and social order the sanction of God and nature; it also provided an accessible model of the state and the social order which was used by villagers in their attempts to impose order on their communities. It is now time to turn from the theories of clergymen and politicians to the actual social relations of English villages: How in practice did families and villages work?

3

Families, Property and Family Economies

The ideological constructs of household manuals defined appropriate relationships within families in early modern England. But the specific social and economic circumstances of a particular family, and the regional economy in which they participated, provided the immediate context. Furthermore, at any given moment, a family was shaped by its own position in the course of development followed by families over the period of their existence. Couples married, children were born and as the children came of age and themselves married, the family shrank again to the earlier structure of husband and wife, if both still lived. An understanding of this process and its social implications is central to comprehending the place of the family in the social order of early modern England. We must therefore examine families as institutions: how they were formed, how they survived and how they dissolved. We must then review the process for regional variations, differences between social groups and different roles and experiences of women and men throughout the course of a family's existence. In this chapter we will focus on the family as an economic institution – as the means by which property and status were transmitted from one generation to the next; in the next we will examine the family as the foundation of all social relationships and discipline.

The families described by the household manuals were independent, property-holding households. Few writers who described early modern families had much to say about the many households which were not independent, and even not property-holding. Such households did not – at least for the theorists – exist. Because of the dearth of direct evidence on such households, this chapter will focus on property-holding households, although it will illuminate the experience of the poor and propertyless as much as possible.

The advice manuals assumed that the family was a productive as well as reproductive unit; and until at least the middle of the eighteenth century, most production – agricultural and industrial – took place in family settings. The family in this sense – the sense most familiar to early modern English women and men – included not just a married couple with children, but also servants, apprentices and sometimes even day labourers. One of the aspects of English society most frequently commented on by foreigners was the practice whereby children were sent away from home between the ages of ten and fourteen to work in the homes of others, to be disciplined and to learn a trade. In the sixteenth century, the practice still extended into the upper reaches of the gentry and aristocracy, although it was on the wane; it remained the practice among lesser gentry, tradesmen and yeomen – as well as their poorer neighbours – at least through the seventeenth century. It is this household whose economy we will examine.[1]

The household manuals described the family economy and sexual division of labour in schematic terms. Some authors divided the roles of husbands and wives into getting and spending (clearly a more urban conception), but others saw the division as a spatial one of outside (men) and inside (women). Writers on farming and husbandry gave more detail; women were responsible for the house, the dairy, the brewhouse, poultry and the kitchen garden; men were responsible for livestock and field crops. In general, it was assumed that each partner was responsible for the sale of any surplus produced in their area of the enterprise; Fitzherbert insisted that both husband and wife be ready to give one another a full accounting of their doings at the market. Women often had a closer and more regular connection to the market than did their husbands: the produce of the wife's domain – eggs, butter, cheese and even vegetables – had a more extended season than did that of a

[1] Peter Laslett, *The World We Have Lost*, 2nd edn (New York, 1971), pp. 1–3; Ann Kussmaul, *Servants in Husbandry in Early Modern England* (Cambridge, 1981) is the most thorough study of servants: chapter 1 discusses the conceptual problems involved in studying servants; Alan Macfarlane, *The Family Life of Ralph Josselin* (Cambridge, 1970, reprinted New York, 1977), pp. 92–3; and Macfarlane, *Marriage and Love*, pp. 82–5; Chamberlayne, *Angliae Notitia*, pp. 435–6, suggests that nobles still apprenticed children, and he did not approve.

husband's domain, and women's connection to the market was sustained by their obligation to provision their households.[2]

The meaning of this sexual division of labour varied according to regional economies. A wife's responsibility for the dairy was unlikely to lead to major involvement with the market in an arable farming village like Cawston, but would have done so in pastoral regions. Such differences in the meanings of sexual divisions of labour suggest that women might have higher status in pastoral areas, and might be more closely involved with the work of the household. The importance of women in pastoral economies is suggested by the 'skimmington' ritual in cheese areas of the west country: the ritual, directed against women who beat their husbands, included a re-enactment of the incident with the skimming ladle used in cheese-making as the weapon. Implicit in the ritual was the assumption that cheese production was a source of female independence and insubordination.[3] Direct evidence of women's status is always difficult to come by, but we can unravel the role of women in their families' lives.

The sexual division of labour was shaped not only by regional economies, but also by the level of wealth of a household, and the sources of its wealth. Alice Clark was certainly right in positing an inverse correlation – at least generally – between the wealth of the family and the economic contributions of the wife. We have already seen Thomas Platter's surprise at the leisure of merchants' wives in London; and by 1723, servants on a Norfolk farm assumed that the work done by a servant and that done by the sister of the farmer were quite different: the servant did more.[4] Because a higher proportion of women than men were illiterate, contracts and financial transactions that involved written records were the preserve of men; the more a family was engaged in such transactions, the greater the exclusion of the wife from the family's central economic activities.[5]

---

[2] See Fitzherbert, *Booke of Husbandrie*, esp. pp. 177–8; Brathwaite, *The English Gentleman*, passim; also Gervase Markham, *The English Housewife*, ed. Michael R. Best (Kingston and Montreal, 1986).

[3] David Underdown, 'The taming of the scold'; Idem, *Revel, Riot and Rebellion*, pp. 99–103.

[4] DEP/60, Childerhouse con Carpenter, esp. testimony of William Finch.

[5] Cressy, *Literacy and the Social Order*, esp. pp. 119–21.

The role of the household as a productive economic unit – not merely a unit of consumption – makes its property a central consideration. Whether property took the form of capital, of a business or of land, its nature and amount shaped the character of the family. In pre-industrial England, the most important and secure property was land, and most capital was rapidly turned into land. There were two moments in the life of a family when property commonly changed hands: at marriage and at death. Marriage in England almost always meant setting up an independent household. There is indirect evidence that many parents turned over at least part of their estate to children at the time of their marriages, but the paucity of marriage contracts for those below the gentry makes it impossible to determine the extent of this practice, or to connect such settlements with the later disposition of property by parents.[6] Property was a central concern in family formation. It also played a role in the final dissolution of the household, at the death of the household head. At this time, those who had not already distributed their property to their children did so, and their wills record the decisions they made. We have a far better idea of how property was distributed at the time of a man's death than we do of how it was brought together at the time of marriage, but both are important points in the life of the family.

There is, however, extensive evidence of the importance of property considerations in decisions about marriage, both from prescriptive literature and from marriage litigation in the church courts. Such considerations are scarcely surprising, as the amount of property at the beginning of a marriage usually placed limits on the amount of property that could be accumulated during the marriage. William Gouge advised that partners be equal in 'estate', and most other writers agreed – though they all made property secondary to love and respect. In real life it is somewhat more

---

[6] Laslett, 'Mean household size'; Macfarlane, *Marriage and Love*, chapter 3; cf. Lutz K. Berkner, 'The stem family and the developmental cycle of the peasant household: an eighteenth century Austrian example', *American Historical Review*, 77 (1972), pp. 398–418; for earlier settlements, see e.g. ANF Wills 1617 16, John Trolop of Stow Bardolph; ANW Wills 1691 126, John Lombe, Gent. of Cawston; ANW Wills 271 Rawling, John Bradye, Sr of Cawston, plowright; ANF Wills 1651–2 116, Humphrey Wilson of Winfarthing; NCC 1661 OW 23, Henry Alden, yeoman of Winfarthing.

difficult to disentangle motivation, but property was still critical. In the early 1590s, Elizabeth Purkey's master, Robert Dey, wanted to find a husband for her rapidly, as she was pregnant with his child. In the negotiations leading up to her marriage with Robert Bate, Bate and his father were assured that she was well dowered: she expected £10 as a legacy and she had two cows and several sheep, as well as 40 marks. Robert Bate and his father Edmund felt betrayed when the £10 proved fictitious, and as a consequence Elizabeth publicly accused Robert Dey of fathering her child.[7]

The case of Robert Bate and Elizabeth Purkey is extreme, because the marriage was arranged by outsiders who wanted Purkey to be married at the time she gave birth. But even in more 'normal' courtships, under the control of the couple, financial considerations were important, though sometimes resented. When John Turner was courting Mary Baldrye in 1566, she said to him that 'she would go first and see his lands and house and as she liked them so would she do'.[8] In 1579, Joanna Mors of Otley, Suffolk agreed to marry Edward Cleve if he entered a bond with her that he was worth 100 marks, and several years earlier Cicely Paynter had made her agreement to marry John Payne conditional on his granting her a house and land in Brinton for life, and £40 in goods or money. In 1572, Susan Mychells of Norwich was frankly sceptical of Christopher Pamplyn's claims; she refused to respond to a marriage proposal until she discovered whether he really did have an office worth £40 a year and £110 in ready money – even though he had promised her a jointure of £10 a year.[9]

Concerns about the property of potential spouses were shared by families. In 1581 Edward Planden of Badwell Ash, Suffolk, refused to follow through on a contract to marry Francys Brooke because of his fear of his father's displeasure: his father, who claimed the title of 'gentleman' – though it was not recognized by neighbours – had a landed income of £40 a year, while Francys' portion was but £10. A similar problem led William Baker to

---

[7] Ex Officio con Robert Dey, DEP/28, ff. 235–42, 244–5v, 247–51v, 253–6; e.g. Gouge, *Dometicall Duties*, pp. 188, 190; Tilney, *Flower of Friendshippe*, f. Bii.

[8] DEP/10, Bk. 11a, Personal answers of Mary Baldrye to the libel of John Turner, f. 120v.

[9] DEP/13, Christopher Pamplyn con Susan Mychells, ff. 302–3, 306; DEP/16, Bk. 17a, John Payne con Cicely Paynter, ff. 241–2; DEP/17, Edward Cleve con Joanna Mors, ff. 87–8.

refuse to marry Agnes Whistlecroft in 1592; she was worth less than £30, while his father was worth at least £50; her father was merely a farmer while his was a landholder.[10]

Widows were among the most careful in negotiations about their own marriages. Experience had taught them the importance of property; those with children also sought to protect their inheritance. In 1583 Joane Wilson broke off her discussions of marriage with John Clifford when she discovered that he was more deeply indebted than she had known; in 1639, a similar problem led Agnes Thirlby to pull out of marriage negotiations with Willian Paine. In 1560, Alice Pekesse of Swaffham asked John James to enter bonds to fulfil her late husband's will, and to give her children £20 which she herself had intended for them; when James refused, she assumed the marriage negotiations were closed. In 1573, Rose Plumb made a similar move, and William Ringold agreed, but after entering the bonds he cancelled them, so she assumed that he was no longer interested in marriage.[11]

Women were particularly likely to worry about property at the time of their marriage because according to English law they ceased to exist as legal individuals when they married. They retained possession of their land, although their husbands enjoyed the profits, and it could not be sold without their consent. Attempts were made to ensure that consent was freely given, but coercion was always possible. If a woman's title to land was reasonably secure, her title to movable goods – money, furniture and the like – was non-existent. As soon as she was married, movables became the property of her husband. The concern of women was realistic: since women most often brought their portions in money, it was important that a prospective husband had sufficient property and was responsible. Only through caution could wives escape the fate of a Skoulton woman in 1623: neighbours complained that Robert Kirby had married a 'poor man's daughter', but by 'extraordinary spending' 'he hath almost

---

[10] DEP/19, Francys Brooke con Edward Planden, ff. 378–84v; DEP/26, Agnes Whistlecroft con William Baker, ff. 437–42, 471–9.

[11] DEP/16, Bk. 17b, John Clifford con Joane Wilson, wid., ff. 81–3; DEP/44, William Paine con Agnes Thirlby now Cricke, ff. 88–9v, 193v–94; DEP/8, Bk. 7d, Personal Answers of Alice Pekesse, May 1560; DEP/15, Bk. 15, William Ringold con Rose Plum, wid., f. 15. Second marriages were always difficult, though also necessary: the role of wicked stepmothers in fairy tales is one sign of this.

spoiled all his poor wife's portion'. Kirby had already forced his
wife to sell some of her land, so the town asked that the remaining
£33 of her dowry be paid directly to them for her use, so that
Kirby could not spend it.[12]

Property was clearly central to decisions about marriage, but it is
impossible to quantify its importance. Historians have recently
stressed the mobility of the English population in the early modern
period, and the time of greatest mobility was young adulthood,
when people moved from place to place as servants. Young people
rarely married in the parishes where their parents lived or held
land, and it is very difficult to work from marriage to landholding
records. Marriage records provide at best a minimum estimate of
the importance of property in marriage decisions. Such an estimate
is possible in Stow Bardolph and Wimbotsham; parish registers
survive from both parishes, and in the 1620s a full survey of
landholdings was made, and can be compared to a series of court
books for the fen at Salter's Lode.[13]

During the 1620s, sixty-six marriages took place in the two
villages. Of those, the partners in seventeen (25.7 per cent) are
known to us only from entries in the parish register. The other
forty-nine all have some other evidence of residence in the villages
for at least one partner or member of their families – from wills,
inventories, court cases or landholding records. Of the group for
which such independent evidence exists, in sixteen (32.7 per cent)
both families have property in one of the two villages. Other
marriages undoubtedly were made between one partner with
property in the villages and another with property elsewhere. Such
is probably the case, for instance, with the marriage of Alice
Watton, widow, and Jeffrey Fideman. In 1625 Fideman, who had
married Watton in 1620, held a messuage and forty acres of the

---

[12] C/S3/24, Complaint of Skoulton against Robert Kirby: if the remaining portion of her
dowry was £33, his wife was not that poor; for the legal status of women, see Smith, *De
Republica*, pp. 123–5, 127–8.

[13] The decade chosen was selected because the 1625–6 survey (Hare 3351) makes it possible
to get a complete picture both of those who held customary lands in the villages (copy and free
holders) and those who held leases; it is also the only time acreages are generally given. The
rentals – Hare 3314 (1615) and Hare 3318 (1634) – provide additional evidence. The parish
registers used were Turner Deposit 8.1.79, Q187D for Wimbotsham, checked against the
original in the parish, and the copy of the Stow Bardolph parish register in PD 305/1. David
Souden, 'Pre-industrial English local migration fields', Cambridge University Ph.D., 1981,
chapter 3, finds that only about one-third of those marrying in a parish were baptized there.

demesne of Stow Bardolph, and ten years later be paid £6 10s. rent. There is no evidence of his presence in the village before his marriage to Watton, nor of the presence of any relatives. There were other Wattons in Stow however, perhaps relatives of Alice's first husband. It is unlikely that the capital which acquired Fideman's land came entirely from his wife: William Watton had a half acre on the east side of the Ouse in Stow in 1625, and John Watton paid a mere 15½d. rent in 1634. On the other hand, Fideman's will mentions a messuage in the nearby village of Runcton Holme.[14]

In addition to the marriages in which both husband and wife came from property-holding families, in twenty-eight others the family of at least one partner held land. In two of these only the husband's surname is known, but of the others, in sixteen it is the husband's family which is known, and in ten the wife's family. This suggests a slight, but not pronounced, tendency to patrilocal residence. In these two villages, a minimum of one-quarter of all marriages took place among the propertied, and it is likely that the families of at least some of the others were also both propertied. The choice of marriage partner was not merely a matter of fancy.

The accumulation of property could take place through serial marriages, common enough in an age of early mortality. When Beatrice Legate, widow of Stow Bardolph, married John Fenton, widower of Wimbotsham, in 1629, it was her fourth marriage and his third. Beatrice Barker came from an established local family, as did her first husband, John Bosse. She inherited £10 from her father just before they were married in 1614, but John Bosse died in 1617 before any children were born. He left her his tenement and lands for life. Her second husband, William Bayes, does not appear in local records before his marriage to Bosse, but his marriage to her was his second one, and his will – by which she received £10, some grain, five cows and various goods – implies that he had land elsewhere settled on his children. Bayes died in

---

[14] Edward Watton married Alice Barker in Stow Bardolph in 1603; PCC PROB 11/238 25R, Alice Fideman, refers to her son Christopher Watton and her 'Daughter Vincent': Richard Vincent married Katherine Watton in Stow Bardolph in 1633; also NCC 20 Battelle 1650–1, Jeffrey Fideman, linen-weaver; there is no trace of Christopher Watton after his mother's death. Surnames are sometimes, of course, shared by those who are unrelated, but the relationships missed by serial marriages and changes of surname are probably underestimated at least as much as they are overestimated with the use of surnames as a test.

1621, and a year later his widow had married again, this time to Richard Legate, who paid 2s. 7d. rent in 1615, and had a tenement and seven acres in Stow Bardolph in 1625. He died in January 1629, leaving her with one child; by October she was married to Fenton. Beatrice Barker/Bosse/Bayes/Legate was clearly an attractive marriage partner, with property of her own, and until her third marriage, no children. At the same time, as a young woman she was unlikely to have the experience to manage her holding, so marriage was also desirable for her.[15]

Her fourth husband, John Fenton, had had an only slightly less dramatic marital history. His first wife, Elizabeth Rockley, whom he married in November of 1625, gave birth to a daughter early in 1627, but the daughter was buried immediately, and Elizabeth several months later. In November of that year Fenton married Elizabeth Dennis, probably the widow of Henry Dennis, who had died in April 1627; she died in 1628. Fenton was evidently a householder, because in 1626 or early 1627, he and his wife had been charged in the Salter's Lode court with illegally having inmates in their house. In 1635, at least some of the rent paid by John Fenton was paid in right of his wife. When she made her will in 1643, Beatrice Fenton entrusted Robert Bosse – evidently a kinsman of her first husband – with the upbringing of her son Thomas, then about twelve years old; and her first husband's brother, John, left her daughter Elizabeth Legate a cupboard when he died in 1642. It is possible to examine the career of Beatrice Barker/Bosse/Bayes/Legate/Fenton in some detail because she held property and stayed in one place. Property added to her desirability as a wife, and it also may have made marriage more necessary; although the arrangements cannot be traced, the surviving evidence does suggest that Beatrice was careful to safeguard her property in each of her marriages.[16]

Property was a central component of decisions about marriage, although it was not the only one. Economic resources were necessary to set up a household, and disregard of property

[15] Evidence from the parish registers of Stow Bardolph (1614, 1618, 1621, 1623, 1629) and Wimbotsham (1625, 1627, 1628); ANF Wills 1614, Bk. 41 331, Christopher Barker, yeoman; ANF Wills 1617 92, Robert Bosse; ANF Wills 1621 29, William Bayes, yeoman; ANF Wills 1621 38, John Bosse the Elder, husb.; ANF Wills 1629 6, Richard Leggate.

[16] NCC 1642 OW 32, John Bosse, yeoman; ANF Wills 1649 49, Beatrix Fenton; Hare 3314, 3315, 3351, and 3318; Hare 4186, 2 Charles I.

considerations was foolish. But property was a secondary consideration: few got to the stage of worrying about property if other attractions were absent; and it was considered inappropriate to make property too important. In 1565, Margaret Underwood admitted that Thomas Deynes had talked of marriage with her, but 'he said if he might enjoy the house and land in her mother's possession that he would be content to marry with her, wherefore for that he would have had her for her land's sake as she conjectured, she made him an answer that she would no more talk with him in any matrimony [sic] matter'.[17] To stress the economic role of the family is not to deny its other aspects.

Marriage created a family by bringing together resources from both spouses to make a new economic unit; that property was used to raise children, and then would be – eventually – used to provide children with property for their marriages, property which might be supplemented by the earnings of the children as servants or labourers. Unfortunately, transfers to children at marriage are rarely recorded, and we have only indirect evidence of them – when fathers note in wills, for instance, that some children have already been provided for. More often we can examine the devolution of property at the death of parents, and incidentally gain insight into the family economy that had existed before death. It is to this evidence, recovered from wills, that we now turn.

Before we examine the evidence from wills, we should note some of the difficulties with this evidence, for wills do not provide straightforward evidence of the distribution of property from one generation to another. First, wills often record not the complete process, but the end point in the distribution of property from parents to children. This is especially true for parents some of whose children are grown and married; great disparities in the bequests to different children may reflect earlier gifts rather than parental displeasure or the absence of property. Wills are characteristically more complete – and more revealing – for those whose children are underage and still need to be provided for. The

[17] DEP/10, Bk. 10, Personal answers of Margaret Underwood to allegations of Thomas Deynes, 7 June 1565; cf. Macfarlane, *Marriage and Love*, esp. chapter 7; Gouge, *Domesticall Duties*, pp. 197–205.

language of the will may indicate whether provision has already been made for some children, but certainty is never possible.[18]

Wills are also legal documents, shaped by the demands of both common and customary law. Those who merely wished to follow the legal rules of inheritance did not need to make wills; others might enter joint tenancies with children before their death. The failure to mention land in a will does not necessarily mean that there was none. This situation is further complicated by the existence of different legal rules for freehold and copyhold land: in Cawston the custom of the manor for copyhold land was partible inheritance (the equal division of land among sons) while on all other manors involved in this study, and for freehold land, the custom was primogeniture.[19] This confusion is balanced by the almost complete testamentary freedom of English landholders. Copyhold land could usually be devised by will if the testator had previously paid a fee and surrendered the land to the lord to 'the use of his last will and testament'; the Statute of Wills in 1540 made it possible to devise freehold land absolutely freely, though unless she renounced it a widow had a life interest in one-third of all freehold land. When Edward Chamberlayne commented on the testamentary freedom of fathers, he noted the power it gave them, and said that it 'kept the children in great awe'.[20]

Wills were not only shaped by the legal context, which is at least evident to us; they were also shaped by the person who wrote them. This influence is clearly present in the style of the wills, and also often in the preambles. Manuals on how to write wills were available in early modern England, and were consulted. The influence might reach beyond the style, as a will writer – especially if the testator were dying – might remind the will maker of obligations or expected behaviour. It is unclear how far such

---

[18] Margaret Spufford, 'Peasant inheritance customs and land distribution in Cambridgeshire from the sixteenth to the eighteenth centuries', in *Family and Inheritance*, ed. Goody et al., p. 171; Bayley, *Practise of Piety*, pp. 811–12, 814–15; ANF Wills 1651–2 116, Humphrey Warner of Winfarthing, yeoman, states that he has already given legacies to three children.

[19] Alan Macfarlane, *The Origins of English Individualism* (New York, 1979), pp. 81–4; Cicely Howell, 'Peasant inheritance customs in the Midlands, 1280–1700', in *Family and Inheritance*, ed. Goody et al., pp. 112–55, also discusses legal traditions.

[20] Macfarlane, *Origins of English Individualism*, pp. 83–4; Warnes 19.12.68, Shelfanger Court Books for bequests to 'use of will'; Chamberlayne, *Angliae Notitia*, pp. 458–9.

suggestions might go; the variety of arrangements made by testators indicates that they retained their discretion.[21]

Another problem with wills is that although social status and occupation are generally given, they are not always precise. Some might claim a higher status in their will than they were accorded by their neighbours, but wills also reveal the inadequacy of the social categories with which we approach early modern society. William Gamble, a worsted weaver (by his own description) from Cawston, left 15½ acres of land in addition to the messuage and tenement in which he lived, and another acre and one rod was given in lieu of a bond for £30 when he died in 1662; he could as well have been described as a husbandman. A year later, Thomas Alden, Sr of Winfarthing described himself as a linen weaver in his will; he left lands 'in his own occupation' and 'occupied by Thomas Pilgrim', and his executors and those who inherited land were bound to pay legacies totalling more than £250. To classify either of these men as a 'craftsman' – as one would on the basis of their self-description – clearly does not do justice to their experience.[22] The social descriptions of the wills are crude, and often fail to reveal the variety of economic and social roles occupied by one individual.

The last problem with wills grows out of the previous one: Who in the villages we are examining actually left wills? Although upwards of half the population, representing the poorer husbandmen and all those below them, were unable to pay the hearth tax, this group – and especially the very poor – is severely underrepresented in the collection of wills (see table 1): Stow Bardolph and Wimbotsham had the highest proportion of labourers among will makers, but even if we assume that all those who gave no occupational description were labourers, still only just over 20 per cent of the will-making population were labourers in Stow and Wimbotsham. Women were also underrepresented among the will makers; only ninety-one of the 562 wills left in the five villages between 1590 and 1750 were made by women, and most of those women were widows (see table 2). Married women could not make a will without the consent of their husbands, and there are only three such wills in the sample. The men who made

---

[21] Spufford, *Contrasting Communities*, pp. 321–3.
[22] ANW Wills 64 Wilson (1662) William Gamble; NCC 1663 OW 19, Thomas Alden, Sr.

Table 1 Status or occupation of male testators (%)

Status	1590–1659	1660–1750	1590–1750
Cawston			
None	23.2	9.1	15.0
Labourer	3.6	2.6	3.0
Husbandman	3.6	6.5	5.3
Yeoman	21.4	27.3	24.8
Gentleman	3.6	2.6	3.0
Single	3.6	2.6	3.0
Textiles	8.9	23.4	17.3
Retail trades	8.9	1.3	4.5
Clerk	3.6	2.6	3.0
Other crafts	19.6	20.8	20.3
Service		1.3	0.8
Number	56	77	133
Winfarthing and Shelfanger			
None	16.9	6.0	11.1
Labourer		3.0	1.6
Husbandman	13.6	3.0	7.9
Yeoman	45.8	46.3	46.0
Gentleman	3.4	6.0	4.8
Widower		1.5	0.8
Single		3.0	1.6
Textiles	5.1	9.0	7.1
Retail trades		4.5	2.4
Clerk	1.7	3.0	2.4
Other crafts	13.6	14.9	14.3
Number	59	67	126
Stow Bardolph and Wimbotsham			
None	16.2	15.8	16.0
Labourer	8.5	1.1	5.2
Husbandman	25.6	9.5	18.4
Yeoman	29.9	48.4	38.2
Gentleman	2.6	2.1	2.4
Textiles	5.1	1.1	3.3
Clerk	1.7	1.1	1.4
Other crafts	7.7	18.9	12.7
Service	2.6	2.1	2.4
Number	117	95	212

Note: All percentages are rounded to the nearest 0.1, so totals do not always add up to exactly 100%.

Table 2   Sex and marital status of testators (%)

	Women	Men
Cawston		
Single	11.8	15.8
Married	8.8	67.7
Widowed	79.4	16.5
Number	34	133
Winfarthing and Shelfanger		
Single	24.0	14.3
Married		66.7
Widowed	76.0	19.0
Number	25	126
Stow Bardolph and Wimbotsham		
Single	12.5	11.8
Married		71.2
Widowed	87.5	17.0
Number	32	212
All Villages		
Single	15.4	13.6
Married	3.3	69.0
Widowed	81.3	17.4
Number	91	471

wills were predominantly married or widowed, fulfilling their final responsibility to their children in providing for their future. In general, property holding accompanied marriage, and so single women and men rarely had much property – especially land – to dispose of. The will-making population mirrors the property-holding population, not the whole population, and its evidence is therefore of necessity partial.[23]

---

[23] For other discussions of this problem, see Evans, *Linen Industry*, pp. 4–5; Spufford, 'Peasant inheritance customs', pp. 169–70 argues that smallholders were proportionately more likely to leave wills than large landholders, but her estimates leave out the landless. The following discussion is based on all the wills registered in the NCC, the ANF and the ANW, between 1590 and 1750, from the five sample villages. All wills filed in the PCC, now in the PRO from 1590 to 1700 were also studied. The Hares, and those who are obviously not part of the community, have been excluded from the statistics.

These disadvantages of wills are outweighed by what they do include. A will allows historians to view the distribution of movable goods, and to see how testators dealt with land outside the village of residence. The evidence from wills provides the minimum distribution of property, but without them, we would know nothing about the gifts of goods or money, the obligations on those who inherit land to their siblings or kin, or even what land was owned outside the village of residence. As long as their limitations are kept in mind, the evidence of wills provides an invaluable glimpse at the ways in which property was passed from one generation to another.

The family economy – wealth, economic activities and farming type – was an important factor in decisions made by will makers. Although personal feelings might affect individual cases, the patterns revealed by the wills in particular villages are a product of specific family economies. The decisions made by male testators illuminate the sexual division of labour, the importance of land and the conception of social hierarchy in these different economies.

The sexual division of labour is suggested by the two decisions made by married men concerning their wives: whether or not to appoint them executor, and whether to give them land or an annuity for the remainder of their lives. The choice of a wife as executor indicates that a husband believed that his wife could satisfactorily wind up his earthly business; the decision to join her with someone else suggests that she is not familiar with at least some of his activities; and the exclusion of her altogether suggests her inability to comprehend the business he had in hand. Similarly, a husband would be less likely to leave his wife land if he believed that she would not know how to manage it, so the legacy of land becomes a quick test of the involvement of the wife in the family agricultural enterprise. We would expect all these decisions to vary by both region and social class.

Both in their choice of executor and bequests of land, men in our sample villages confirm our assumption that women were more actively involved in pastoral economies, and that their involvement declined as one moved up the social scale (see tables 3 and 4). The choice of executor was the first made in most wills. A high proportion of married men in all villages chose their wife alone as executor, and an overwhelming majority chose their wife as at least

Table 3 Executors of married men (%)

	Wife	Wife and other
Cawston		
All (90)	63.3	10.0
1590–1659 (40)	67.5	5.0
1660–1750 (50)	60.0	14.0
None (15)	86.7	6.7
Yeoman (22)	31.8	9.1
Textiles (14)	71.4	7.1
Other crafts (18)	72.2	11.1
Winfarthing and Shelfanger		
All (84)	51.2	21.4
1590–1659 (39)	61.5	18.0
1660–1750 (45)	42.2	28.9
Yeoman (40)	45.0	22.5
1590–1659 (15)	60.0	13.4
1660–1750 (25)	36.0	32.0
Stow Bardolph and Wimbotsham		
All, 1590–1750 (151)	66.2	11.9
1590–1659 (94)	67.0	11.7
1660–1750 (57)	64.9	12.3
1660–99 (31)	70.1	6.5
1700–50 (26)	57.7	19.2
None (20)	80.0	10.0
Labourer (9)	88.9	11.1
Husbandman (28)	82.1	10.7
Yeoman (61)	45.9	19.7
Other crafts (19)	94.7	
All villages		
All (325)	61.5	15.0
1590–1659 (173)	65.7	11.6
1660–1750 (152)	56.6	19.0
None (45)	82.2	11.1
Labourer (14)	92.9	
Husbandman (44)	75.0	13.6
Yeoman (123)	43.1	18.7
1590–1659 (56)	46.4	14.5
1660–1750 (67)	40.3	26.9
Textiles (23)	60.9	8.7

Table 3 continued

	Wife	*Wife and other*
Other crafts (51)	76.5	9.8
1590–1659 (21)	81.0	9.5
1660–1750 (30)	73.3	10.0

Note: 'Wife and other' includes any combination which includes a wife as executor; 'other' is usually a son or male relative or friend, but 1.5 per cent of the men joined their wife and daughter as executors, and these are included in this column.

Table 4   Major bequest to widow, married men with land (%)

	1590–1659	*1660–1750*	*1590–1750*
Cawston			
Land	72.5	66.0	68.9
Earlier settlement		4.0	2.2
Money	15.0	10.0	12.2
Goods	12.5	20.0	16.7
Number	40	50	90
Winfarthing and Shelfanger			
Land	67.7	66.7	67.2
Earlier settlement	22.6	21.2	21.9
Money		12.1	6.3
Goods	3.2		1.6
House room	6.5		3.1
Number	31	33	64
Stow Bardolph and Wimbotsham			
Land	78.8	71.1	75.6
Earlier settlement	7.7	2.6	5.6
Money	9.6	15.8	12.2
Goods	1.9	10.5	5.6
House room	1.9		1.1
Number	52	38	90

Note: All percentages are rounded to the nearest 0.1, so totals do not always add up to exactly 100%.

one of their executors, if not the sole one. Most families followed the injunctions of the household manuals and operated as genuine economic partnerships between husband and wife.

The variations deserve some comment. Overall, the smallest proportion of men chose their wives as executors in Winfarthing and Shelfanger, although the proportion choosing their wife with someone else brings the total number who included their wife up to the same level as that in Cawston. This, at least initially, seems surprising, as we would expect that the pastoral economy of Winfarthing and Shelfanger would give women a greater role; certainly the practice of men in Stow Bardolph and Wimbotsham suggests this, with large numbers choosing their wife as executor. The explanation is found in the social composition of testators in Winfarthing and Shelfanger: almost half of the married men in the villages were yeomen, who in all villages were less likely than other groups to choose their wives as executors. When yeomen alone are compared, the greater role of women in the pastoral economies is evident; in all the pastoral villages, about 45 per cent of the yeomen chose their wife alone as executor, while in Cawston less than one-third did so. Women played a more limited role in the agricultural economy of Cawston than in those of the other villages. The high overall proportion of wives chosen as executors in Cawston reflects the predominance of social groups – like textile workers and other craftsmen – in whose family economies women played a larger role.[24]

The patterns of choice of executor changed over time, reflecting the increasing importance of market production and capitalist agriculture in the villages. In all villages the drop in women being chosen as sole executors is at least significantly compensated for by a steep rise in the proportion of wives joined with others as executors. The process is especially clear in Stow Bardolph and Wimbotsham, where a large number of wills exist along with fairly detailed information about changes in agricultural practice. Before the drainage of the fen in the early 1660s, it was available to everyone in the villages, even though not all had legal rights to its use. The decision by so many labourers and husbandmen to leave

---

[24] Less than one-quarter of the married men who left wills in Cawston were yeomen, while more than 40 per cent of those in Stow Bardolph and Wimbotsham were, and almost half (47.6 per cent) of those in Winfarthing and Shelfanger were.

wills – at least in comparison to the other villages – indicates that the existence of the fen provided them with sources of wealth not available elsewhere. When the fen was drained, this source of wealth disappeared, and the change is recorded in the wills of men from the villages. If the period under consideration is divided at 1660, the change is not dramatic: 67 per cent before 1660 chose their wives alone as executors, 64.9 per cent after; but after 1700, it is quite marked: the proportion dropped to 57.7 per cent. The draining of the fen led to an increase in the importance of both arable farming and of stock production – not dairying – for the market, both of which involved men more than women. The reification of use rights for the fen at Stow Bardolph and Wimbotsham reduced the role of women in local family economies.[25] Still, one must not exaggerate the withdrawal of women from productive work: most women were involved in production, and their role is shown by the extent to which husbands continued to choose wives as executors. Yeomen were more likely to be involved in activities with which their wives were unfamiliar, and in Cawston the ignorance of wives in these matters appears to have been far greater than in the other villages. However, yeomen never constituted a majority of villagers, so most women played an important role in the economic life of their families even at the end of our period.

Men's bequests to their wives (table 4) suggest a similar conclusion, although in this case we must infer from wills that men had already settled land on their wives when land was to pass to a child after the wife's death. It can also be assumed that prosperous men who made no provision for their wives in their wills had already provided for them, most often with land. Women in Winfarthing and Shelfanger were most likely to be thought capable of managing a landholding, and those in Cawston the least likely to be so trusted. But once again, the change in Stow Bardolph and Wimbotsham after the draining of the fen is remarkable, from 86.5 per cent either leaving land or having made an earlier settlement, to only 73.7 per cent after 1660. This brings the behaviour of men in Stow Bardolph and Wimbotsham far closer to that of men in Cawston in the second part of our period. The draining of the fen was a major event, which had ramifications not just for agricultural practice, but for the whole life of the community.

[25] Cf. Thompson, 'The grid of inheritance', esp. pp. 337–40.

The decisions men made about their wives reflect the sexual division of labour in early modern English families, and the extent of women's involvement in the productive enterprise of those families. Bequests to children reveal other aspects of family economies: the role of land in defining status, the amount of property necessary for survival, the availability – and acceptability – of non-agricultural occupations, and expectations about the treatment of children. The decisions made by fathers about their children reflect far more complex imperatives than do those made about wives, and provide less clear-cut evidence. A father was torn between conflicting demands: on the one hand, most fathers wanted to ensure that their children would have enough to prosper, and landholders usually wanted to ensure a viable holding. For those whose property was small to start out with, the desire to provide adequately for children and to maintain the viability of a holding was in tension with the desire to provide for all children. Some fathers would find it impossible to provide adequately for all children, and were torn between giving each child some property, or providing adequately for one child and giving less to the others. Furthermore, a father might use his property as a method of disciplining unruly children – a concern which is manifested in at least some of the wills. The decisions made in these cases were simultaneously influenced by, and influenced, the social structure and agricultural economy of the village.[26]

For the wealthy such decisions were relatively straightforward: like Edward Hammond, they could give all the property they held in one village to one son. Hammond had land in seven parishes, and only three sons. Those who had purchased several holdings in the course of their lives could give one to each son – as was also done by several yeomen in Winfarthing and Shelfanger.[27] For others, such decisions were more difficult. The first choice to be made was whether or not to make a more or less equal division of property among children (see table 5). Men in Cawston were most

---

[26] The best discussion of the impact of inheritance on village social structure is in Spufford, *Contrasting Communities*, chapters 3–5; Thompson, 'The grid of inheritance', pp. 341–5.

[27] NCC Wills Hudd (1621) 44, Edward Hammond; cf. NCC 265 Morse (1633) Elles Baron, pailmaker of Winfarthing; NCC 91 Spendlove (1636) Robert Homes, yeoman of Shelfanger; PRO PCC 289 Pell (PROB 11/291, 324R) 1659, Thomas Firmage, yeoman of Shelfanger; ANF Wills 60 1665 82, William Richards, tailor of Winfarthing.

Table 5 Equal division of estate, men with more than one child

	Equal division (%)
Cawston	
1590–1659 (31)	51.6
1660–1750 (48)	54.2
1590–1750 (79)	53.2
Winfarthing and Shelfanger	
1590–1659 (41)	19.5
1660–1750 (42)	26.2
1590–1750 (83)	22.9
Stow Bardolph and Wimbotsham	
1590–1659 (66)	45.5
1660–1750 (52)	38.5
1590–1750 (118)	42.4
All villages	
1590–1659 (138)	39.1
1660–1750 (142)	40.1
1590–1750 (280)	39.6

likely (53.2 per cent) and those in Winfarthing and Shelfanger the least likely (22.9 per cent) to do so. It may be significant that the custom of the manor in Cawston – and in no other village – was partible inheritance; even those men who overrode custom in the division of their land were still influenced by the norm of equality. Furthermore, in Cawston – and Stow Bardolph and Wimbotsham – land was not as necessary to survival, as common land and non-agricultural occupations made skills at least as important as land. The fen and the market provided alternative employments. In Winfarthing and Shelfanger, on the other hand, the integrity of the holding was critical; there were few employments for those without land, and fathers were reluctant to burden the holding with large bequests for non-inheriting children.

Once a decision had been made as to whether or not property should be divided equally, fathers had to decide how to make the division: land could be divided among all children, or one child could inherit and pay legacies to the others (see table 6). Men in Cawston were the least likely to leave all their land to one son: 35.6 per cent did so, as against 43.5 per cent in Winfarthing and

Table 6 Bequests of land, men with more than one child (%)

	1590–1659	1660–1750	1590–1750
Cawston			
One son	25.0	42.9	35.6
Several, all sons	20.9	14.3	17.0
One daughter	8.3	8.6	8.5
Several, all daughters		11.4	6.8
Sons and daughters	12.5	2.9	6.8
All children	25.0	5.7	13.6
Other	6.7	6.7	6.7
Number	24	35	59
Winfarthing and Shelfanger			
One son	41.9	45.2	43.5
Several, all sons	16.2	29.1	22.6
One daughter	6.5		3.2
Several, all daughters	6.5		3.2
Sons and daughters	12.9	9.7	11.3
All children	9.7	12.9	11.3
Other	6.5	3.2	4.8
Number	31	31	62
Stow Bardolph and Wimbotsham			
One son	45.7	44.7	45.2
Several, all sons	22.9	7.9	14.0
One daughter	5.7	10.5	8.2
Several, all daughters	2.9	13.1	8.2
Sons and daughters	11.4	2.6	6.8
All children	5.7	18.4	12.3
Other	5.7	2.6	4.1
Number	35	38	73

Shelfanger and 45.2 per cent in Stow Bardolph and Wimbotsham. However, Cawston fathers were not significantly more likely to divide their land among all their children than those in other villages. Fathers in Cawston distributed a combination of land and money. In Winfarthing and Shelfanger, the importance of land is shown by the frequency with which yeomen fathers left land to several sons, establishing each on an independent holding. When Robert Eldred, Sr died in 1624, he left land to four of his six sons; two received land in Winfarthing purchased of four different people, one received land in Shelfanger, and the fourth lands in Fersfield and Bressingham. His two remaining sons each received cash bequests of 200 marks.[28]

The pattern of bequests in Stow Bardolph and Wimbotsham once again reveals the significance of the division of the fen. Once access to the fen was restricted by draining, fathers were three times as likely to leave land to all their children: scrounging for a living on the fen was no longer possible, so land compensated for the loss of informal pasture rights. When John Chickoe, a Wimbotsham yeoman, died in 1705, he left most of his land to one son, but each of his two daughters received a fen common lot.[29] The increasing proportion of Cawston fathers who left land only to one son after the Restoration also indicates major social changes. Two factors played a role in this change: first, the stocking-knitting industry, which had provided employment, collapsed in the 1680s, and made land far more important; the second was the gradual increase in the importance of the London market for Cawston's corn, which encouraged agricultural improvement and more systematic exploitation of the fields and heath by larger landholders, and undermined the ability of smallholders to keep cattle or sheep.[30] In Cawston, as in Stow Bardolph and Wimbotsham before the draining of the fen, fathers knew that children with little land could supplement the holding with the use of common land, a certainty never present in Winfarthing and Shelfanger.

Fathers who decided not to divide their land were equally careful not to burden the holding with a heavy load of legacies. In cases where land was left to only one child, legacies were spread out over a much longer time than when land was divided.[31] The consequences of overburdening were evident to all at the time; they are illustrated by the abstract of title made for Mr John Atthill

---

[28] PRO PCC Wills 34 Byrde (PROB 11/143, 267r).

[29] ANF Wills 1705 9 (7), John Chickoe.

[30] Penelope J. Corfield, 'The social and economic history of Norwich, 1650–1850: a study in urban growth', University of London Ph.D., 1976, pp. 86–7; Joyce Appleby, *Economic Thought and Ideology in Seventeenth Century England* (Princeton, 1978), p. 196 for some other factors affecting the Norfolk cloth industry; Amussen, 'Governors and governed', p. 77.

[31] Those who left land to one son allowed an average of 3.6 years for the payment of bequests, those who left land to some other combination of children an average of 2.1 years and those who left no land an average of 0.9 years.

of Cawston in 1802 tracing the history of his holdings. One piece of land had been owned by Francis Colls at the time of his death in 1724, when it was inherited by his son Francis to pay legacies. By 1728 the land was mortgaged, and by 1742 it had been sold.[32] Most will makers sought to avoid such a fate for their land with a complex balancing act.

Decisions about bequests to children also reflected the role of land in defining social position in the community. The yeomen in Winfarthing and Shelfanger, eager to provide their sons with adequate holdings, show this most clearly. Land was the source of social importance in the villages, but the elite was relatively broadly defined, and especially after 1660 fathers did not feel that the division of a large holding damaged the interests of their sons. Their practice reminds us of the broad elite revealed by the hearth tax: a large group, but not really dominated by any one person. To a certain extent the opposite happened in Stow Bardolph and Wimbotsham. There fathers were just as likely to leave land to one son as in Winfarthing and Shelfanger, but after 1660 the proportion leaving land only to sons declined sharply, while the number leaving all children land rose sharply – though those gifts might be relatively small; after the draining of the fen, men worried less about the status of their children, and more about their survival.[33]

If bequests by fathers shaped the family economies of their children, we would expect them to reflect the family economies of the parents. But they also reflect the values of the parents; as mentioned previously wills could be used as a method of discipline. This use of property was rare – explicit in only two of the wills in the sample. It was likely to have been used more as a threat than a reality: the Essex parson Ralph Josselin regularly threatened to disinherit his son John, but never did.[34] The freedom of testators was real, and we do not know how often they advantaged a younger rather than an elder son, but the evidence from these villages

[32] NRS 17774 70x3.

[33] Obviously these decisions were shaped largely by the amount of land held by any one individual; in Stow Bardolph and Wimbotsham they may also have been affected by the availability of the demesne for lease.

[34] PRO PCC Wills 131 Cope (PROB 11/128, p. 516L), 1616, William Raye of Wimbotsham; ANF Wills 92 1687 (138), William Land of Winfarthing; cf. DEP/41, Super Testament of Stephen Burrell: Stephen Burrell, executor con John Burrell, Anne Hoare alias Burrell and Margaret Burrell alias Buxton; Macfarlane, *Family Life of Ralph Josselin*, pp. 120–3.

suggests that fathers used their property as best they could to provide as many children as possible with what was thought necessary for at least economic survival, and if possible, prosperity.

The decisions made by men in writing their wills reflected their role as head of the family, its representative to the community, and the official holder of most family property. Because of their position they had to provide for their children. Men made the important decisions on the distribution of most property, and usually provided for all their children. Their widows, when they left wills, had very different considerations. With the major decisions about property already made, widows did not need to establish their children. It is then not surprising that only one-sixth of the women with more than one child made an equal division of their property among their children – less than half the proportion of men who did so. What kinds of decisions did women make in their wills and how do these wills help us to understand their perspective on the family and the family economy?

In some ways the most intriguing decisions made were made by women with land. Although they are relatively few, their behaviour is suggestive. Only 13.7 per cent of the men who left land left it to one daughter; however, 34.6 per cent of the women did, and of those with more than one child mentioned in their wills, only 6.7 per cent of the men, but 30 per cent of the women chose one daughter as the recipient of land. By contrast, 41.8 per cent of the men with more than one child left land to only one son, but only one-quarter of the women did. Even among those who left land to more than one child, women were far more likely to favour daughters than were their husbands, and were more likely to favour daughters than sons; 42.3 per cent of the widows left land only to daughters, and only 34.5 per cent left land only to sons. There are two conclusions which we can draw from this evidence – conclusions which are necessarily tentative because of the small numbers involved. First, while men generally assumed that land was more important for sons than daughters – and may have believed that land left to daughters left the family – women saw land as important for their daughters, and expected their daughters to be able to profit from it. Women offered a subtle critique of the patriarchal assumptions of the period by giving more authority and power to their daughters than their husbands did.[35]

Women also assumed that their daughters were capable of transacting business, an assumption far more rarely made by men. If widows are compared to men with children who did not choose their wives as executors (since a comparable choice was not available to widows) they were far more likely to choose daughters, or indeed other women, as executors than were men. Only 6.2 per cent of such men, but 21.1 per cent of the women chose daughters as executors; only 14.4 per cent of the men who did not choose their wives as executors included any woman as executor, but 29.9 per cent of the women did. Thus, although women still were more likely to choose their sons than daughters as executors, the differences between women and men indicate that women saw each other as more able than did men.

From their different position in the process of inheritance, women were much more likely than men to favour particular children. Such favouritism did not necessarily advantage daughters; rather it favoured selected children. While two-thirds of the men who did not favour sons over daughters divided their property equally, less than a quarter of the women did so; sometimes daughters and sometimes selected children benefited.[36] Some of these choices may reflect the nature of the property left by women: clothing, cooking utensils and furniture are the stuff of women's wills. The clothing would obviously pass to other women, and household goods would go to those children in need of them at that time. The benefit might be to younger children who were just getting settled, or even to grandchildren. If wills reflect – as they must – the needs of children, women could respond to those needs with more flexibility than could their husbands.

[35] The one question that must be for ever unanswered is whether husbands and wives decided in advance on the distribution of property; it is possible that when this was done, women were more likely to be given the responsibility of providing for daughters. There is no evidence regarding this possibility either way.

[36] 40.1 per cent of the men, and only 16.7 per cent of the women, divided their property equally among their children; while men and women favoured sons at more or less the same rate (41.7 per cent of the women, and 44.5 per cent of the men, who had both sons and daughters favoured sons), women who did not favour sons were far more likely to favour daughters.

The behaviour of women in writing their wills opens a small crack in the patriarchal facade of early modern England. Women did not just accept the valuation of them offered by the writers of sermons and advice manuals, but shaped their wills according to their experience and perceptions of need. From their experience they knew of the abilities and competence of other women – recognized by men in their wives but not in their daughters. This suggests that the descriptions we have of experience in household manuals are inadequate guides to reality: life was lived in tension with prescription.

This small crack gives us some insight into the experience of women, but wills give us even less assistance in understanding the experience of the poor and propertyless. They rarely left wills because they rarely had anything to leave. The evidence on such families is sparse, but they probably survived through a combination of agricultural labour and industrial outwork.[37] A list made in 1603 of 'such as live by their hand labour with their children . . . in Alvington Street' in Cawston, lists seven households, three of knitters and four of spinners. All but two worked independently, and the children who worked with them ranged in age from eighteen years to six months – although it is unlikely that this youngest contributed much to the enterprise![38]

The best evidence about the economy of the poor comes from Stow Bardolph and Wimbotsham. There we have a suggestion of a different economy in the wills of labourers who left everything to their wives, with perhaps some token gifts to others. It is possible that the will transferred a de facto right to use the fen to a wife – a right that would be critical to her survival.[39] The higher proportions of labourers leaving wills in those villages is only explicable in one of two ways: one, that they more often had something to bequeath, or two, that there were simply far more of them there. Since the evidence from Cawston would challenge the second theory, the first

[37] Clark, *Working Life of Women*, pp. 64–92, 107–19 passim.

[38] This list, from the papers of George Sawer, is in the possession of Mrs Janet Hammond; a microfilm copy is available in the Norfolk Record Office.

[39] E.g. NCC 148 Smyth (1638), John Harwick, weaver, left everything to his wife, and ANF 1621 22, John Homes, bricklayer, left everything to his wife with a legacy of 5s. to each of his six children; also ANF 1625 72, John Farrow, labourer; NCC 217 Spendlove (1636), John Walker, labourer; NCC 143 Smyth (1638), Thomas Landrick, labourer; NCC 95 Green (1639), John Boncke, husbandman.

explanation is likely to be the correct one. Labourers in Stow and Wimbotsham clearly saw the bequest – even if it was only 5s. – as an important act.

We know little about the poor beyond the fact that their family economies, even more than those of their wealthier neighbours, depended on the cooperation of all family members; no one was allowed leisure. Olwen Hufton has called these 'economies of makeshifts'. But we must not fall into the trap of assuming that financial obligations were the only things that held families together. Even after children had left home to work, they sometimes returned to help their parents: in 1659 the justices of the Northern division of Norfolk made an order to regulate gleaning and make it more orderly, because 'poor people draw home to them their children and others to glean'.[40] There was no way poor parents could compel grown children to return; the decision to do so reflected either affection or a sense that even though living separately, everyone still contributed to the family. Although there is little evidence in England like that from the continent of children in service sending wages home, working assistance may have been more possible and more common.[41]

The family in early modern English society was not just an institution of ideological importance as described in the social and political theory of the time. It was also an economic institution, the centre of most production throughout this period. Because of its economic role, property was a central factor in family relations, from decisions to get married to the distribution of property at the time of death. Family economies varied by region and by wealth, and the views of mothers and fathers of the family economies also differed. As women and men lived out their lives in early modern England, they took for granted the family as a political and economic institution; it was in this context that families were formed, lived and died. It is now time to turn to the family in process, and to look at the use of authority in families, and the regulation of them, in early modern England.

[40] C/S2/2, July 1659, Fakenham Sessions: this suggests non-economic ties between parents and children unsuspected by Macfarlane, *Marriage and Love*, pp. 108–15.

[41] Kussmaul, *Servants in Husbandry*, pp. 75–7; Macfarlane, *Marriage and Love*, pp. 83–5; cf. Joan Scott and Louise Tilly, *Women, Work and Family in Europe, 1750–1950* (New York, 1978), pp. 109–16 passim.

4

Gender Order
in Families and Villages

The assumptions made in political and social theory about the family and sexuality were simple: a clear subordination of wives to husbands provided the model for all relationships between women and men, and order in both family and community was obtained by restricting sexual relationships to marriage. As the wife was subject to her husband, children and servants were subject to the couple which headed the household. This ideal was never fully realized, but it was the vision which early modern villagers

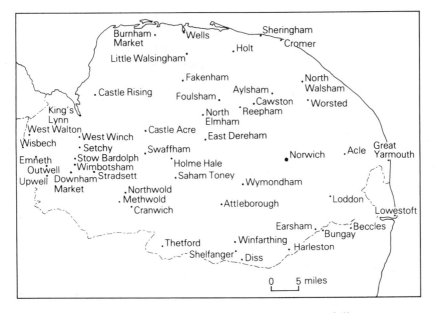

Map 5   Selected villages and towns in Norfolk

struggled to uphold. To this end they used all the tools at their disposal, both informal and formal, to shape their own behaviour and that of their neighbours. The values they demonstrated were parallel to, but not always identical with, those of the theoretical writers we have already examined.

The social control of family life came primarily from within the village. The structure of government, and particularly local government, in England, made it very difficult for anyone in authority to impose standards or policies that did not receive approval in the localities. The tradition of 'self-government at the King's command' required at least the acquiescence of local notables for any kind of enforcement. The gender order of families and villages thus reflected the values – and the problems – of villagers themselves.

The ideal of the orderly family, in which a responsible husband and wife guided and corrected their erring children and servants, was a powerful one. Some of these responsibilities were even enshrined in law. By law, household heads had to ensure that their families came to church each Sunday, that children and servants were catechized and that all observed the Sabbath. Such requirements could be difficult to comply with. Young children – in an age before Sunday school removed them from church – did not readily submit to Sunday discipline: some played in the streets and insulted the parish officers, while others ran about the church during the sermon. Parents who attempted to solve these problems by remaining at home found themselves before the ecclesiastical courts for absence from church.[1] Even in its most mundane aspects, reality fell short of the ideal.

Responsible household heads were necessary for village order. Many villagers suspected that in the same way that the legal immunity of married women was exploited by food and enclosure rioters, so the disruption of society by wives or children might be

---

[1] By 'An Acte to retain the Queen's subjects in Obedience' (35 Eliz I cap. 1), harbouring recusants was made an offence; this probably included wives, though Parliament resisted such an interpretation and later attempts to make husbands responsible for recusant wives: J.E. Neale, *Elizabeth I and her Parliaments, 1584–1601* (New York, 1958), pp. 280–94, 396–405; Amussen, 'Gender, family and the social order', p. 200; ANW/6/8, 1639–40, Great Yarmouth: January 1639/40, John George, and February 1639/40, John Sparkes; ANW/2/74, 1639 Francis ux. Thomas Ixford of Cawston; ANW 6/6, John Silence of Sparham.

encouraged by irresponsible household heads. Thus, not only did Juliana Rowland of Raynham frequently scold with her neighbours, but, her neighbours complained in 1572, she allowed and encouraged 'her children to call honest women whores'.[2] The problem was compounded if sexuality was involved. In 1573, the townsmen of Little Walsingham suspected the wife of William Davy of 'using herself dishonestly' and William of being 'a bolsterer of her in her wickedness; she could not else be so bold for she have had an ill name a great while'.[3] In Erpingham in 1614, John Friends' neighbours suspected that he was 'corrupted with money' to accept his wife's adultery with William Fuller.[4] Fathers were expected to make their children conform to sexual norms. When John Shuckforth of Gayton Thorpe fathered the illegitimate child of Katherine Arnold in 1581, he left town to avoid the responsibility. In this he had the assistance of his father, and so while John was charged with fathering the child, his father was brought to court for helping him leave. In 1662, the inhabitants of Burgh St Peter made a three-pronged attack on disorder in their midst. Mary Bramsby lived apart from her husband Robert, and she was 'vehemently suspected' by her neighbours of living incontinently with John Parker. The suits brought against Mary Bramsby and John Parker for fornication and adultery are predictable; the third complaint was against Mary Bramsby's father John Burrough, who allowed his daughter to remain in his house, away from her husband, in spite of her adultery.[5]

A common theme runs through these complaints, all of which arose in response to questions in the visitation articles of the Archdeacon or Bishop. If the head of the household had done his duty, neighbours would not have had to step in. The invocation of

---

[2] ANW 2/8 1572, Raynham presentment; E.P. Thompson, 'The moral economy of the English crowd in the eighteenth century', *Past and Present*, 50 (1971), pp. 76–136, esp. 115–16; Underdown, *Revel, Riot and Rebellion*, pp. 110–12.

[3] ANW/1/7, 1572, Walsingham Deanery; cf. ANW 6/6, 1606, Thursford con Joanna and Oliver Fish.

[4] ANW 2/58, Erpingham: it is ironic that Fuller was able to find compurgators to exonerate him from the charge, but as John Friend was not, he was excommunicated for accepting money from Fuller that Fuller was not guilty of giving!

[5] ANW/2/15, Gayton Thorpe; DEP/46, Offic. promot. per Thomas Burrows con John Parker, ff. 209–13, Idem con Mary ux. Robert Bramsby, ff. 214–18v, and Idem con John Burrough, ff. 232–7.

powers from the outside to control behaviour in families *ought* to have been unnecessary, and was a last resort. In the presentment of 'third parties', communal disapproval of the household head is evident. Neighbours did not like the task of keeping order in other households, but they would do so when necessary. These presentments, although answers to specific questions from the Archdeacon, represent choices by villagers. They did not have to present people, and especially in the late seventeenth century, they often did not. Instead, they answered the articles with an undoubtedly fictitious *'omnia bene'*. Few presentments of lax household heads were made after 1660; the reasons for this are best discussed later.

The order that heads of household were to maintain in their homes was based on a rigid moral code. Much of this code is revealed by the way in which family and sexual behaviour shaped reputation. Reputation derived its significance from the nature of the village community. The absence of extensive kin networks in many villages and the high degree of geographical mobility did not grant anonymity. People were constantly observed by their neighbours, and the limited range of most geographical mobility meant that reputation followed them when they moved. In 1618 Agnes Ayers alleged that Anne Leight was a whore, and 'was rung out of Hilborough and Swaffham with a basin'[6]: she said this in Shropham, eleven miles (as the crow flies) from Hilborough, fourteen from Swaffham. When Thomas Brabon insulted Mary Tite in Norwich in 1701, alleging that she cuckolded her husband, he added that 'the report you left behind you at Denton where you lived last was an impudent woman'.[7] Denton is about twelve miles south of Norwich. The scale of local society made it possible to know and judge the behaviour of neighbours, even new arrivals.

Reputation shaped the attitudes of neighbour to neighbour as much as did social position. Existing reputation – 'common fame' – determined one's ability to contest further assaults on one's

[6] Macfarlane, *Origins of English Individualism*, pp. 70–6, 139–40; cf. Miranda Chaytor, 'Household and kinship: Ryton in the late 16th and early 17th centuries', *History Workshop Journal*, 10 (1980), pp. 25–60; David Cressy, 'Kinship and kin interaction in early modern England', *Past and Present*, 113 (1986), pp. 38–69; Amussen, 'Féminin/Masculin', pp. 286–7; DEP/37, Anne Leight con Agnes Ayers, f. 363 ff.: a charivari is implicit in the insult.

[7] DEP/53, Mary ux. James Tite con Thomas Brabon, 27 March 1702.

reputation. Reputation also affected dealings with official bodies. When John Nicholls of Cawston was presented to the archdeaconry court in 1615 for allowing drunkenness and bawdry in his house, he was able to avoid ecclesiastical penalties by purgation. Purgation gave reputation legal standing: those who could get three, four or more of their neighbours (the number was based on the severity of the offence) to swear to their honest life and conversation could avoid penalties.[8] Reputation could discredit accusers; in 1590, the questmen of Attleborough presented Martiall Barker to the archdeacon's court for fornication with Thomas Chamberlain, but only after they were warned that if they failed to do so they would have to 'wear papers' (i.e. do penance). In the litigation which followed, it emerged that the presentment was based on rumours originating with Ralph Cooper, who was eighteen and 'a lewd boy'. It was not 'publicly reported of credible men'. The story was not given credence by 'honest and grave' inhabitants of Attleborough because both Thomas Chamberlain and Martiall Barker had always been known to be honest.[9] Thus good reputation was almost self-perpetuating; if rumours of misbehaviour became too frequent, no doubt reputation could crumble, but accusers of the respectable were more suspect than the accused. Reputation was important enough that Martiall Barker – like many others – went to court to defend hers. The sources of reputation, however, differed for women and men; we will focus on those relating to family and sexuality.

Reputation is, of course, not absolute: it exists in the eye of the beholder. It was a social judgement, as we shall see more clearly in the next chapter. The assessment of reputation by villagers can be traced in the evaluations of witnesses in court cases; the defamation cases brought before the various courts of the Diocese of Norwich reveal the aspects of their own reputations that villagers valued. At the centre of reputation, particularly for women, was sexual

---

[8] ANW 2/58, Cawston, John Nicholls; Ralph Houlbrooke, *Church Courts and the People During the English Reformation, 1520–1570* (Oxford, 1979), pp. 45–6; Wrightson and Levine, *Poverty and Piety*, p. 101; for common fame, see Richard Wunderli, *London Church Courts and Society on the Eve of the Reformation* (Cambridge, Massachusetts, 1981), pp. 63–4.

[9] DEP/24, Martiall Barker con Richard Stokes, Archdeacon of Norfolk, Richard Thayne, William Hill and Simon Dowe, ff. 354–65, esp. 355, 362.

behaviour. In 1581 Cicely Lee of Edgefield was presented to the Archdeacon of Norwich for 'suspicious living' with William Baker, Gent. She rejected the charges against her, and described how Baker had attempted to seduce her at least half a dozen times. He 'didst watch his time' and came by her house when her husband was absent. She always resisted his seduction, 'saying that she did set as much by her honesty as he did by all the goods he had'. Eventually, however, he got her in her house, barred the doors and raped her.[10] The key word in Cicely Lee's account is 'honesty', used to describe her fidelity to her husband, but giving it broader implications. The linking of sexual behaviour to general honesty was by no means unusual. In 1566 Thomas Barne of Girston sought to undermine a witness's credibility by noting that she was a servant of the plaintiff's husband (and thus a dependant) and that she had borne an illegitimate child and had not yet done penance for the fault. Barne assumed that one could not trust a woman who did not at least do penance after bearing an illegitimate child.[11] Sexual behaviour was one component of 'honesty' in early modern England, and cannot be segregated from other social questions.

Sexual behaviour was not the only component of reputation. Relationships within families were observed and evaluated. When Thomas Hardy testified about the will of Robert Hawes in 1566, he was sharply criticized by later witnesses; he was a man of 'lewd conversation, false, ungodly, and unnatural', who had denied his own father money and goods to sustain himself. He was 'a scape thrift, a disobedient child crassly deceitful, injurious and false in his saying'. He had once threatened to have his father put in the stocks, and had alleged that 'the gallows was too good for him [his father]'.[12] The focus on Hardy's treatment of his father indicates that villagers assumed bonds of obligation between children and parents. Hardy's father expected help from his son when he was in need, and his neighbours found nothing odd in his expectation. Hardy's behaviour in his own family helped to discredit his

---

[10] ANW/2/15, 1581, Edgefield con Cicely ux. James Lee.

[11] DEP/10, Bk. 11a, 1566, Mrs Agnes Brown con Brown, f. 249v.

[12] DEP/10, Bk. 11a, 1566, Testament of Robert Hawes, ff. 54v, 64v, 65v; cf. ANW/2/58, 1617, presentment of John Graie, singleman of Cawston, 'that he have undutifully behaved himself to his natural mother, reproaching her with reproachful terms and words'.

testimony on unrelated matters. Respect was, predictably, also expected from wives to husbands. Eloise Sutton, William Palmer and Thomas King agreed in 1567, was 'a common make bait and sower of strife between party and party, a common and notorious liar, an unquiet partner with her husband and among her neighbours of no reputation or credit . . . and will be persuaded with a pot of beer to say and depose what any man will have or procure her to say'.[13] The connections made between quarrelling with her husband, setting strife among neighbours and lying are not necessarily obvious. These connections, made with such ease, indicate the significance of behaviour within the family.

This evidence demonstrates the importance of reputation, but it only shows how others judged reputation. We must also look at how people constructed their own reputations. This can be systematically examined in the defamation cases brought before the Consistory Court of the Diocese of Norwich. In theory, the ecclesiastical courts had jurisdiction over defamation cases only when the offence alleged was punishable in those courts: thus we should expect a concentration on sexual offences; charges of theft, perjury and the like would be heard in the common law courts. In practice, a much broader range of insults appears.[14] The person who brought a defamation case sought to protect a reputation that had, they thought, been damaged by an allegation. The insults and allegations complained of reveal the assumptions and fears of early modern villagers.

The most noticeable characteristic of defamation cases between 1560 and 1725 is that they were increasingly brought by women against other women. Between 1574 and 1640 men brought more than half (54.8 per cent) of the defamation cases in the deposition books of the Consistory Court; after 1660 they brought just over a third of the cases (35.1 per cent). It should not surprise us that men were more often defendants than women: in a patriarchal society the words of men would be taken more seriously than those of women. Until 1590, the behaviour of women and men is similar in this regard: 31.1 per cent of the suits brought by women were

[13] DEP/11, Bk. 11b, Tolk con Goslynge, exceptions, f. 22.
[14] See e.g. J.A. Sharpe, *Defamation and Sexual Slander in Early Modern England: the church courts at York*, Borthwick papers No. 58 (1980), pp. 3–8 passim for the law, 11–15 for practice.

against other women, as were 35.4 per cent of those brought by men. After 1600, their behaviour diverged: only one-third of the suits brought by men between 1600 and 1640 were against women, but almost half (48.4 per cent) of these brought by women were directed at other women. After the Restoration the proportion of men's cases directed at women dropped to one-fifth. At the same time, the Consistory Court was becoming increasingly a local court: the proportion of defamation cases arising in Norwich and its immediate suburbs, and Great Yarmouth and its suburb Gorleston, rose from only 13.5 per cent before 1590 to 50 per cent after 1660.[15]

The subjects of litigation reveal additional differences between women and men. While sexual insults predominated for both women and men, even the vague insults of 'whore', 'jade', 'bitch' and 'drab' complained of by women had more concrete sexual implications than the equivalent insults – 'whoremaster', 'rogue' and 'knave' – for men. Such insults became increasingly common for both women and men over the period, but throughout, (if the general charge of being a whore is included), they were of greater concern to women.[16] The insults complained of by men concerned a much broader range of activities than those complained of by women. Men complained of being called thieves, drunkards and blasphemers, as well as of critical assaults on their social position. The sexual insults they challenged should be understood in the context of their social implications were they true. To be a cuckold – or to cuckold another – threatened household order. Fornication with an unmarried woman threatened the village with a bastard and bastards often became drains on the parish poor rates. The position of men in the social order of their communities was a product of a complex combination of sexual behaviour, familial

---

[15] This analysis is based on DEP/15, 16, 17, 18, 19, 20 (Bk. 21a), 22, 23, 24 (156 cases); DEP/35, 37, 40 (154 cases) and DEP/46, 49, 53 (114 cases); many cases were settled before depositions were taken, but only the deposition books allow a consistent comparison of the causes of defamation cases.

[16] Before 1590, such insults were alleged in 52.7 per cent of the cases (thirty-nine of seventy-four) brought by women, and in 13.4 per cent (eleven of eighty-two) brought by men; after 1660 in 77 per cent of the cases brought by women, and 60 per cent of those brought by men (fifty-seven of seventy-four cases brought by women and twenty-four of forty cases brought by men). Vague insults account for 64.6 per cent of the cases brought by women and 32.9 per cent of the cases brought by men between 1600 and 1640: cf. Martin J. Ingram, 'Ecclesiastical justice in Wiltshire, 1600–1640, with special reference to cases concerning sex and marriage', Oxford University D.Phil., 1976, p. 277.

relations and relations with their neighbours. Women's reputations were far more narrowly rooted in sexual behaviour. Women protected their sexual reputations from charges of being a whore, cuckolding their husbands, bearing illegitimate children or keeping a bawdy house. Only a few women, all before 1640, complain of insults that are not specifically sexual, but six of the seven who do so were accused of being a scold or of having been ducked as a scold. Scolding had implications both within and outside the household. It involved stepping out of the meek and passive role assigned to women. In popular images of disorderly women, scolds were bracketed with women who beat or cuckolded their husbands. So although scolding itself is non-sexual, it was connected with sexual misbehaviour. And women could disrupt communities in very few ways: sexual disorder was one, but scolding and quarrelling was the other.[17]

What are we to make of these patterns? First, women's reputations were more easily threatened than were men's. The charges they complained of were far more likely to be vague allegations of wrongdoing than were men's – although vague insults were more frequent causes of complaint by both women and men later in our period. At the same time, the pattern of litigation – an increase in the proportion of cases brought by women against other women, and the slight decline in the proportion brought by men against women – suggests that the social worlds of the sexes were becoming more distinct; women, it would seem, had a smaller role in the world of men, and the absence of charges of scolding in the later period suggests that the impact of their behaviour on their neighbours had diminished. Sexual reputation became relatively more significant for women as they had more limited roles in their families. This same pattern holds for men as well, but with a slightly different emphasis. The growing vagueness of the terms of abuse complained of by men suggests an increasing superficiality of reputation: what mattered

[17] Scolding never accounted for more than 10 per cent of the cases brought by women, and six of the seven scolding cases were brought before 1590. The one non-sexual insult alleged by a woman that is not scolding involves a religious lapse: DEP/18, Cowper, wid. con Kenderwell, Cler.: he said at visitation that she was a 'busy woman and did trouble him and interrupt him in his service', and also that she had not received Communion for two or three years: these offences were all punishable in the ecclesiastical courts, so the defamation case may have been Cowper's way of defending herself against the accusation. For scolds, see Underdown, 'The taming of the scold'.

was what people thought you were, not what they thought you did. Significantly, when men brought suits against women after 1660, they were more than twice as likely to complain of specific sexual allegations than they were against men: the social distance between women and men meant that a woman could dent a man's reputation only with details. Finally, while the general insults for women have sexual connotations, those for men have social ones.[18]

The defamation cases suggests that 'honesty' had one meaning for women and another for men. Women's honesty was determined and judged by their sexual behaviour; men's honesty was judged in a wide variety of contexts with their neighbours, and bore a closer relation to our notion of honesty as 'truthful'. Reputation was a gendered concept in early modern England.

Reputation demonstrates that appropriate behaviour in early modern villages was defined by gender. Because of its importance, villagers payed close attention to the sexual and social relations of their neighbours. The nature of that attention, the values it reflected and the concerns it embodied differed along the life course of individuals. This interest first focused on individuals during courtship. The role of the household in the social order of the village made stable, valid marriages critical: if the marriage was for any reason invalid, the village might find itself responsible for the woman and any children involved. The law made marriage a minefield for the unwary. The centre of confusion was the 'promise' to marry. A promise to marry someone in 'words of the present tense' (*'verba de praesenti'*) was legally binding, although consummation was not supposed to occur until after the marriage had been solemnized in the church. Yet not everyone knew what constituted a legally binding promise. One reason for reading the banns in church was so that anyone who claimed a prior contract could speak up. Matrimonial litigation often occurred when one party discovered they had unintentionally entered into a legally binding contract of marriage.[19] Genuine – and understandable – confusion about the law was common: Elizabeth Lord agreed to

---

[18] In half the cases that men brought against women after 1660 there are specific allegations of sexual misconduct (as opposed to general abuse); this is the case in only 25 per cent of the cases that men brought against other men.

[19] Ralph Houlbrooke, *The English Family, 1450–1700* (London and New York, 1984), pp. 78–9; Howard, *Matrimonial Institutions*, vol. I, pp. 336–8, 377–80.

marry one Harrison when he wrongly said that he could get her discharged from her previous contract with John Davys. Cicilia Hennant suffered from her own apparent passivity; when Edward Bradley came to her house, he 'took her by the hand she thinking nothing and asked her whether she could be content to forsake all men and take him to her husband, to the which she answered nothing, but took the cup and bade him drink and so departed'.[20] Her behaviour – by her own account – was ambiguous, but Bradley and his witnesses took her silence as consent. The promise was usually accompanied by an exchange of tokens, but participants often argued about what was a gift and what a 'token'. In 1581 Mr Thomas Gyrlinge sought to force Mrs Anne Skippon to follow up an alleged promise of marriage, noting that he had sent her some gifts. She had refused the gifts, although he had placed no conditions on their acceptance, and it turned out that the messenger had kept them![21]

Confusion was one major source of matrimonial litigation; the absence of social approval was another. Marriage was not just the business of the couple. Decisions to marry inevitably balanced prudence and affection. Prudence extended beyond the considerations of property we examined in the last chapter to the approval of family and community. Many young people accepted – or made – an offer of marriage conditional on the consent of parents or 'friends'. In 1563 Anne Sponer told Stephen Gurney that 'she would make him promise if he could get the good will of most of her friends',[22] while three years later Annice Thurlow told Robert Wade that 'if he could obtain her friends' good will she could find it in her heart to love him'.[23] Parental judgements included, but were not limited to, financial concerns, though the precise concerns are not always specified. Suzan Ives of Norwich was convinced by her mother not to go ahead with a planned marriage

[20] DEP/13, n.d. Personal answers of Elizabeth Lord to allegations ex parte Harryson, f. 111; DEP/10, Bk. 11a, 1565/6, Personal answers of Cicilia Hennant of Norwich to allegations of Edward Bradley, f. 16 and Bradley con Hennant, ff. 18v–20.

[21] DEP/18, 1581, Mr Thomas Gyrlinge con Mrs Anne Skippon, ff. 338–40 and Anne Skippon alias Mather con Thomas Girling, ff. 256–8.

[22] DEP/10, Bk. 10, Personal answers of Anne Sponer of Walberswick (March 1563/4).

[23] DEP/10, Bk. 11a, 1566, Personal answers of Annice Thurlow to libel ex parte Robert Wade, f. 169v; cf. Guildhall Library Ms. 9189, v.1, 1622/3, Edward Locke con Sara Johnson, ff. 26v–7v, 36v–40v; DEP/19, 1581/2, Francys Brooke con Edward Planden, ff. 378–84v; DEP/16, Bk. 17a (1576) Clara Bateman con Robert Pernell.

to Richard Richardson. More dramatically, Elizabeth Cocke, a widow from Tivetshall, was allegedly locked up in her brother's house in East Dereham to prevent her marriage to Ralph Thompson.[24]

Household manuals all stressed that children should heed their parents' advice in decisions about marriage. The families of marriageable women and men often had strong ideas about whom they should marry, but those involved always sought to uphold their independence. In 1566 Elizabeth Browne's father favoured her marriage to Robert Keene, but Elizabeth claimed she was already contracted to one Gilder, and would marry him even 'if her father and all her friends did what they could to the contrary, and wept bitterly'.[25] Under pressure, she eventually agreed to have the banns for her marriage to Keene read – at which point Gilder publicly objected. Mary Aldham of Shimpling was married to Matthew Cotwin by 'the means and procurement' of her father and uncle in 1577, in spite of an earlier promise to John Russell; by 1579 Aldham and Cotwyn had separated because they 'could not agree together' and Russell sought to marry her. Unfortunately for Russell, his mother had not objected when the banns were read, and while he lived only on his mason's craft, Aldham's father had more than £100 a year, so there was 'a great inequality'.[26] Ellen Thorne of Skeyton was persuaded by her mother and stepfather to entertain Erasmus Crome's suit, although she didn't wish to, because his offer – which included a promise to pay for litigation about her lands – was so good. Crome pulled back in the face of an additional lawsuit, so Thorne promised herself to John Dybolde. She thought that Crome's hesitation left her free, but the marriage was an advantageous one, so he pursued it.[27]

Matrimonial suits came into the courts because of confusion, conditions by one party or other or parental pressure. They could also be a crude form of blackmail. In such cases, the reputation of

[24] DEP/18, 1580, Richard Richardson con Suzan Ives, ff. 8v–11; DEP/17, Ralph Thompson con Elizabeth Cocke, widow of Tivetshall, ff. 268–9v: it is possible that litigation in this case is collusive, to free both parties from the suspicion of an existing contract.

[25] DEP/10, Bk. 11a, Robert Keene con Elizabeth Browne, ff. 177–8, 227v and Gilder con Elizabeth Browne, ff. 212–12v.

[26] DEP/23, John Russell con Mary Aldham, 353–4v, 448–53: at one point in this struggle, Russell tried to kidnap Aldham.

[27] DEP/17, 1579, Erasmus Crome con Ellen Thorne and John Dybolde, ff. 103–6v, 130–5, 154–5v.

witnesses on each side was critical to the outcome. John Barnes persuaded two of his friends to say they witnessed a promise of marriage between him and Thomazine Aldham of Sapiston, Suffolk. Their original testimony suggested a cloak and dagger operation – ostensibly because Aldham's brother had the wardship of her son, and would keep it if he learned of her intent to marry her servant Barnes. Four months later, both 'witnesses' admitted that they had seen no such promise, but had been told by Barnes that the real witnesses lacked sufficient credit to testify. John Barnes would have done quite well for himself had he succeeded in marrying Thomazine Aldham, and he hoped the report of the promise would succeed where persuasion had failed.[28] The absence of witnesses was a serious problem, often recognized too late; when Margery Robinson was served with a citation from William Robinson, she commented that all their talks had been private, so the court would have to weigh her word against his. Without witnesses reputation was central.[29]

Suits for breach of contract could, however, be constructive efforts to sort out the position of those involved in the tangled webs of talk and promises, often to make another marriage possible. When Mary Woods of Beeston St Lawrence sued William Drake in 1617, it was alleged that Drake had wanted to marry Woods, but had been beaten by his father-in-law so that he would marry his present wife. Woods obviously wanted to know where she stood. Six months after her wedding to John Thurston in 1567, Katherine Balle brought a suit against her husband in which it was alleged that Thurston had made a prior contract with Anne Banyard. Whether Katherine wanted to be free from her marriage or to quiet gossip is not specified, but only a lawsuit could establish the validity of her marriage. John Wright brought a suit against Elizabeth Inglebright apparently with the intention of disproving the rumoured promise; in her personal answers, Inglebright acknowledged the contract, however, and said she

---

[28] DEP/20, Bk. 21a John Barnes con Thomazine Aldham, 358–61, 362–4v, and also DEP/16, 17b, 1583, ff. 72–7: Barnes spread a rumour of a promised marriage to him within one month of her husband's death; Aldham had since married Mr Thomas Kighlie.

[29] DEP/16, William Robinson con Margery Robinson, ff. 168, 183v–4.

would do anything in her power to prevent Wright's marriage to anyone else.[30]

Marriage was too important to be left to the contracting parties. Parents, 'friends' and neighbours acted both to further and to prevent matches. William Browne's mother, a widow from Bradfield, Suffolk, was said to have promoted his marriage to Margaret Farrington in 1576 hoping that Farrington's father 'would be a good guide unto her son';[31] on the other hand, Prudence Barrett's promised marriage to Henry Quashe so offended her friends that they threatened to waste her portion in fighting it.[32] The concerns of parents and families were obvious – wealth, character and position – but neighbours had a more complicated set of concerns. In 1606 one witness alleged that Catherine Drayne was an appropriate wife for Henry Billingford (who had promised to marry her): although she might 'be thought' to be inferior – 'for her parentage being a yeoman's daughter' and for having earlier borne an illegitimate child – because of the 'comeliness and feature of her body, and honest comeliness and qualities', she was a good wife 'for a better man than Henry Billingford'.[33] Neighbours could be swift to depress pretension: when William Baker sought to avoid his promised marriage to Agnes Whistlecroft on the grounds of disparity of fortune, some witnesses denied any inequality.[34] The 'truth' of any of these allegations is impossible to determine, but the judgements they express were only partly based on property. Husband and wife were also expected to 'agree quietly together' and to work well together. Fortune was one part of the equation, but neighbours might also be concerned that a particular young man or woman marry, or marry a particular type of person; character and abilities were important.

[30] DEP/37, Mary Woods con William Drake, f. 13v; DEP/11, Bk. 11b, Katherine Balle con John Thurston, ff. 78v–80v; cf. DEP/13, Roger Archer con Audrey Gilley, ff. 161v–4v, 281–2v, 288v and Roger Stocks con Audrey Gilley, ff. 301–1v, 304v–5, in which a promise to Archer is alleged, although he was not free from prior contracts: the suits sought to determine whether Gilley's marriage to Stocks was valid; DEP/13, John Wright con Elizabeth Inglebright, f. 345.

[31] DEP/16, Bk. 17a, Margaret Farrington con William Browne, ff. 82–3.

[32] DEP/19, Henry Quashe con Prudence Barrett, ff. 254–60, 407–10; Richard Flatman con Prudence Barrett, ff. 392–6: Flatman had married Barrett without either banns or a marriage licence.

[33] DEP/33, Jermy con Billingford, ff. 557r–v.

[34] DEP/26, Agnes Whistlecroft con William Baker, ff. 437–42, 471–9.

Disputes over marriage contracts occurred frequently in court records of the late sixteenth century, but less often in the seventeenth century. This is not because betrothal was less important; the movement of the betrothal into the wedding service was a much later development and cases of pre-nuptial fornication indicate that the promise to marry remained a recognized stage in the courtship process. Why did this stage of courtship cease to be a subject of conflict in the courts? There are two possible explanations. The first is that conflicts over marriage really did disappear, and that young women and men were completely free to make their own decisions, suffered no intervention from parents or friends and never changed their own minds. If this is so, the seventeenth century is indeed unique in history. The alternative explanation is that the informal control of courtship was more effectively exercised in the seventeenth century, so that litigation became less necessary. The 'freedom' that historians have seen in the choice of partners by young people in early modern England was exercised within closely defined limits. A lawsuit only occurred after a courtship had progressed to a certain point; in the seventeenth century fewer young people reached that stage without social approval. Not every courtship ended in marriage, but fewer inappropriate courtships came close enough to marriage to make legal action possible. The informal supervision of courtship both encouraged and discouraged marriages. The informality and invisibility of much of this control does not signify its absence, and the glimpses we have of the working of the informal system suggest its ubiquity. Such informal controls are more consonant with what we know of early modern English society than is complete freedom on the part of unmarried women and men.[35]

The legal definition of marriage made doubts about who was married or free to marry possible and even probable; it also made marriage a subject of public concern. The differences between legal and popular definitions of marriage remind us that English

---

[35] The betrothal ceremony or 'promise' only lost its role with the passage of Lord Hardwicke's Marriage Act in 1753: Gillis, For Better, For Worse, pp. 140–1; Ingram, 'Ecclesiastical justice', pp. 112–14; Stone, Family, Sex and Marriage, pp. 628; Macfarlane, Marriage and Love, pp. 132–47 passim; Amussen, 'Féminin/Masculin', pp. 273–5; cf. DEP/16, Bk. 17b, Ex Offic. promot. per Agnes Drake con Thomas Poyer, ff. 60–v; and DEP/35, Augustine Ransome con Agnes Lincoln, ff. 368–71.

villagers did not blindly accept standards offered by official institutions, but shaped them to meet their own needs. Katherine Salter summarized popular opinion when she asserted (more loudly than her neighbours were wont to do) 'that after a couple have talked of matrimony it is lawful for them to have carnal copulation'.[36] This popular view encouraged pre-nuptial fornication, and also made the promise of marriage a common ploy in seduction. Yet fornication before marriage remained an offence in the church courts; the charge was never common, and those charged with it were often surprised. Edmund Barker of Watton was presented for fornication with Mary Beckerton, since deceased, in 1663. He admitted the offence, but said that they had contracted marriage, and he 'had the carnal knowledge of her body as of his wife before God'; he would have proceeded with the wedding had she not died.[37] The intermediate position of the betrothed – legally bound but not fully married – served only to confuse those involved in courtships.

The easiest way to escape betrothal was geographical mobility: knowledge of marriage contracts was limited to a small area. George Hunter was contracted to Helen Hathwat in York; the entire wedding was planned, guests invited and clothes bought, when George left for London, never to return. Helen was pregnant when he left; George married another woman, and settled with her in Essex. Helen Hathwat suffered from social conditions which enabled a man to move away from those who knew his past.[38] Women could also move, but they did so less often than men.

Helen Hathwat's experience is instructive, because it reminds us that early modern England was a mobile society, while its matrimonial law assumed a geographically stable agricultural society. As an increasing number of villagers were cut off from the land, it became more difficult to enforce betrothals: there was no

[36] ANW/1/4, 1564, Wighton con Katherine Salter; Martin Ingram, 'The reform of popular culture? Sex and marriage in early modern England', in *Popular Culture in Seventeenth Century England*, ed. Barry Reay (New York, 1985), pp. 129–65, esp. 146–50, suggests greater ambivalance about pre-nuptial fornication, but I have seen no evidence that it was frowned on after a public promise of marriage.

[37] ANW/2/78, 1663, Watton con Edmund Barker; Quaife, *Wanton Wenches*, pp. 59–62; Gillis, *For Better, For Worse*, p. 52; Peter Laslett, 'Long-term trends in bastardy in England', in *Family Life and Illicit Love in Earlier Generations* (Cambridge and New York, 1977), pp. 128–30.

[38] Guildhall Lib. Ms. 9189 v.1, Helen Hathwat con George Hunter, ff. 128v–30v (1623/4).

way to ensure compliance by a labourer who could leave more or less at will. It was not, however, until the passage of Lord Hardwicke's Marriage Act in 1753 that betrothal lost its legal validity. Until then – and even afterwards in popular culture – the ambiguities and confusion, as well as community concern, remained an important part of gender relations.[39]

The confusion surrounding marriage shows that the clarity of definition sought by household manuals never existed. The challenges to the norms of the household manuals were, however, more often tacit than explicit; even a bigamous marriage was a back-handed acceptance of them. It was the everyday behaviour of women and men that undermined the theoretical definitions of household order. Those who clung too firmly to the image of sermons, household manuals and social theory had nothing but disappointment awaiting them.

The problems raised by the birth of 'illegitimate' children are a perfect illustration of the indirect nature of challenges to the gender order. The birth of an illegitimate child created a household with neither communal approval, financial security nor a father to govern it. Illegitimacy rates peaked between 1590 and 1610 but remained a problem throughout the period. The rates alone, however, tell us little about what it meant to bear (or father) an illegitimate child. The charge of bearing or fathering a bastard was a regular, though not frequent, cause of defamation cases throughout the period. And while it was really the relation between the parents that was illegitimate, not the child, 'bastard' is a term of abuse frequently complained of by men. A bastard lacked legal status in inheritance, and the insult may have originally been used to question rights to property.[40]

The undesirability of bearing or fathering a bastard is demonstrated by the behaviour of those in danger of being discovered. The experience of women and men was different, however; most women's pregnancies were discovered by observation, but the designation of putative fathers depended both on the accusation of the woman involved and the observation of neighbours. In 1601 Agnes Haddon's neighbours in Neatishead, Norfolk, were

---

[39] Gillis, *For Better, For Worse*, pp. 139–42.
[40] Laslett, 'Long-term trends in bastardy', pp. 111–14, 151–4.

convinced that John Brende, Gent. was the father of the child she was carrying, because his 'familiarity' with Haddon 'was very offensive unto the said neighbours ... and ministered cause of suspicion unto them of their incontinent living together'.[41] Agnes Haddon was unable to charge anyone else with fathering the child, although she tried to. Such attempts were not unusual, and were often encouraged by the actual father. When Mr Poynter, the minister of Blakeney, got Elizabeth Reve with child in 1605, he told her to quickly seduce another man in order to charge him with the bastard. Reeve obligingly did so, but changed her story when she was asked to repeat it under oath.[42]

The fathers of illegitimate children were joined by their families and friends in pressuring women to supress information. Matthew Goodwin of Little Walsingham offered £5 to Elizabeth Freeman to not charge his stepson William Gasely with fathering her child. When Alice Parish was questioned by her mistress Mrs Bacon, she readily denied that the child had been fathered by Bacon's eldest son, but remained silent when asked about the younger ones. 'And therewith her mistress was so much moved, and fell down upon her knees; And this examinant to content her did then say that it was none of her younger sons.'[43] Alice Parish was initially vulnerable to her mistress's pressure, but later did charge William Bacon, one of the younger sons, with fathering the child. In 1608, Elizabeth Stewarde of North Walsham continued to name William Cates of Cromer, a married man, as father although he and his friends offered her £6 13s. 4d. – equivalent to four years' wages – to charge someone else. Stewarde recognized the stakes, and insisted that she would not 'wrong any man with false reports' both for the harm it would do his reputation and her soul.[44]

Men did everything in their power to avoid paternity accusations. Thomas Fayerweather, a blacksmith from Roydon, Suffolk, fled to Norwich when faced with one. In 1640 John Call found patronage more useful: Francis Parlett, a justice of the peace

[41] DEP/31, Ex Offic. con Thomas Haddon and Agnes Haddon, ff. 433–41v.

[42] RAY/262, 1605, Examination of Elizabeth Reve; the curate of Wiveton tried to arrange a marriage with William Sayers, but he would only marry her with the consent of the town.

[43] C/S3/44, 1661, Examination of Elizabeth Freeman; NRS Accn. Christie 14.5.82 Q 190A, 1616, Examination of Alice Parish of Heydon.

[44] DEP/34, Ex Offic. con William Cates of Cromer, ff. 7v–8; women over twenty working as servants in husbandry were to receive 30s. in wages plus 10s. for livery in 1613: AYL/1, 1613, justices' wage rates. .

who employed Call's father as his brewer, wrote the Archdeacon that when the civil authorities had examined the case they had found no evidence against Call, and since the child had died shortly after birth and the mother left King's Lynn, there was no need for further punishment of the unfortunate lad. The inferential nature of evidence against them – being seen with a woman – provided some men with protection, and meant that women who were seen with several men had difficulty making convincing accusations.[45] Their desire to avoid accusations, and the lengths they would go to avoid them, indicates that men's relations with their neighbours deteriorated as a result of an accepted accusation. A bastard was always a potential charge on the rates; those who fathered them won no popularity contests.

Men might avoid paternity accusations, but it was far more difficult for women to deny their impending maternity. Mary Goodchild, a servant in East Dereham in 1676, did so by disappearing: she asked her mistress for permission to see a doctor about her illness, but instead went to London where she bore her bastard, and then returned to service, leaving the baby in Shipdham, where it was maintained by its father, Edward Mason.[46] Others attempted to hide a pregnancy, not telling anyone of their predicament. Prosecutions for infanticide are directed primarily at servants, and occur frequently in the surviving assize records for the county. The women involved wore heavy clothes, and often moved during the course of pregnancy. They gave birth alone, and usually claimed that the child was stillborn. When Elizabeth Michell of Wilton was in labour in 1673, she asked a neighbour for something to ease her pains, which she claimed were from her 'monthly courses'.

> The said neighbours did get some water and herbs and warmed
> them and put them in a pail . . . and set it under a wicker chair

---

[45] AYL/16, Thomas Rous to William Blennerhassett, 9 July 1592; ANW/2/74, 1640, 17 December 1640, Francis Parlett to Dr Tallbott; see also e.g. C/S2/5, Norwich Sessions July 1703, Thomas Cock of North Walsham and Norwich Sessions January 1704/5, Philip Panke of Skeyton.

[46] DEP/49, Mr John Greene con Edward Mason, file 25, 167[6]: the reason this case is in the courts is unclear, though it may be significant that Goodchild's infant was born in one Quaker household, and was being cared for in another. Cf. Guildhall Lib. Ms. 9189, v. 1, 1623, Offic. dmi con Dye alias Dive Hall of Acton, who fathered a child on his servant Elizabeth Carter, hid her from her parents, took her to Westminster to give birth and then apprenticed her in Charing Cross, ff. 115–17.

for her the said Examinant to sit over . . . she finding ease she removed herself unto another chair just by . . . and when her pains came again she removed herself unto the aforesaid wicker chair and there she was delivered; at which time she was not sensible what came from her until she was a little recovered; And afterward she looking into the pail found a dead child.[47]

Some mothers were more aware of what was happening, but still asserted that the child was born dead.[48] The unwillingness of juries to convict for infanticide suggests that they saw the choice as the lesser of two evils, and that they were unable to condemn those who did not try to keep their child alive.

Women also sought to avoid bearing illegitimate children through abortion. Their lovers or even their mistresses often provided the necessary information. The practice was not always condemned, as most people believed that the soul only entered the foetus at the time of 'quickening', usually the fifth month. In April 1627, Joan Thorpe, a servant in Burnham Sutton, who had become pregnant at Christmas,

finding her ordinary monthly courses ceased demanded of her mistress . . . what were good for her to take, and her mistress told her; she thereupon received as was directed, and upon the taking of the same being first a posset of hyssop, and another of wormwood and saffron, she grew very sick therewith and her courses returned and brake out very powerfully upon her and so continued until her delivery as aforesaid.[49]

She was delivered of a 'very little' child, which she kicked into a muck hill so that no one would see it; she never checked to see

[47] PRO ASSI 16/26/4, Examination of Elizabeth Michell, late of Wilton.
[48] E.g. PRO ASSI 16/27/4, Information of Susan Barker of South Burlingham; ASSI 16/19/4, Information against Francis Tills; ASSI 16/22/3, Information against Mary Pooley; ASSI 16/23/3, Information against Mary Williams; ASSI 16/13/4, Information re. Elizabeth Cullyer of Tibbenham and ASSI 16/14/5, Information re. child found in a pond in North Lopham; see also Amussen, 'Governors and governed', pp. 278–80; Keith Wrightson, 'Infanticide in earlier seventeenth century England', in *Local Population Studies*, 15 (1975), pp. 10–22, and R.W. Malcolmson, 'Infanticide in the eighteenth century', in *Crime in England, 1550–1800*, ed. J.S. Cockburn (Princeton, 1977), pp. 187–209.
[49] C/S3/26, Information re. Joan Thorpe of Burnham Sutton, 2 May 3 Charles I.

whether or not it was alive. Thorpe's mistress had a knowledge of abortifacients that no one found surprising. When Mary Lambe bled during an illness in 1605, some people suspected her of aborting a pregnancy. At the end of the 1670s, Nicholas Todd was responsible for the pregnancy of Elizabeth Turner, and gave her a recipe (made up by an apothecary in King's Lynn) which Elizabeth took to abort the child: it made her very sick, but the child survived.[50] Abortion provided one way that unmarried women could avoid the obloquy and shame of an illegitimate child – and perhaps also that married women could avoid unwanted children.

During the seventeenth century, there appears to have been a shift in attitudes towards infanticide. In Sussex in the period up to 1640, 53 per cent of the women accused of infanticide were convicted and 88 per cent of those convicted hung; by the end of the century in Norfolk, most women accused of infanticide were acquitted. Yet the only legal changes during the period served to make conviction easier rather than more difficult, as bearing a dead child without witnesses was defined as infanticide.[51] The still-birth defence used by most mothers was legally untenable. Juries apparently recognized that given the position of mothers of illegitimate children, the decision to allow a child to die was a rational one; they may have also reasoned that the death of the child was preferable to the dependence of mother and child on parish relief. The trial would impress the mother with the power of the law, the verdict of its mercy.

[50] DEP/33, Lomax con Lambe, esp. ff. 280–2 and the counter-arguments in ff. 434–44; DEP/51, Turner con Todd, 1680, esp. ff. 389–90; see also C/S3/23A, Articles against Henry Eaton of Holme Hale, who tried to make his servant abort the child she carried. I have found no evidence of the use of coitus interruptus as a method of birth control, and it seems likely that abortion was more common than has hitherto been acknowledged by most of those who have discussed family limitation: see e.g. Wrightson and Levine, *Poverty and Piety*, p. 55, where they cite breast feeding and coitus interruptus as the basis of low marital fertility; but see Angus McLaren, *Reproductive Rituals: the perception of fertility in England from the sixteenth century to the nineteenth century* (London and New York, 1984), chapter 4.

[51] 21 Jas. I cap. 27; Cynthia B. Herrup, *The Common Peace: Participation and the Criminal Law in Seventeenth Century England* (Cambridge, 1987), pp. 144, 176; in the Norfolk Assizes found in PRO ASSI 16 and ASSI 35, as well as those found in NRO C/S3 there are twenty-four identifiable infanticide prosecutions, and the outcomes are clear in twenty. Of those twenty, one accusation was not returned as an indictment, six (30 per cent) were guilty, 65 per cent not guilty; only two appear to have been hanged. Cf. Peter C. Hoffer and N.E.H. Hull, *Murdering Mothers: infanticide in England and New England*, Linden Studies in Anglo-American Legal History (New York, 1981), pp. 19–27, 68–71.

While the behaviour of men suggests that they suffered social ostracism after fathering illegitimate children, evidence of how mothers were treated is more direct. When Robert Breaman of Brancaster discovered that his servant Jane Taylor was pregnant in 1661, he fired her. Taylor then began a journey more remarkable for being recorded than for having taken place. She left Brancaster and returned to Creake, where she had been born, and from there was sent to Thornham, where she had been in service. Thornham sent her back to Brancaster, which sought the advice of a justice of the peace and had her returned to Thornham. The journey, of at least twenty miles, left Taylor a mere two miles from her starting point.[52] The social ostracism of bastard-bearers is even more explicit in the case of Elizabeth Rix of Winfarthing, pregnant with her third bastard in 1712. At that time the putative father, along with Rix's former master and several other townsmen, decided that Rix should be married to someone from outside the parish. They found a rather sickly young man named Smith from Diss, who worked as a wool-comber in Norwich. He accepted the offer of £10 to marry Rix, though he did not know that she was eight months' pregnant. The day after the wedding the townsmen of Winfarthing had Elizabeth Rix moved to Diss, although her husband disappeared the same day. Diss complained, and Rix was eventually returned to Winfarthing, but only after Winfarthing had spent more than £10 on court battles. Her homecoming could not have been a very friendly one.[53]

There has been extensive debate in recent years over the causes of illegitimacy, but the discussion has generally ignored the treatment of bastard-bearers. Many of the women who became pregnant alleged that they consented to sexual relations only after a promise of marriage; given the treatment of bastard-bearers, they undoubtedly relied on the promise. In the 1570s, Helen Hawke of Denton was courted by Nicholas Rushman. They had spoken of marriage, and 'being sure together' Nicholas 'requested divers and sundry times to have his pleasure of her'. She agreed, but when she became pregnant he sought to deny his responsibility – though he

[52] C/S3/45, Jan 1661/2, Examination of Jane Taylor.
[53] PD 100/23, Complaint from Diss; C/S2/6, Norwich Sessions, July 1712; also PD 78/48, 1712–13.

admitted that he had 'lain in naked bed with her'.[54] Consent to sexual relations may have been the last best hope of poor girls seeking to marry, but for every girl who used it successfully there were many others for whom it failed. The attempt to get married by becoming pregnant was a high-risk enterprise, and it is unlikely to have been deliberately risked by many. Certainly no girl could have come of age in early modern England with illusions about the treatment of those who bore bastards. They were tolerated only in rare, extenuating circumstances. When Agnes Drake became pregnant in 1583 everyone assumed that Thomas Poyer was the father, since he had been Drake's suitor for three years, and their marriage was expected. When the child was born Poyer refused to marry Drake because her mother would not give him her house in Dilham.[55] Drake's behaviour was explicable and normal; the problem was Poyer's refusal to go through with the marriage. Unless there was a very good excuse, however, the single pregnant women was condemned and ostracized.

Women who bore bastards posed an implicit challenge to social and familial order by creating a 'family' without a head: such families were not included in household manuals. The behaviour of women and men within marriage could also challenge the social order, although these challenges – like those brought by bastardy – were usually indirect. These challenges fall into two major groups: the first involves the treatment of husbands by wives, the second marital breakdown, which often involved men who transgressed expectations within marriage.

The primary challenge to social expectations within marriage arose when women interpreted gender in ways that differed from the prescriptions of social theory. According to that theory, women had two equally important duties: obedience and sexual fidelity. There is extensive evidence that women believed fidelity was important, obedience secondary. The insults alleged in

[54] Wrightson, 'The Puritan reformation of manners', pp. 56–7: 20 per cent of Lancashire mothers and 27 per cent of Essex mothers claimed a promise; Quaife, *Wanton Wenches*, gives figures for Somerset of 60 per cent claiming a promise during the Interregnum; DEP/15, Bk. 15, Margaret Cuckoo con Nicholas Rushman, ff. 111–13 (Cuckoo was mother to Helen Hawke).

[55] DEP/16, 17b, 1583 Agnes Drake con Thomas Poyer, ff. 60–60v; for possible changes in attitudes to bastardy, see Ingram, 'Reform of popular culture: sex and marriage', pp. 150–6.

defamation cases where relations between husband and wife were at issue almost always refer to sexual offences; when women had to evaluate other women's treatment of their husbands, they defined obedience vaguely; and women involved in East Anglian charivari were less likely than men to emphasize obedience.

The charivari evidence is the most sketchy, but still suggestive. The two offences were most often led to charivari – the wife who beat her husband and the wife who was unfaithful – were closely connected in popular consciousness. In 1615, Alice Kemp of Cawston made the connection when she told Faith Docking that 'if you beat Cuckold your husband again about the horns we will have a better riding than we had before'.[56] The usual ritual of the skimmington ride in the west country – directed at a couple in which the wife beat the husband – had the leader of the procession carrying horns, the common symbol of the cuckold. The most fully documented charivari in East Anglia, in Wetherden, Suffolk in 1604, was directed at Nicholas Rosyer and his wife, who had beaten him one evening when he came home drunk from the alehouse. There is no other allegation of misbehaviour in that case, and the charivari was organized and carried out by men. Men, not women, were concerned with the phenomenon of the domineering wife.[57]

The other kinds of evidence of women's rejection – at least tacitly – of the duty of obedience are equally indirect, but give substance to the charivari evidence. The insults complained of by women in defamation cases are significant. When women defended

[56] ANW/7/3, 1615, Faith Docking con Alice Kemp.

[57] PRO STAC 8/249/19, Complaint of Nicholas Rosyer against James Quarry et al. Another charivari, in Holt, Norfolk, in 1661, is more confusing: the chief witness against the actors, a servant named Amy Hinde, describes mock copulation in the ritual, although she had heard that the cause of the riding was that one Wildgosse's wife had beaten him (C/S3/44); there may have been religious issues involved, because the riding took place on Shrove Tuesday, and the victims were described by John Bond, ejected minister of Holt in 1660, as 'honest sober persons': AYL/1, John Bond to Sir John Palgrave, 4 March 1661; for Bond, see Blomefield and Parkyn, *History of Norfolk*, vol. IX, p. 399. E.P. Thompson, '"Rough music": Le Charivari Anglais', *Annales ESC*, 27(1972), pp. 285–312; Idem, '"Rough music" et Charivari' and Martin Ingram, 'Le charivari dans l'Angleterre du XVIe et du XVIIe siècle', in *Le Charivari: actes de la table ronde organisée à Paris (25–27 avril 1977) par l'Ecole des Hautes Etudes en Sciences Sociales et la Centre National de la Recherche Scientifique*, eds Jacques Le Goff and Jean-Claude Schmitt (Paris, 1981), pp. 273–83, 251–64; Martin Ingram, 'Ridings, rough music and the "reform of popular culture" in early modern England', *Past and Present*, 105 (1984), pp. 79–113; Underdown, 'The taming of the scold'.

their own reputations, they worried about sexual reputation. Whenever mistreatment of a husband is alleged, so is sexual misconduct. Thus, when Thomas Rayner of Cawston charged that Margery Suffield 'didst spear thy husband out of the doors in his shirt', the allegation followed his statement that 'thou art a drunken sottish whore and thou are drunk and if one had not saved thee from the fire thou hadst been burnt and there was a man in thy chamber with thee'.[58] The insults make her treatment of her husband a result of her drinking and infidelity.

Although this pattern may partly be a response to the jurisdiction of the court over sexual offences, the variety of offences that men complained of make jurisdiction an insufficient explanation of the pattern. If people did hurl insults like 'filthy housekeeper', 'sloppy cook' or 'disrespectful wife' at women, the damage they did to reputation was sufficiently limited that a defamation case was not necessary. Women apparently centred their own interpretation of their reputations on chastity rather than on obedience to men. Why?

The most likely explanation lies in the family economy and women's role in it. Although, as we have seen, that role differed between the regions, it was always important. The economic activities of women in the dairy, garden and brewhouse, and as spinsters, brought necessary income to their families. And although both married and unmarried women worked in textile manufacturing, the agricultural roles of women were a function of their marital status. They could not be carried out by a passive woman. A meek woman would be unable to bargain effectively at the market. The wives of early modern England could not successfully fulfil their obligations to their families were they too demure. Women thus received contradictory messages: in the market they should be assertive, at home obedient. The transition between the two could not have been easy; it was certainly a source of tension in the household manuals, and it provides an initial explanation for the nature of defamation cases.

Women's economic role inevitably conflicted with expectations of obedience to husbands. A discussion between husband and wife over market strategies might be perceived as insubordination. Chastity, however, was relatively straightforward, and involved

---

[58] DEP/39, Suffield mul. con Rayner, ff. 333–33v, 336–36v.

women in fewer contradictions. It was less likely to conflict with other social expectations. The subordination of women was far more important to men than to women. Inasmuch as the standards for women's behaviour were defined by men, submissiveness was central, but when women defined the appropriate dimensions of their own behaviour, they made it tangential.

The values women expressed in their defamation cases are confirmed by their testimony when they judged each other. Once again, women resisted the emphasis on submissiveness. In 1633 Mary London brought a suit against her stepson George to obtain a portion of her deceased husband Thomas's estate. The first witness, Christopher Layer, Armiger, testified that Thomas had disinherited his wife because her estate was smaller than had been promised before their marriage. Her children by her first marriage had thus been a charge on him, and Layer also alleged that Mary London and her children did not treat Thomas London with sufficient respect – or at least so London had thought. Mary London, Layer added, had refused to care for her son Thomas London after his father's death. On the other side, the clergyman who wrote the elder Thomas London's will asserted that Mary 'showed a very careful and motherly love to her said son notwithstanding that her said husband had not left her the wherewithall to relieve him'. He seconded the two neighbours – women – who said that Mary 'did by all the time of their said intermarriage carry and behave herself loving and in good and dutiful manner towards the said London . . . and had a very due care and respect of him'.[59] 'Due care and respect' is the crucial phrase, but it depends on what is 'due'. The allegations on both sides in the case could be true; there are two different sets of expectations. One set of expectations was held almost exclusively by men, the other almost universally by women.

The conflict between the demand of subordination and work was particularly acute when women were actively involved in the family economy. Sketchy evidence from the early eighteenth century suggests that by then some women were more willing to emphasize obedience in judgements of the behaviour of other women. By this time, women's activities within the family

[59] DEP/40, London con London, ff. 272–3v, 295, 302v–8 and continuation in DEP/41, f. 148 (also ff. 138v–9v, 147v).

economy, especially in that of the wealthier farmers and yeomen, were far more limited. Testimony in several early eighteenth-century separation cases is somewhat less ambigious than earlier evidence. When Samuel Bridgewell of Great Yarmouth accused his wife of adultery in 1706, a servant testified that 'she never saw her commit or omit anything whereby her said husband . . . might be justly provoked to treat her roughly or unkindly, or whereby he might become jealous of her virtue and chastity'.[60] This is less positive than 'due care and respect', though 'justly provoked' is still ambiguous. A case involving a couple from Norwich and Framingham Pigot in 1724 outlines the new standards explicitly. Mary Hubard sued her husband Peter for 'divorce', alleging that he had left her at her father's house after she gave birth to their child. He countered with witnesses (women) who testified that he had treated Mary very well, but that she had refused to follow him to his 'country house', although she was well enough to do so.[61] This is the only case I have found where women testified in support of a husband when no sexual infidelity was alleged. The expectation that a wife would do whatever her husband asked is clear; it accompanies Peter Hubard's high class position, and Mary's evidently limited economic role. The decline in the economic role or wealthier women – like Mary London and Mary Hubard – made it easier to expect them to be passive and obedient. This change took place only for a small social group of mostly urban, middle-class women. For the majority of women, whose economic contributions remained important, there was little change.[62]

Women re-defined their proper relation to their husbands in order to minimize its contradictions and difficulties. This process was not a conscious one on their part, nor does it represent a desire for independence from their families. Women's independence and autonomy were critical to their success as wives and mothers. But the contradictions between women's economic roles and their expected subordination were so severe that they posed a challenge to the most carefully conforming wife. As a result, they elevated

---

[60] DEP/54, 1706, Mary Bridgewell con Samuel Bridgewell, testimony of Elizabeth Gay.

[61] DEP/58, July 1724, Mary Hubard ux. con Peter Hubard vir: especially testimony of Mary ux. Lawrence Bonde and Elizabeth ux. John Sporle.

[62] For the continuing vitality of the family economy, see Cooperative Working Women, *Life as We Have Known It*, ed. Margaret Llewelyn Davies (London, 1931, reprinted New York, 1975).

the importance of sexual behaviour, more than they neglected obedience. The implicit assumption – the contrapositive of that made in the skimmington – was that women who were sexually faithful to their husbands fulfilled all their other wifely obligations. This failure to examine women's non-sexual treatment of their husbands too closely reflected necessity; when the contradictions between women's subordination and the demands of the family economy decreased, as they began to do for middle-class women after 1700, the willingness to focus on obedience increased.

Only one group of women was consistently punished for repudiating feminine meekness. These were scolds. Scolds brought their rejection of women's 'quiet' and obedience out of the household and into public view. Their offence, to the church courts, was a 'breach of Christian charity' that required penance; to the secular courts – mostly manorial ones, but also some urban courts – it was a public disturbance for which the penalty was the cucking stool. Scolds disturbed not just their own households, but the whole neighbourhood. The prosecution of scolds was most common before 1640; while accusations of scolding, abusing neighbours, brawling in church and other forms of quarrelling usually make up between a tenth and a quarter of the offences in sample Act Books of the Archdeacons of Norwich and Norfolk before 1640, they do not appear in the sample books after 1660. This mirrors the pattern of defamation cases involving accusations of being a scold or having been ducked.[63] What are we to make of this? At a time when the emphasis on female obedience within the family was increasing – albeit only in particular social groups – why is the emphasis on quietness outside the family decreasing?

One possible explanation is that prosecutions became unnecessary because scolding ceased. The complete disappearance of scolding in a mere twenty years is, needless to say, improbable. If the answer is not in the behaviour itself, it must be in those who responded to it. After all, the fear of disorder, and anxiety about its presence, so striking in the period 1560–1640 not only reflected

[63] The sample is made up of the following books: Visitation Act Books, ANW/2/8 (1572), ANW/2/15 (1581), ANW/2/27 (1589–90), ANW/2/58 (1614–15), ANW/2/66 (1626–8), ANW/2/74 (1638–40), ANW/2/84 (1678, 1681), ANW/2/85 (1678) and ANF/1/1 (1560–1), ANF/1/2 (1590), ANF/1/5 (1667); Visitations Presentments, ANW/6/1 (1578–9), ANW/6/6 (1605), ANW/6/7 (1610–11, 1622), ANW/6/8 (1639–40), ANW/6/10 (1680), ANW/6/12 (1680) and ANW/6/13 (1681); cf. Underdown, 'The taming of the scold'.

real disorder; it also reflected the anxiety of those in authority about the potential for disorder. Anxiety was understandable for those in authority in the eighty years before 1640: a rapidly growing population, an increase in the number of poor and vagrants, and the economic crises brought about by inflation, bad harvests and the collapse of the cloth trade fostered instability, and made social control more difficult. In addition, social mobility meant that many of those in authority had only recently achieved their current position.[64] Scolding women disappeared from the courts when social mobility had virtually halted, population stabilized and the economy begun to improve. These changes began in the 1650s, and made the courts unnecessary for controlling disorderly women; disorderly women themselves became less of a threat to order. Scolding ceased to be a problem when disorder ceased to be an obsession. Scolds were part of the problem of public order; they demonstrate once again the significance of gender in the social order of early modern England.

Scolding was the subject of public concern for only part of our period; marital conflict and marital breakdown received attention throughout it. Relations within marriages were constantly observed, and the only major change after 1660 was that some forms of legal intervention – presentments to the church courts and petitions to the justices of the peace – disappeared. When the villagers of Little Barningham presented John Warner for adultery with one Graunt's wife in 1607, they added that her adultery had led her to 'greatly disagree together' with her husband.[65] In the same year the questmen of East Winch were disturbed that after receiving Easter Communion Robert Galicon went home and beat his wife. More than twenty years later William Markall of Mileham was presented to the Archdeacon for being so drunk on the night of 10 November 1639 that 'he beat his wife about the street so as the neighbours could not rest in their beds he kept such a disorder'.[66] Such presentments reflect the interest of the village in marital relations, and a willingness to intervene, using the law when necessary.

[64] Lawrence Stone, 'Social mobility in England, 1500–1700', *Past and Present*, 33 (1966), pp. 16–55; see below, pp. 140–3 for other consequences of social instability.

[65] ANW/6/6, 1607, Barningham presentment of John Warner.

[66] ANW/6/6, 1607, East Winch; ANW/2/74, 1639, Mileham vs. William Markall; this attitude is also apparent in petitions to JPs: see below, pp. 166–70.

Bringing warring couples before the justice of the peace or the church courts rarely provided an effective solution to marital conflict. One popular solution to marital discord was ad hoc: one partner simply left. In 1577, it was reported that thirty-seven years previously (1540) John Ballesdon had married Cicely Lowndes in Martham; when they were living in Yarmouth ten or twelve years later (c. 1552) she went to Antwerp, and then lived in Essex and London; she was gone until about 1568, when she was found and brought back to Norwich. Ballesdon, having heard that his wife was dead, had married Agnes Raven in Norwich, a marriage which ended with Cicely's re-appearance in 1568. Agnes married someone else, and brought a lawsuit after Cicely's death to ensure the validity of her second marriage.[67] This case is unusual only in that the partner who left was the wife; the timing and locations of Cicely's travels also suggest Protestant sympathies. The frequency of informal separations is impossible to compute, but they were certainly fairly common. In 1603 Cicely Kymer, 'widow', reported that her husband had gone overseas, and in 1619 Dorothy Padge reported that her husband had left her about seven years earlier, and she had heard that he was in the East Indies. In 1623 King's Lynn ordered that John Ousloo leave town within a fortnight to return to his wife in Dartford, Kent.[68] The tone of discussions about such separations was matter-of-fact; desertions were an accepted, if not desirable, aspect of family life.

Desertion solved the problem of the bad marriage, and made possible bigamous second marriages, but those marriages were not secure. Distance provided some protection: when Richard Flynt, then rector of Winfarthing, was asked about the marriage of Henry Farthing alias Boston to Margaret Asshley in April 1574, he said that since Farthing had moved to Winfarthing from Needham Market, more than sixteen miles away, he had no idea whether or not he was already married.[69] Rumours of the death of absent spouses were frequent, but unreliable and difficult to verify. Richard Rockley of Dersingham had been deserted by his first wife

---

[67] DEP/16, Bk. 17a, 1577, Agnes Raven con John Ballesdon, f. 250 ff.

[68] NRS Accn. Christie 14.5.82, Q 190A, Examination of Cicely Kymer, wid., 7 November 1603; Examination of Dorothy Padge of Wells, 22 September 1619; cf. ANW/6/6, Margaret Heynes of Dersingham: in all these cases we only know of the desertion because of a pregnancy; KL C/21/1, 20 James I.

[69] DEP/15, Bk. 15, 1574, Personal answer of Richard Flynt, Rector of Winfarthing, f. 147.

in about 1579; he had 'never heard from her neither do he know whether she be [dead] or no'; he had heard she had been hanged, so in c. 1587 he married Margaret Thorpe, a Dersingham widow. Rockley's neighbours were not all convinced that his first wife was dead, and doubted the validity of his second marriage.[70]

Geographical mobility was simultaneously a source of flexibility in the marriage system, and of additional confusion. There was no way of telling whether someone was married elsewhere, yet this was a practical concern of neighbours worried about the potential stability of marriages. In about 1570 Gawen Brown's neighbours in Cley, on the north Norfolk coast, heard that he had another wife in the north, although he had lived as husband and wife with John Webster's daughter for at least six years; when some of the Cley sailors were in Berwick, they went to Brown's home town, and met his first wife and children. Nothing was done at the time, since Brown's northern wife asked that he not be harmed, but it was remembered when his testimony on another matter was evaluated in 1577.[71] Curiosity impelled Brown's neighbours to check the story, yet because his current marriage appeared stable, they did nothing.

This flexibility, and interest in stability over strict legality, almost matched the flexibility with regard to pre-nuptial fornication. As legal divorce or re-marriage were impossible for most people, alternatives were tolerated. The town of South Lynn did nothing about John Lebie's bigamous marriage to Margaret Peach, but when he ran away and left her, and she contracted herself to another man, the potential confusion became too great, and she was presented for the offence. A double standard may have been encouraged by concern over the legal status of, and responsibility for, children. The villagers of Stratford, Suffolk, in 1675 questioned whether Robert Barrett and Elizabeth Felgate were legally married when Felgate bore a child and Barrett failed to take Communion; they wanted to be certain that Barrett was responsible for the child. Nearly twenty years later the inhabitants of

---

[70] ANW/2/27, Richard Rockley of Dersingham.

[71] DEP/16, Bk. 17a, John Webster con John Bartholemew, ff. 155–63; even London was not a good hiding place: DEP/34, Borowghes con Brooke has evidence of a wife paying a husband so that she can remarry in London, where she is later seen by former Norwich neighbours: ff. 386–7v, 61, 65, 119, 120, 121, 190, 383–5; Amussen, 'Governors and governed', pp. 238–41; Gillis, *For Better, For Worse*, p. 99.

Haddiscoe, Norfolk had to sort out the status of Elizabeth Youngs and John Holmes, both widowed. Holmes claimed they were married in order to sit in the church seat 'which belongs to the master of the house she lives in' and to vote in parish elections at Easter. Their marriage was denied when Youngs brought a suit against a third person for trespass, so that Holmes could testify on her behalf.[72] Disorder resulted from such uncertainty about who was married. Marriage entailed a particular set of relations and behaviour within the community; those who fulfilled those roles were regarded as married, those who did not were suspect.

The story of Margaret, the wife of William Least of Cawston, illustrates the issues raised by marital breakdown, desertion and re-marriage. Margaret Least was presented to the Archdeacon of Norwich in 1625 for having two husbands living. She told the court that her first husband, William Lightfoot, had left her nineteen years earlier and she had heard rumours that he was dead. In 1619 she contracted herself to William Least; the banns were published in Cawston Church, and they were married. No one in Cawston raised any objection. William Lightfoot returned to Cawston in the spring of 1625 for a few weeks. His brief appearance was enough to demonstrate that Margaret had not actually been widowed.[73] Until then there has been no ambiguity in anyone's mind about Margaret Least/Lightfoot's position. And it is probable that after Lightfoot's departure the neighbours continued to treat Margaret and William Least as lawful man and wife. Time had made Lightfoot's death probable, but there was no certainty. Margaret Lightfoot's re-marriage was a gamble, but not an unreasonable one.

Desertion and bigamy were extreme responses, and the story of marital breakdown usually began long before either occurred.

---

[72] ANW/6/6 (1607) South Lynn con Margaret Peach; DEP/49, 1675, bundle 18: Offic. promot. per Mr William Dewsing con Mr Robert Barrett; CON/41, Libels and Allegations con John Holmes and Elizabeth Youngs of Haddiscoe, DEP/53, 1694, Offic. Dmi. promot. per Mr Nathaniel Smith Cler. con John Holmes, and Idem con Elizabeth Youngs, wid.

[73] ANW/2/66, 1625, Margaret ux. William Least of Cawston; she appears in the 1611–12 Poor Book (NRS 2604 12 B 2) as 'William Lightfoot's wife' on a list of those to receive doles; the list indicates the extent of desertion: it includes thirty-one men, eighteen widows, three single women and four deserted wives (including Lightfoot). Lightfoot's problem is common: cf. Guildhall Library Ms. 9585, May 1588, Super testament of John Harris of Stepney: he had been gunner on the ship 'Primrose', but there was disagreement as to whether he had been killed or captured by the Turks, ff. 117v–18v, 123–4.

Villagers often attempted to reconcile feuding couples before presenting them to the church courts. When Elizabeth Granger left her husband William in Terrington in 1642 and went to stay with her mother in South Lynn, she was returned to her husband by the officials in South Lynn. Those who testified about the marriage of John Dey and Katherine Miles – who had been separated for about twenty years – agreed that neighbours attempted a reconciliation. Yet to focus on attempts at reconciliation masks the popular acceptance of separation. When John Dunne of Mintlyn was presented to the Archdeacon of Norwich in 1572 for harbouring another man's wife in his house, he seems to have thought that the explanation that 'he did not keep her against her husband's will' would be acceptable.[74]

Family breakdown was usually a gradual process, whose existence was recorded only when it became relevant to later events. There was a formal procedure for separation in the church courts; while it was rarely used, it allows a more systematic look at marital breakdown and the community's attitude to it. Both women and men sued for separation, but more women did so than men. The separation formalized living arrangements most couples had long since made; but it gave neither the right to re-marry. The grounds for separation were gender specific. When men sued for separation, the ground was invariably adultery. When her husband sued for separation, Margaret Gardiner had lived for a year in the house of Mr Gibson, in Tyd St Mary, Lincolnshire. During that time she reportedly slept with Gibson every night; when Mr Gibson called her a whore, she did not deny it but said that 'she was his whore and no man's whore else'.[75] Joanna Bland was 'put away' by her husband, a King's Lynn sailor, in 1575 when he returned from a voyage to find her pregnant. Robert Skynner was jealous of his wife, and so forced her to confess that she had once 'had to do with . . . carnally' John Gricks, Jr; although she made the confession under pressure (and on her knees before witnesses) Skynner still sought a divorce.[76] Only a few husbands cited other complaints: Thomas West feared violence from his wife

---

[74] KL C21/2, 2 March 17 Charles I, f. 32: here the issues also involved the burden of poor relief; DEP/19, 1581, Offic. Dmni promot. per Mr M. Hawghe con John Dey and Audrey his present wife, ff. 291–4; the marriage of John and Audrey Dey is again at issue thirty-six years later: DEP/37, 1617, Audrey Dey, wid. con Edmund Smith, ff. 167 ff.; cf. DEP/28, Felmingham ux. con Felmingham vir, ff. 401–3, 502; ANW/2/8, John Dunne of Mintlyn.

[75] DEP/15, Bk. 15, John Gardiner con Margaret Gardiner his wife, ff. 190–1v.

[76] DEP/17, 1580, Henry Bland con Joanna Bland his wife, ff. 243r–v; DEP/23, 1588, Robert Skynner con Elizabeth Skynner his wife, ff. 333–5.

Amy's lover after she had left and gone to Yorkshire, while Bridget Grime (it was alleged) not only had various lovers but sought to poison her husband Thomas.[77] All these cases focused on the behaviour of the women, usually apart from the marriage itself. Cases brought by men against their wives reflect little on the nature of the marriage before or apart from the alleged infidelity.

The separation cases brought by women are strikingly different. While many of the women had been abandoned by their husbands, and often alleged the husband's infidelity, witnesses more often focused on the marriage before the separation or desertion. Richard Hall, it was alleged in 1565, was 'a cruel man to his wife in words', he beat her, and six years before, 'in the dear year of corn' compelled his wife and their children to eat bread made of 'Tytters [potatoes] and acorns'. Richard Hall now wanted to marry another woman, and had told her 'he would find a way for his wife'.[78] Hall's failure to support his wife, and his attempt to marry another women were critical from the legal point of view, not the history of the marriage; marital history was relevant to the witnesses because it legitimated the separation. When Joane Barrett sought a separation from her husband Henry in 1590, she produced not only evidence of his adultery (he had fathered the child of Alice Love) but also evidence that he was 'so fierce and cruel a man towards her that she dare not dwell with him'.[79] Most of the men who were sued for separation by their wives had already left them: in 1590 Thomas Seffold had gone to London, been arrested for debt and in King's Bench prison had married another woman before his first wife took action.[80]

Women who sought separations from their husbands alleged that they had been deserted, but they also generally alleged cruelty: in the early eighteenth century Samuel Sad tried to strangle his wife Elizabeth, while a century earlier Constance Boston complained of her husband John's excessive violence. On at least one occasion Thomas Felmingham had severely beaten his wife, dragged her about the house and threatened her with a pistol. These men had gone beyond the acceptable level of violence in marriage: one of

[77] DEP/34, Thomas West con Amy West, 1608, ff. 525v–9v; DEP/37, Grime vir con Grime mul., ff. 131v–6, 137r–v, 176v–9.
[78] DEP/10, Bk. 10, Katherine Hall con Richard Hall, June 1565.
[79] DEP/24, Joane Barrett con Henry Barrett, ff. 17–20, 99v–100v, 130–1.
[80] DEP/24, Elizabeth Seffold con Thomas Seffold, Gent., ff. 242r–v, 342–4v.

the neighbours told John Robinson in 1696 that 'he was a very ill man to beat his wife *at that rate*' [my emphasis].[81] Other evidence suggests a similar tolerance. When Mary Becke sought a separation from her husband William on the grounds of cruelty, several witnesses denied the allegation. According to a servant, 'she never heard nor saw Mr Becke use any cruelty to the same Mary but that any women might well bear at her husbands hands'. And although Mary sought a bond for his good behaviour from a justice of the peace, he was never 'so cruel or to hate her so much that she should require further security of her life for mutilation of her members than other honest wives have'.[82] Anne Goslinge's family knew that her husband John beat her, but they did nothing to intervene until she had been knocked unconscious and kicked.[83] Too much violence threatened a woman's life; up to that point some violence at least was tolerated.

We know of conflict in families because of the observation of friends, family and neighbours. Families were not islands, isolated from the world, but were tightly bound into the village community. The observation of courtship and marriage by neighbours reflects this, but we must also examine the process of intervention in family affairs. How did villagers control 'private' behaviour? Did these mechanisms change over time? If so, what is the significance of these changes?

The easiest controls to identify are the formal ones, although they were a last rather than a first resort. The legal apparatus of England – both ecclesiastical and secular – could be brought to bear on the sexual and social transgressions of early modern villagers. Bastard-bearers and begetters could suffer in both civil and ecclesiastical courts. The visitations by the archdeacons, when the churchwardens and questmen presented offenders against a variety of canons, provided an ideal opportunity to discipline errant villagers. The visitation articles suggested fornication, adultery, bastard-bearing, harbouring an unmarried pregnant

---

[81] DEP/58, 1719, Elizabeth Sad con Samuel Sad; DEP/34, Constance Boston con John Boston her husband, ff. 101–7v; DEP/28, Felmingham ux. con Felmingham vir, ff. 401–3, 502; DEP/53, Hannah Robinson mul. con John Robinson vir, 1696.

[82] DEP/10, Bk. 10, June 1565, Maria Becke con William Becke.

[83] AYL/17, 45–7, Examinations re. the death of Anne Goslinge the wife of John Goslinge of Bedingham, 1600.

woman, scolding and brawling with neighbours and living apart from a spouse as offences to be presented, as well as absence from church, working on the Sabbath and failing to receive Communion. Villagers whose behaviour – toward family or neighbours – was particularly intractable could also be complained of in petitions to justices of the peace. Those presented to the ecclesiastical courts often did penance for their offences; those presented to the justices could be whipped, fined or bound over to keep the peace.[84]

These formal mechanisms of control were rarely used after the Restoration: post-Restoration presentments for sexual misdemeanours almost always involve a pregnancy; petitions to the justices of the peace in quarter sessions decline in the 1660s, and in Norfolk the last extant petitions against disorderly neighbours date from 1670.[85] For practical reasons, bastard-bearers were still examined about the paternity of their children, but otherwise regulation of 'personal behaviour' almost disappears. Yet it would be absurd to imagine that there was little illicit sex, no domestic violence, no scolding and no separation of couples after the Restoration. What happened?

The answer can be found if we turn to the process of informal control, which began long before formal complaints were made. The constant observation by villagers of each other was central not only to the definition of reputation and to the defence of women in suits for separation, but was also a tool of social control. Criticism need not go through the courts to shame those involved, and might be just as effective if it did not. One reponse to misbehaviour was gossip: many defamation cases can be seen as attempts to stop a rumour before it became 'common fame' to the discredit of the victim. In 1590 Thomas Corpe alleged in Hethel that Roger Watson had been whipped in Norwich for living with a whore. Before Watson could stop the rumour, it was repeated by Thomas Newark in Hethersett and Thomas Richardson in Swainsthorpe, and the defamation suits brought by Watson have an increasingly desperate air about them. Deliberate gossip, with the intent of

---

[84] Wrightson and Levine, *Poverty and Piety*, chapter 5, for the range of court use in one village; J.A. Sharpe, *Crime in Seventeenth-century England: a county study* (Cambridge, 1983), pp. 167–8.

[85] PRO ASSI 16/20/3, Articles vs. Henry Parker of Downham Market; Articles vs. Henry Gay of Wymondham; Amussen, 'Gender and the social order'.

damaging someone's reputation, could be an effective informal method of control: it indicated communal disapproval, and shamed its subject. If the subject of gossip did not stop the behaviour, at least everyone else knew what to think of it.[86]

People could be shamed without recourse to words: in 1605 Ralph Furnice of Carbrooke was presented to the Archdeacon of Norwich after he went 'out of the parish church of Carbrooke when one William Maies was married and set up horns upon the camperland rails where the said Maies and his wife should come, and for making of puppets to the disgrace of the said Maies'.[87] Although William Maies and Widow Dawsing were presented for fornication before their marriage, there was no suspicion that Maies might be a cuckold, so the display was inappropriate. In East Braddenham in 1590, Christopher Hawes and Mark Hendry were suspected of throwing a horn (the symbol of the cuckold) into John Clarke's yard – though it turned out that the horns were placed there by Clarke's son John; the gesture, if unchallenged, would have undermined Clarke's reputation.[88] In neither of these cases were actual words involved, but the insult was understood by all.

By its very nature the informal regulation of familial and sexual behaviour is rarely visible; it surfaced only when there was disagreement about its necessity, or when the victim and perpetrators did not share the same code: although Nicholas Rosyer described the charivari directed against himself and his wife as 'unlawfully, riotously and tumultuously' undertaken, one of the witnesses described it as 'an old country custom used in merriment upon such accidents'.[89] When there was consensus about who ought to regulate behaviour, and the standards used, conflicts about sexual and familial behaviour rarely reached the courts. Informal sanctions were more effective in controlling behaviour after 1660; the relative scarcity of rural labour in the late seventeenth century ensured that those who rejected local standards could more easily move away than they could earlier in the century.

---

[86] Amussen, 'Féminin/Masculin', pp. 272–9; DEP/24, Roger Watson con Thomas Corpe, ff. 97–8; Ibid. con Thomas Newark, ff. 174–5, 314r–v; and ibid. con Thomas Richardson, ff. 180–1v, 183–4.

[87] ANW/6/6, 1605, Carbrooke vs. Ralph Furnice.

[88] ANF/1/2, 1590, East Braddenham con Christopher Hawes and Mark Hendry.

[89] PRO STAC 8/249/19, Complaint of Nicholas Rosyer against James Quarry et al., response of Susan Hamond, wid: Hamond also says that Rosyer lived 'with much dissention' with his wife.

The one area in which we have relatively reliable evidence about behaviour throughout the whole period is bastardy. The illegitimacy rate peaked in the early seventeenth century, plummetted in the 1650s (probably due to underrecording) and then slowly increased in the second half of the seventeenth century. It is difficult to say what changed: there may have been less pre-marital sex, but it is equally possible that men became more willing to accept communal pressure to marry the woman they had made pregnant: there is some evidence of an increase in rates of bridal pregnancy, certainly after 1700. As we have seen, it is unlikely that women – who faced loss of employment and reputation, who were driven from home by gossip and hostility, or even by fines against their parents – had ever deliberately sought pregnancy while unmarried.[90]

Other aspects of familial behaviour are more difficult to measure, and leave us with a final problem. The disappearance of the formal control of gender relations after the Restoration does not (and cannot be interpreted to) mean that all behaviour could now be swiftly made to fit expectations by a bit of gossip, indirect shame or a warning from a local notable. There are too many signs of continued disorder for such a supposition to be plausible. Rather, most aspects of gender relations ceased to cause concern about community disorder. Scolding is the best example of this; similarly, it is possible that village elites, although still very concerned to ensure the subordination of their own wives, were less concerned about the couples who quarrelled. They were participating in a re-definition of the social nature of marriage, as it came to be seen less as a public economic partnership, more a private affective one. Although this transition occurred only for the wealthier members of village society, they were the ones who governed. This re-definition of marriage was an ideological change; real families still had an important economic and public role. However, ideological change transformed the regulation of family life.

Gender order was clearly defined: women and men belonged in families governed by a benevolent *pater familias* who guarded their

[90] Laslett, 'Long-term trends in bastardy', pp. 115–19; Ingram, 'Reform of popular culture: sex and marriage', pp. 151–6; Wrightson, 'Puritan reformation of manners', pp. 66–7; P.E.H. Hair, 'Bridal pregnancy in rural England in earlier centuries', *Population Studies*, 20 (1966), pp. 233–43.

morals and directed their behaviour. Even the father in this scheme only did God's will, and helped his subordinates to do the same. In practice, this did not always work quite as comfortably as it should have done. Young women and men had their own courtships; they sometimes refused to conform to expectations of them, and often no one could force them to. To bear a bastard was not to reject the gender order; but it did disrupt it. After marriage, there was great flexibility in relations between husband and wife, and women often had considerable independence. Marital breakdown was a constant reminder of the failure of life to conform to expectations.

This flexibility in familial and marital relations was possible because the underlying assumptions were rarely challenged. Everyone agreed that men were superior to women, that husbands ought to govern their households and that the household was the basis of order.[91] In resolving the frequent disruptions and quarrels, village governors never had to defend the gender order itself.

Gender relations were challenged implicitly, not explicitly, and one can only speak of gender disorder insofar as the failure of social relations to conform to the ideal constitutes disorder. After 1660 women still bore bastards, men still left their wives; bigamy, domestic violence and sexual infidelity did not disappear. Yet they ceased to be a major subject of concern to those responsible for village order. The visitation articles had not changed, but the answers had; the role of justices of the peace remained what it had been, but not those brought before them. Gender became less tied to other aspects of the social system; the family became less central to political and social order. Locke's separation of the family from political discourse is best seen as a recognition of social experience that had become a reality by his time, not an innovation. But to fully explain the earlier concern with the gender order we must turn to the hierarchy of class and the political order of society. By examining the strains and conflicts in that order, we can better understand the significance of the family for seventeenth-century English women and men.

[91] Challenges to the patriarchal order in the Civil War were very rare: see Hill, *World Turned Upside Down*, esp. chapter 15. Dorothy Osborne, conducting a secret correspondence with her beloved, was shocked that the Duchess of Newcastle had published a book, yet in that same book the Duchess apologized for doing so, and said it was only because she had no household, no children and was separated from her husband: *Letters of Dorothy Osborne*, ed. G. C. Moore Smith (Oxford, 1928), p. 37; Margaret Cavendish, Duchess of Newcastle, *Poems and Fancies* (London, 1653, facsimile ed. Menston, Yorks, 1972), f. A7.

5

The Ordering of Society

Children who stand in little awe of their parents, and have even less fear of the wrath of God, readily set at defiance the authority of magistrates. . . . It is therefore impossible that a commonwealth should prosper while the families which are its foundations are ill-regulated.

Jean Bodin, *Six Books of the Commonwealth*

The bonds of deference and responsibility which were supposed to hold the family together also operated throughout society. In the village, hundred and county (as well as the nation) those of higher status were to govern and care for their inferiors, and in return receive obedience and respect from the governed. The enforcement and construction of such relations is more obvious outside the family than inside it. Relations within families were only discussed when things went very wrong. This is not because the family was more 'natural' than the larger social units, but because conceptual parallels could not reproduce in a village the same sexual, emotional and economic bonds that held a family together. The different interests of villagers were more obvious than those of family members. Villages were manifestly social constructs.

Local government in England depended on the cooperation of many people, including the governed. The officers of local government were unpaid, and there was no police force. In such circumstances, communal solidarity was constantly sought and maintained. A bored gentleman wrote two days after Christmas in 1704 that 'I'm just come from Ipswich to drink ale with the tenants, and as soon as that ceremony's over, shall return from whence I came'.[1] Such a

---

[1] B.L. Egerton 2720, f. 46, John Rouse to O. LeNeve, 27 December 1704; cf. E.P. Thompson, 'Patrician society, plebeian culture', *Journal of Social History*, 7 (1974), pp. 382–405; James Obelkevich, *Religion in Rural Society* (Oxford, 1976), pp. 58–60.

ceremony – obviously an interruption of his own Christmas festivities – was disliked but necessary. It sustained an image of a vertically integrated local community, of paternalistic concern and elite condescension.

One inducement to cooperation with local government was the tangible benefits it offered. County and village government was not just disciplinary: the patronage extended by governors to governed was extensive and easily accessible. The 'governors' were not too distant – or different – from those they governed. Within villages the offices of overseer of the poor, churchwarden and questman remained within a small group. A different group – somewhat less well-to-do – served as constables. Landholders selected and served as parish officers, and approved rating lists and accounts. Officeholders were neighbours, friends or employers; they were open to influence. When some leading parishioners of Swaffham disliked the seat given to Robert Theodorick, they complained to the churchwarden, who moved him.[2] The processes of government were not alway formal.

In such a situation, the support of wealthier neighbours could be critical. Intervention – either positive or negative – was most often recorded when it involved the legal difficulties of poor neighbours. In 1600 Augustine Stywarde, Gent., wrote to Bassingbourn Gawdy, JP, about Margaret Fraunces, who was charged with betwitching Joane Harvey. Stywarde asserted that Harvey suffered from a disease, 'the mother', which led to fits. The disease had a natural rather than a supernatural origin, so he asked that Fraunces be released from prison. Support was also available in more mundane cases. In 1640, William Emerson alias Anderson of Wiggenhall St Peter was presented for absence from church. His minister, Robert Jackson, wrote that Emerson lived more than a mile from the church, and while he always came to morning service, he sometimes attended evening prayer in a church closer to his home. According to Jackson, Emerson 'doth not absent himself from his own church out of faction but in a manner upon

---

[2] DEP/43, Robert Theodorick con John Bride, ff. 78v–80v, 81v–4, 98–102v; Wrightson and Levine, *Poverty and Piety*, pp. 106–7; Amussen, 'Governors and governed', pp. 66–7; see above, pp. 26–9.

necessity'.[3] In a situation like this, a minister's support might be crucial.

Neighbours also identified malicious accusations for the courts. In 1643, William Stanton of Fakenham alleged that Rachel Merrye had said 'that it is no matter what she said for now there is no king, no laws, nor no justice'; many in Fakenham refused to believe the charge because Stanton's wife competed with Merrye as a midwife. Merrye was an honest poor woman, whose husband had left her many years before and she 'taketh great pains and labour for to maintain herself and child, without the relief or help of any'.[4] When two poor widows from Runton were charged with unlicensed alehousekeeping in 1664, Robert Flynt, the Rector, suggested the accusation was malicious, adding, 'Sir, It becomes not me to patronize alehouses but I do assure you that although I live very near them, yet I do not know of any abuses in them'.[5] Such intervention was not without self-interest, of course: Alice Robotome, a widow from West Lynn, was in Swaffham Bridewell in 1655 after the birth of her second illegitimate child. The town asked for her release because she supported not only her first illegitimate child, but also a legitimate one and her aged mother; while she was in the Bridewell, 'a great Charge lies weekly upon the town'.[6]

These procedural interventions all served to help the person in trouble, but the most important evidence that neighbours gave about one another was about the reputation of those in difficulty. In 1621, Henry Tisdale of Shouldham, the town herdsman, was charged with some offence at the instigation of Elizabeth Charrington and her mother. The townsmen protested that Tisdale had 'ever since we know him been of honest life and good behaviour and one that hath been both careful and diligent in keeping and looking to the charge which he hath had under his hands'.[7] Sixty years later the

[3] B.L. Egerton 2714, f. 104, 20 December 1600, Augustine Stywarde to Bassingbourn Gawdy: the 'mother' is presumably a form of hysteria; ANW/2/74, 1640, Certificate of Robert Jackson re. William Emerson alias Anderson.

[4] C/S3/34, Fakenham, 20 July 1643, Petition re. Rachel Merrye; this case also suggests the political awareness of the countryside: see Underdown, *Revel, Riot and Rebellion*, pp. 218–19.

[5] AYL/190, Robert Flynt to Robert Doughty, JP, 17 February 1664/5: there is no challenge here to the charge of being unlicenced; Flynt assumes the only problem would be disorder.

[6] C/S3/43A, 1655, 16 July 1655, Petition of West Lynn re. Alice Robotome, wid.

[7] C/S3/23, Petition of Shouldham re. Henry Tisdale: struck out in the original is the allegation that Elizabeth Charrington and her mother don't know 'what belongeth to an oath'.

significance of reputation is even more evident. Margaret Willis of King's Lynn was excommunicated in 1684, on what some believed was false evidence. Some signed the testimonial with a note that 'upon the credit of those who have subscribed, I do believe the contents of it to be true'.[8] The support of honest people was a proof of honesty. With the support of social superiors, poorer villagers could survive enormous difficulties. And each time they did, the prestige of local notables was increased, and advantages of local reputation were emphasized to those who were vulnerable to authority.

The expected reciprocity of the social hierarchy of early modern England tells us nothing of the hierarchy's nature and structure, or of changes in it. The economic changes of the sixteenth and seventeenth centuries made shifts in the social order almost inevitable. The polarization of villages, and the gowing prosperity of village notables, undermined the existing structure, and social hierarchy was often heatedly contested. How were people defining the social hierarchy? What conflicts emerged around it? And how are these related to the economic changes we have already defined?

The best place to begin such a discussion is in the parish church. The church was the main gathering place in every village, and Sunday services the one time at which everyone was supposed to be present. The Church fostered its role as supporter of social order and hierarchy, and helped to reify it by the assignment of church seats. In 1633, Clement Corbett, the Vicar General of the Bishop of Norwich, wrote to the rector and churchwardens of West Walton in response to a complaint by two parishioners:

> Finding that the parishioners of the said parish of West Walton of both sexes men and women do sit in the seats or stools of the said church ... promiscuously together, whereby there is no decency or order observed, but mere confusion and disorder; I have therefore decreed and ordered ... to the end that all things may be done in decent and good order in the church, that forthwith you place all the parishioners of your parish ... on the North side of the said Church, and all their wives or women ... on the south side of

---

[8] TES/3, August 1684, Testimonial for Margaret Willis of King's Lynn.

the said church having an especial regard to the degrees and qualities of the persons so by you to be removed, displaced and placed, that there may be no just cause of complaint.[9]

Corbett assumed that the Church should reflect the social order – with 'especial regard to the degrees and qualities'. Villagers should have, as they did in Cawston, seats which reflected their social position. The Church mirrored the social structure of the community. Men and women sitting 'promiscuously together' undermined decency and order. The men were the parishioners: the household was represented by its (male) head. Corbett tied together the class and gender hierarchies.

The placement of people in church was the visible representation of the local hierarchy. Because of the symbolic importance of seats in the church, conflicts often emerged about where people sat. Events at church on Sunday encapsulated the social and personal tensions of villages. Many conflicts about church seating emerged because of the social transitions taking place in villages. In theory, status – whether one was a gentleman, a yeoman, husbandman or labourer – was fixed, as was position in the social hierarchy. But men like George Sawer of Cawston, who accumulated land and money, wreaked havoc with the theory. Many of the minor gentry, like Sawer, acquired their status on the basis of their wealth, not because they owned a manor in the parish.[10] Yet whatever the source of the treasured 'Gent.' after their name, they had to be placed in the church. The grounds on which seats were assigned were thus extremely important, and could be explicitly contested, as they were in East Bilney in 1668. The chief inhabitant of the parish, Christopher Crowe, Gent., a justice of the peace, sat in the first seat; William Breame sat in the seat behind him, along with some of Crowe's servants. William Wiscard's family was assigned the third seat, immediately behind Breame and Crowe's servants,

[9] FCB/1, f. 2v, Clement Corbett to Rector and Churchwardens of West Walton, July 1633; cf. Methwold P.D. (uncat) letter from Corbett in April 1631, 'that you place the men on the one side of the church, and the women on the other, they being placed according to their several degrees and quality'.

[10] Spufford, *Contrasting Communities*, pp. 76, 81–3 for the activities of Thomas Dillamore, Sr, of Chippenham, an engrosser; for George Sawer, see Amussen, 'A Norfolk village, 1595–1615'; conflicts over church seats are similar to those among the gentry about placement on the Commission of the Peace: see A. Hassell Smith, *County and Court: government and politics in Norfolk, 1558–1603* (Oxford, 1974), pp. 71–2; Stone, 'Social mobility'.

but his family was large and 'overflowed' into the seat in front. While Crowe and Breame made claims of ownership to the second seat, Wiscard countered that he was far wealthier than Breame, and was the second wealthiest inhabitant of the parish. Wiscard asked that the claims of wealth override the claims of tradition in the assignment of church seats.[11]

William Wiscard was not unusual in his recognition of the significance of the seat in church, or in his struggle to establish his 'proper' social position. Litigants sought to have their status acknowledged, or to denigrate others. In a 1623 petition against Simon Keeper of Newton next Castle Acre, it was said that 'out of an insulting and proud mind and stomach albeit he be a poor man will put the chief of the parish out of their seats in the church belonging to them'. By sitting in seats to which he had no 'right', Keeper symbolically rejected the social order.[12]

Those with prominent seats were expected to acknowledge their significance. In 1636, Robert Theodorick had been given a seat in Swaffham Church, 'contrary to the liking and approbation of divers of the best men in the parish, he being an oatmealmaker and a man of no great credit, and the stool in which the said Theodorick was placed being a seat fit for the best man of the parish aforesaid, and in which such men had and do sit'. In spite of their reservations, the churchwardens did not move him until a year later, when Theodorick took 'into the seat aforesaid a man of mean condition, a barber by profession'.[13] When the churchwarden moved him, Theodorick took him to court for removing him from his place in the church. Theodorick's experience is instructive. The leading inhabitants of Swaffham, an important market town, accepted his placement, even though they thought it inappropriate, until he sought to shape the symbolic hierarchy of the town against their standards.

Many humbler parishioners shared Theodorick's awareness of the significance of church seats. In 1608 the churchwardens of

---

[11] DEP/48, William Breame con William Wiscard, Mr Christopher Crowe con William Wiscard, ff. 113–19v, 129v–32.

[12] C/S3/24, Petition vs. Simon Keeper of Newton next Castle Acre.

[13] DEP/43, Robert Theodorick con John Bride, ff. 78v–80v, 81v–4, 98–102v; Robert Theodorick may have been a kinsman of Thomas Theodorick, who served as churchwarden on several occasions and also as feoffee of the Swaffham town lands: he was part of the local oligarchy. Robert Theodorick is recorded as the town soldier, being paid for attending militia drills in 1636–7; in 1643 a Robert Theodorick was bound to appear at quarter sessions: PD 52/72, Swaffham churchwarden's accounts; C/S3/34.

Bawdeswell sought to move Margaret Skener into 'certain new seats . . . where the poor and such as took alms did sit', but she refused, 'in regard her husband did contribute to the maintenance of the poor and all other charges'. Skener's neighbours, however, thought it inappropriate that she, 'living as an inmate in the parish within another man's house should be ranked and seated with others much her betters'.[14] Here are two separate sources of social position. The payment of town charges gave one a stake in the town. But as we saw in Winfarthing, this stake was considered ephemeral unless accompanied by landholding; as an inmate, Skener lacked status.

In Cawston George Sawer distinguished between the poor and those who were unable to contribute to the town charges. Margaret Skener's defence of her place underlines the fine social gradations in early modern villages. These gradations are shown again in the complaint of Prudence Clark of Earsham against Susan Gyrney in 1633: Gyrney had pushed into her seat so she could not sit there. Prudence Clark sat in 'the lowest seat of the women's seats near unto the maids' seats on the south side of the Church'; Susan Gyrney, a servant, sat in the maids' seat. Clark sought to maintain the distinction between herself and the maids. Because the maids' seat was too crowded, some women in Prudence Clark's seat allowed the maids to sit on their seat to rest, but Clark found her status endangered by such a proceeding.[15] Clark's suit indicates that the fine distinctions were not always insisted on; as with Robert Theodorick, they became a source of contention in conjunction with other conflicts.

Lawsuits about who should sit where, and the pushing and shoving to keep one neighbour or another out of a particular church seat, occurred regularly throughout the period. There is, however, another kind of conflict that especially suggests the tension surrounding social position in early modern villages. In these conflicts one party claimed control or ownership of particular seats. The first of these conflicts to come before the Consistory Court of Norwich in our period occurred in 1617 in the busy port of Great Yarmouth; the other cases of this sort come predominantly from wood–pasture villages, half of which are also

[14] DEP/35, Skener con Leman and Pescod, ff. 202b–202c, 247v–9.
[15] DEP/41, Prudence Clark con Susan Gyrney, ff. 260–1v, 263v–4v, 337–9.

market towns. An examination of several of these cases explains this distribution.

One of the best documented cases comes from the village of Fressingfield, a large parish in the wood–pasture region of Suffolk. In 1634, a dispute emerged between Francis Sancroft, Sr and his nephew Francis Sancroft, Jr, on the one hand, and William Grudgefield on the other. All three were gentlemen. About ten years before, the Sancrofts had (with the permission of Grudgefield's mother) partitioned off half of the maids' seat belonging to Grudgefield's house, which was near the front of the church. In 1634 Grudgefield decided he needed the seat, asked the Sancrofts to move, and they refused. Although their class position was similar, the Grudgefields were newcomers, while the Sancrofts had reportedly lived in the same house in Fressingfield for 300 years. The Sancrofts represent the rising gentry: while Francis Jr's father had styled himself a yeoman, his son William became Archbishop of Canterbury. The Sancrofts were respected members of the community, and as in Winfarthing and Shelfanger, the differences between the wealthiest inhabitants of Fressingfield were not great. Grudgefield's request, if complied with, would have symbolically diminished the Sancrofts' status, and created an image of greater social distance than actually existed.[16]

This kind of conflict was far less likely in arable areas, where parish elites tended to be more sharply differentiated. In pastoral villages and market towns, the social distance between the numerous prosperous yeomen and minor gentry was minimal. The timing of these lawsuits is as significant as their geography. They appeared in the second decade of the seventeenth century, when the land market was less active and class structure becoming less fluid, and their records are scattered through the surviving Deposition books. The conflict over control of seats was most likely to occur in a community with a broad elite and relatively stable social structure. If the community was not changing

---

[16] DEP/41, William Grudgefield, Gent. con Francis Sancroft Sr, and Francis Sancroft Jr, Gents., ff. 524–65; Fressingfield, WEA, *Looking Back at Fressingfield* (Fressingfield, 1979), pp. 29, 33, 35–6; I am grateful to Mrs Nesta Evans for information on Fressingfield.

significantly, the best way to enhance status was to control a seat in the church, preferably as close to the chancel as possible.[17]

The nature of the class system of early modern England is shown by the way in which decisions about church seating were made. The records available for Norfolk show no evidence of pew rental in rural parishes. In the countryside, large seats were sometimes built and maintained by leading families, but most were assigned by the churchwardens; when a family built its own seat, it was attached to the family's house or tenement. In Fressingfield the Sancrofts' seat had been built about fifty years earlier for Mr Lawrence, whose house William Grudgefield owned. In a dispute in Framingham Pigot in 1635, James Witherell's family had held the same seat for half a century. The churchwardens, he argued, had no right to place people in that seat, but only the Witherells and 'such as have been allied unto them or otherwise out of courtesy have been permitted so to do'.[18] When Thomas Pecke, Jr bought his house from John Keeble in Stowmarket, Suffolk some time before 1665, Keeble sought to reserve his wife's right to its seat in church. Pecke refused, even when offered 'four or five pieces'. The seat belonged to the house, and the wife of a former owner was 'buried in the said seat'.[19] Those who sympathized with Keeble did so because the seat was one of the chief seats in the parish, and Keeble was a 'better' man than was Pecke. A complicated set of issues thus came into the designation of seats for particular inhabitants. The assignment of a seat to a house assumed a stable society, but would undermine the use of the Church as a mirror of the social order in a period of social change. The frequent shifts in seating implied in the litigation were responses to such change.

Because church seating balanced past and present, whenever possible churchwardens and others sought flexibility in order to mirror the social relations of the village. Sir Ralph Hare wrote to

[17] L. Stone, 'Social mobility'; I am grateful to Mrs Nesta Evans for sharing her maps of the distribution of yeomen wills in Norfolk and Suffolk. See N. Evans, 'Community of the South Elmhams'.

[18] DEP/41, Grudgefield, Gent. con Sancroft Jr, and Sancroft Sr, Gents., ff. 524–65; Fressingfield WEA, *Looking back at Fressingfield*, p. 36; DEP/42, James Witherell con Martha Harnie, ff. 5–8, 9–11v; seats were also attached to houses in Myddle: Gough, *History of Myddle*; payments are recorded in Great Yarmouth in 1669: DEP/48, Mr Joseph Waller con Thomas Wolfson, Idem con Thomas Bayes, ff. 136–43v, 183–91v.

[19] DEP/47, Pecke Jr con Keeble, ff. 243–7.

the churchwardens of Brancaster in 1655. He noted that there was no seat suitable for Mr Samuel Nash or his tenant Mr William Blomefield in the church, but there was a 'fitting' place for a new seat; the churchwardens were asked to allow Nash to build a seat for his house.[20] In 1672, when Robert Bathoe of Beccles claimed that a particular seat belonged to his house, the churchwardens responded that as they maintained it, they could place and displace those who sat there. Changes ought to reflect communal consensus, not unilateral decisions. Thus Nathaniel Burrell, the Rector of Letheringsett, testified against Mr Thomas Girdleston of his parish in 1726. Girdleston had removed the seat which had been 'erected, built, and adorned' by the previous owner of Mr James Hunt's house at her own expense. Girdleston had then enlarged his own seat, 'without the consent of any person that he knows of'.[21] Such behaviour, like Robert Theodorick's, made the definition of status an individual, rather than collective, decision. Villagers were reluctant to fix the assignment of seats in the church too rigidly, or to relinquish control of the process of defining and reifying the social order.

The separation of women and men in churches appears to have become more common in the seventeenth century, though its origins are obscure. While practice was quite rigid in some churches, in others women and men continued to sit together. The separation of women and men – and indeed married women from maids – helped to prevent the church service from becoming a setting for too many secular activities. It also reinforced the subordination of women to men, unmarried to married, and accompanied Arminian attempts to emphasize hierarchy and holiness in worship. When local gentry built large seats for themselves in the later eighteenth century, they were shared by men and women; at the end of the nineteenth century, the

---

[20] C/S3/42, Sir Ralph Hare to Churchwardens of Brancaster, 1655.

[21] DEP/49, Tirrell and Elmy, Churchwardens of Beccles, con Robert Bathoe, files 22, 24; cf. ANW 2/74, Coltishall presentment of Thomas Palmer in 1640: Palmer had been churchwarden the previous year, during which time he had his name carved in one of the seats in the church which had been built by the town; Thomas Lary, the carpenter, was also presented, and DEP/38, Cremer con Cooke, ff. 59–68; DEP/60, Mr James Hunt con Mr Thomas Girdleston, test. of Nathaniel Burrell. The re-organization of the seats in Myddle took place in 1658 because it was 'unseemly and undecent' that 'young boys . . . should sit above the best of the parish': Gough, *Myddle*, p. 117.

separation of the sexes in Norfolk churches was maintained only among the poor.[22]

The assignment of church seats ensured that the whole community was aware of the social order; there was no question of who belonged where. Church seating emphasized the importance of hierachy in the social order, and made it clear that each had their own place as well as their own duties. It created an illusion of stability in the face of social and economic change.

The ordering of the village in church was especially important because order was being challenged outside the church. Local notables could not take for granted the respect and deference of their inferiors; villagers often challenged the local elite, and refused to respect its members. These challenges ranged from mere rudeness or insulting remarks to or about superiors to claims of equality with them. When Thomas Copping of Kirstead with Langhale called Thomas Spooner, Gent., a 'common drunkard', it was cause for a defamation suit: nothing a gentleman did was 'common', so the use of the word effectively denied Spooner's status.[23] Two servants of Sir Thomas Hare got into an argument with William Collyer and others about the payment of a toll; the servants said that their '"master Sir Thomas Hare would not suffer himself to be so used by them," Collyer replied they "had money enough to go to suit with Sir Thomas Hare and they did not give a fart for him."' Collyer and his companions were indicted at quarter sessions for distraining a beast and for offensive words.[24] Disrespect which went unpunished undermined the local elite's effectiveness.

Simple insults were the most commonly reported refusals of deference; and while a man might have complained in any case of

[22] The distinction was not made in Myddle: Gough, *History of Myddle*; men and women continued to sit together in Longham in 1615 (ANW/2/58), in Great Yarmouth in 1617 and perhaps in Beccles in 1672; the importance of hierarchy when the separation was made is shown in presentments, e.g. ANW/2/58 (1615), Ursula ux. Philip Cooke, of Morston, who refused to sit with the married women, and 'disorderly placeth herself among the maids'; and ANW/2/74 (1639) Paul Rose and w. Ann of Weasenham, who sat together in church; *The East Anglian; or Notes and Queries*, ed. C.H. Evelyn White, NS V, 1893–4, pp. 147, 175; there was considerable variety of local practice: Obelkevich, *Religion and Rural Society*, pp. 109–10 finds no separation of sexes, but it was still the custom in Wells Cathedral in the 1930s (personal communication from David Underdown).

[23] DEP/28, Thomas Spooner Gent. con Thomas Copping, ff. 422, 525–6, 530.

[24] C/S3/57, Examination of Robert Cole of Stow Bardolph, 14 July 1686; also indictments of William Collyer, Thomas Norrice and Ursula Copper.

being called a 'whoremasterly knave', the speaker was being doubly rude when the person addressed was a parson or a gentleman. In 1632 Thomas Layer, a gentleman from Booton, chided Thomas Garrard, the churchwarden, for not paying poor men for work done on the church when almost everyone had paid the rate, and alleged that Garrard made up his accounts in Cawston's alehouse. Garrard responded that Layer 'did not speak truth'; Layer promptly brought a defamation case.[25] In 1631 Mr Robert Blomefield said to Mr Salter, a parson, 'a fart on you', and witnesses believed Blomefield 'ought to have used the said Mr Salter with reverence in respect of his function and calling'.[26] Respect was also due to the wives of parsons and gentlemen. When told that Alice Deye had said that 'Little Snoring was like unto Great Snoring for it was never without whores and thieves', William Malbye told her husband, William Deye, Gent., that she has not 'honestly spoken' in giving 'the town such an evil report'.[27] She retaliated with a defamation suit. The concern with minor slights, slurs and allegations reflects an assumption that virtue accompanied social and economic superiority.

Insults were challenged by defamation cases; other challenges to order were dealt with by the criminal law. Sedition against the government was the most extreme threat. Some sedition was rooted in economic hardship. In 1597, high grain prices led to mutterings in many places. A man in Fakenham was hauled up before the justices for saying that 'There should be a camp at Whissonsett, meaning such as Kett's camp was, and there men should fight for corn ...'.[28] The reference to Kett's rebellion, which held the city of Norwich hostage for a month in 1549, was menacing. That same year, John Curtis of Wiggenhall St Mary Magdalen was told by Thomas Welles that the poor had risen in the west and would arrive in the county in a week; Welles expected four or five people to join him in going to a justice to ask 'that they might have corn cheap for their money and if they could not get

---

[25] DEP/40, Thomas Layer, Gent. con Thomas Garrard, ff. 355–7; this evidence is challenged in DEP/41, ff. 24, 25v, 27v–8v.

[26] DEP/44, Mr Salter con Mr Robert Blomefield, ff. 5v–7v, 162–2v, 232–2v, 410–15.

[27] DEP/11, Bk. 11b, 1567 Anne Deye ux. William Deye, Gent. con William Malbye, Personal answer of William Malbye, f. 74: Malbye refers to her as Alice.

[28] C/S3/12A, 39 Elizabeth, Presentment of Gallow Hundred; for Kett's rebellion, see Diarmaid MacCullough, 'Kett's Rebellion in context', *Past and Present*, 84 (1979), pp. 36–59.

any reasonably for their money then they would arise and get it with strength and that if they did arise they would knock down the best first'.[29] The threat against the gentry of the county was unmistakable, and the information forwarded to the privy council.

Even less menacing comments were taken seriously. When Philip Patrick of Castle Acre called Randall Cooke a 'Scottish rogue' in 1610, adding 'all Scots are rogues and rascals well known', the reference to James I's Scottish background was not lost on Patrick's listeners.[30] In 1668, Thomas Murland was brought before the justices for saying 'His name is but Charles Stuart and there is Charles Robatham'; his listeners assumed that he meant that Charles II was Charles Robatham (rob them).[31] Others were more direct; in 1662 Robert Flower of Wareham was in an alehouse in Wells-next-the-Sea when he refused to pledge to General Monck, saying 'No, he scorned to pledge an hypocrite'.[32] Monck, of course, had used a Parliamentary army to engineer the return of the King in 1660. Such comments were not frequent, but occurred regularly from the 1640s on, and peaked in the 1680s, when many in Norfolk supported the Duke of Monmouth and criticized the Duke of York, long before he came to the throne as James II.[33]

Assaults on authority aimed at those well below the King were taken nearly as seriously, as political theory would require. William Byrde of West Lynn refused to pay an overseers rate in 1615 because of the idleness of Humphrey Guybon, Esq., a justice of the peace. In his refusal, Byrde allegedly said that 'he is as good a

---

[29] The exchange between Curtis and Welles is quoted by Buchanan Sharp, *In Contempt of All Authority* (Berkeley and Los Angeles, 1980), p. 37, although he misquotes the numbers involved as four or five thousand, instead of four or five: PRO SP 12 262, f. 151 I; also reports of disorder in Norfolk in PRO SP 12 262 151, 30 April 1597 and PRO PC 2/22, 1 May 1597; John Walter, 'A "rising of the people"? The Oxfordshire rising of 1596', in *Past and Present*, 107 (1985), pp. 90–143.

[30] C/S3/17, Information of William Thompson, Cler. and Randall Cooke.

[31] C/S3/48, 20 Charles II, Information of Thomas Haillett, 21 May 1668.

[32] C/S3/45, Information re. Robert Flower.

[33] There are eleven indictments for seditious words supporting the Duke of Monmouth in PRO ASSI 16/50/4 (1685); see also PRO ASSI 16/43/4 (1681), Information of Richard Kilby against Richard Smyth; C/S3/55A, Examination of Thomas Ward of Swaffham, Gent. and C/S3/54A, Calendar of Prisoners, March 1684 Assizes, where Simon Olly was held for saying 'The Duke of Monmouth is a Prince and will reign Governor of this Kingdom . . . in spite of thousands such as the Duke of York'.

man as he [i.e. Guybon]';[34] he was brought before the justices. In 1617 John Wither of Brinton compounded his offence when served with a warrant by telling justices that, 'Your worships had not authority to send for him, except it were a felony or treason, and that he would not obey it'.[35]

The most threatening refusal of deference was the claim to judge the social order, which included an implicit claim of equality. When Alice Corkes of Itteringham said in 1589 that 'My Lord Bishop, my Lord Cromwell and all other the Justices were not so good subjects unto their God and prince as was her Uncle Francis Kett/And that Mr [Blenner]Hassett was a very villain and not worthy to be a justice',[36] she questioned all social order. Francis Kett, a grandson of Robert, was a millenarian who had recently been burned for heresy. Claims to social and moral equality were common, as when Henry Weavers told Mr Miles Lynn, a parson, in 1613, 'I am a better man than thou art knave parson a turd in thy teeth'.[37]

Many of the cases involving claims to equality involved parsons, suggesting some uncertainty about their status. Thomas Playforth said to Parson Fuggill in 1599 that he 'was as good a man as the said Mr Fuggill, setting his calling aside'.[38] The place of parsons in disputes opens up some of the murkier aspects of the social hierarchy of early modern England. In 1591, when Alice Nurse of Norwich bore an illegitimate child, she was reluctant to identify the father, '"because he was such a man as he was" then she was demanded if he were a gentleman, she answered, "no, he was a minister."'[39] The minister was respected and feared, but he was not a gentleman. Earlier in the sixteenth century it had been commonplace to give priests the courtesy title 'Sir'; by the end of the century the minister had no specific place in the social order. As a 'clerk', respect was due him, but ministers differed greatly in wealth and education. The parson's position was ambiguous. Ministers often came from yeoman and minor gentry families; they

[34] C/S3/20, Examination of Thomas Anderson of West Lynn, Labourer.

[35] C/S3/21, Petition to JPs against John Wither of Brinton.

[36] ANW/2/27, Itteringham vs. Alice Corkes; there are unfortunately no quarter sessions or assize records for this period to use as a comparison; for Frances Kett, see *DNB*.

[37] DEP/36, Mr Miles Lynn, cler. con Henry Weavers, ff. 124–9.

[38] DEP/30, Bk. 33, Offic. dmi con Playforth, ff. 139, 156, 172; cf. DEP/17, Gurney, Cler. con Mr Francis Trever, f. 371.

[39] DEP/26, Mihell con Rood, Cler., ff. 213–14v.

were rarely wealthier – and often poorer – than their leading parishioners, yet were set apart from them. They were outside the usual social hierarcy, and it was therefore difficult to know where they belonged.[40]

The wealth of the minister was clearly critical. In a society which usually made a loose equation of wealth and status, the special position of less prosperous parsons aroused antagonism, on the part of both the minister and his parishioners. When Mr Ineson, the parson of Tuttington, was reckoning with several of his parishioners for tithes in 1605, he grew angry with their reluctance to pay and took one by the beard and said, 'Hang up all such knaves as have £30 a year by land and have but the tithe of one cow for the poor parson'.[41] Reckoning for tithes was a particularly sore point in relations between clergy and laity. The process was resented by those who had to pay, and Ineson's outburst testifies to the frustration of the clergy with a process that emphasized their dependence on their parishioners. A regular stream of tithe cases before the Consistory Court demonstrates that while many tried to avoid payment, the clergy carefully guarded their rights. In 1667 John Wasse of Harply said that ministers should 'work for their living as he did', and when he separated the tithe wheat and rye from his thirty acres, he gave the parson the smallest sheaves.[42] In some parishes, tithes were the source of considerable profit, but dependence on such an unpopular levy did not lead to a comfortable relationship between clergy and laity.

The rhetoric which enjoined respect for social superiors also led to conflicts over clerical behaviour. If they were so special, some reasoned, it was inappropriate for the clergy to behave as did their neighbours. In 1640 the churchwardens of Wolverstone, Suffolk, complained about their rector both to the Consistory Court and the committee of the House of Commons investigating Bishop Wren, the Laudian Bishop of Norwich; Jonathan Skynner, they alleged, 'followed mechanical works and almost all sorts of husbandry'. He kept his cows and pigs in the churchyard, and 'he

---

[40] See Mary Prior, 'Reviled and crucified marriages: the position of Tudor bishops' wives', *Women in English Society, 1500–1800* (London and New York, 1985), pp. 118–48; L. Stone, 'Social mobility'; Christopher Hill, *Economic Problems of the Church* (Oxford, 1956), esp. pp. 202–4, 206–8.

[41] DEP/33, Ashe con Ineson, f. 187v.

[42] DEP/48, Heyhoe, Cler. con John Wasse, ff. 42v–52.

hath done some offices not fit for his coat as this deponent conceiveth as pitch and load the cart with faggots and peas and help to drive his cows to the bull, and drive his horses and cows to pasture and from pasture'. Inappropriate behaviour was only one of the churchwardens' complaints about Skynner, who had come to the parish after a 'godly' minister, Mr Timothy Dalton, had been ejected. It caused particular resentment because of his use of his power: his presentments had led to the excommunication of a twelve-year-old boy for not answering properly to the Catechism, and a poor woman who

> had six small children and was feign in her husband's absence to stay at home with them; then he threatened and forbade all the parish from coming near her; by which means the poor woman died at last for want of food; and then he caused her to be buried in a field near a ditch side.[43]

The objects of Skynner's hostility were as inappropriate as his agricultural pursuits.

Edmund Gibbs joined social and religious complaints in his suit against John Brookebank, the Rector of Gayton, in 1669; he alleged that Brookebank cursed, and had refused Communion to Gibbs and others for trivial reasons. Brookebank farmed £20 or £30 of land, and spent much of his time on it; one witness had seen Brookebank 'sow barley as an ordinary husbandman'.[44] Something was wrong when a clergyman acted 'as an ordinary husbandman', and yet for many of the clergy nothing else was possible.

Criticism of the clergy for moral lapses like drinking or card playing is understandable, but the general concern about appropriate behaviour emphasizes the peculiar and awkward position of the parish clergy. It is often difficult to unravel the layers of conflict – over tithes, doctrine or personal quarrels – in cases

---

[43] DEP/45, Bk. 48b, Driver and Smith, Churchwardens of Wolverstone, con Jonathan Skynner, Cler., ff. 131–42, esp. ff. 134–4v; *Journal of Sir Simonds D'Ewes*, ed. Wallace Notestein (New Haven, 1923), 30 December 1640, pp. 200–1: the woman referred to was excommunicated from church; Dalton had gone to New England. See Hill, *Economic Problems*, pp. 216–18 for attitudes toward the by-employments of the clergy: the desire that the clergy devote themselves to God rather than mammon was common to most Puritans.

[44] DEP/48, Gibbs con Brookebank, Cler., ff. 151–4v, 285 ff.; also Brookebank con Gibbs, ff. 111–12, for defamation.

between clergy and their parishioners. However, sometimes clergymen themselves reveal the tensions of their position. John Hodgson was the vicar of Stradsett, a village a few miles east of Stow Bardolph and Wimbotsham. In July 1629 Mr Francis Piggott, Gent., charged that after a service a year before, Hodgson had returned to the church and said, 'I am as good a man as you and an honester man than you and that you have cozened me of ten pounds'.[45] Three months later some Stradsett parishioners sent a petition to Sir John Hare and Francis Parlett, Esq., complaining of Hodgson's behaviour: he had insulted various parishioners, was a common railer and brawler 'in base and uncomely terms', he had sued poor parishioners in the church courts for petty offences and on several occasions had insulted his patron, Mr Parlett. As his patron lay dying, Hodgson had railed against him, had called the widow, 'Queen and the filthiest and wickedest woman', and had even prayed for her death. He brought and threatened malicious suits in the ecclesiastical courts.[46] Hodgson's behaviour was that of a quick-tempered and unpleasant man, but these characteristics were exacerbated by his ambiguously elevated social position.

In several defamation cases brought by Norfolk clergy, witnesses state explicitly that the victim's status contributed to the insult. Two of these insults refer to Cawson's rector in the late seventeenth century, Dr John Hildeyard. Hildeyard served as a justice of the peace and was closely connected to the Tory magnates the Paston Earls of Yarmouth. In the middle of an enormous tithe dispute between Hildeyard and the Whig Clement Hyrne, Gent., Hyrne called Hildeyard 'pitiful lousy priest, beggarly priest, a whoremaster and a dunce'. The words, said one witness, 'render not only him the said Doctor, but the priestly office contemptible and ridiculous'.[47] In 1681 Richard Mosse of Briston was alleged to have said that 'ministers were domineering and encroaching and had not need to be made justices of the peace, and that Doctor Hildeyard was more like a just ass than a justice'.[48]

---

[45] DEP/38, Piggott Gent. con Hodgson, Cler., f. 105–7v.

[46] C/S3/27, Articles against John Hodgson, Vicar of Stradsett: these are repeated in C/S3/28A, where he promises reform; Hill, *Economic Problems*, pp. 215, 219–20.

[47] DEP/50, file 14, Hildeyard con Hyrne, evidence of Edward Bradfield.

[48] C/S3/54, Examination of John Talk, worsted weaver, 11 July 1681; for the Paston connection, see Historical Manuscripts Commission, *Sixth Report* (London, 1877), pp. 378, 382; arms were seized from Hyrne after the Rye House Plot: *Norfolk Lieutenancy Journal*, Norfolk Record Society, XXX, ed. Basil Cozens-Hardy (Norwich, 1961), p. 44.

Hildeyard was not alone as the target of such insults. After a complaint by Thomas Gibbs, the Rector of Banham, about Brian Shardelow's alehouse in 1702, Shardelow was reported to have said of Gibbs, 'he take away my license he kiss mine arse . . . he is a rogue and a shitten jackanapes and I care not a turd for him go you and tell him'. The insults – rogue, jackanapes, kiss mine arse – were more insulting than usual when directed at a minister; one witness interrupted Shardelow's colourful invective saying, 'Hold a little . . . don't abuse the minister'.[49]

Cases in which an insult alone was seen as inappropriate are concentrated in the period after 1660; before then, they were usually accompanied by explicit claims to equality. Before 1640, the nature of the social hierarchy, and the basis of class position were contested. After the Restoration, while conflicts over the placement of individuals continued, the general outlines of the social order were clearer. The continued insecurity of those at the top of the class hierarchy is revealed, however, by their swift response to insults; though they no longer had to depress the pretensions of those who claimed equality, an insult was still a challenge to them. Threats to the social order were readily perceived and disciplined.

A parson had no clearly defined place in the social hierarchy because his position was based on the ancient division of society into orders – those who pray, those who fight and those who work – which had long since ceased to reflect social reality. In the hierarchy emerging in the seventeenth century, social position was based on a theoretically fixed status hierarchy, but status in turn largely depended on wealth. English society was undergoing the early stages of a transformation which made it, by the end of the eighteenth century, a society of classes which perceived the opposition of their economic interests. In the seventeenth century this was reflected in the tendency of villagers to rely on wealth as a test of social position. In a later period, the class of professionals which included the clergy was amalgamated with the upper class through education and social background, which then became the basis of respect. In our period, the class hierarchy was more crudely, though by no means exclusively, based on wealth.[50]

---

[49] DEP/53, 1702, Mr Thomas Gibbs, Cler. con Brian Shardelow.

[50] Stone, 'Social mobility'; Edward Thompson, *The Making of the English Working Class* (New York, 1966), esp. preface; problems for the clergy continued in the nineteenth century: Obelkevich, *Religion in Rural Society*, p. 126.

The significance of wealth in the social order is underlined by villagers' discussions of reputation. Social position, determined largely by wealth, in turn qualified men for local government. As officeholders, local notables were responsible for presenting their inferiors to justices and archdeacons for social and moral offences, for granting and withholding poor relief and, through such decisions for determining whether or not a newcomer was welcome; the system assumed that those of higher status were worthier and better able to make such judgements. The equation of wealth and worth was effected through reputation. The key concept in this process was 'credit'. The term is ambiguous: from its Latin root meaning 'to believe' comes its use in court testimony referring to the truthfulness of witnesses; but it had also long been used in trade, where letters of credit assured merchants of buyers' ability to pay. By the late sixteenth century 'credit' described both honesty and solvency; wealth and virtue were joined. Thus, in 1580 Margaret Guybon said in Bury St Edmunds that John Smythe 'was of no more credit than one that was in the alms house'.[51] As the ensuing argument focused on allegations that Smythe had syphilis, it was not only his wealth that was in question. The word might be used with conscious ambiguity; both meanings are certainly contained in this testimony in 1617:

> Susan Wylie is a woman of single ability and dwelleth upon the Common and liveth partly by her own industry and partly by the relief of her neighbours. And such a one as is of very small credit or estimation and one to whom very little or no credit is to be given to her testimony.[52]

Poverty was apparently the only reason for disbelieving Wylie's testimony. When a number of poor women in Suffolk complained about the sexual advances of the churchwarden, the accused brought in several witnesses who testified that the women involved were 'poor needy vile base people of no esteem amongst their neighbours', and 'such as he believe for some small

---

[51] DEP/19, John Smythe con Margaret Guybon, ff. 279v, 280r–v, 281; the relevant definitions (2, 5, 9) in the *Oxford English Dictionary* all cite a first use in the sixteenth century.
[52] DEP/37, Slynne con Wrott, f. 3v.

reward may be procured to swear falsely'.[53] The churchwarden was respected among his neighbours, and given the choice between the testimony of the women and of the churchwarden, those of 'credit and estimation' in the community chose the churchwarden. Credit affirmed the worth of local notables.

The concept of credit meant that the orderly and obedient poor were special cases. When several poor people testified in a Shelfanger tithe case in 1689, they were described as 'honest poor people', who had nothing to gain from the case because those with houses worth less than 40s. paid no tithes.[54] In 1603, William Rugge of Felmingham asked Sir Bassingbourn Gawdy for relief for Francis Flewdes, a carpenter who had lost his goods in a fire, because 'he is very honest, well given, and a very good workman, and no loiterer, gamester, nor alehousehaunter but a very painful daily and diligent labourer'.[55]

Credit and reputation were self-reinforcing concepts. It is rarely possible to see how they were established, but a case in Shelfanger allows us to disentangle some threads of the discussion. In 1635 Katherine Fuller brought a defamation case against George Cooper, who had called her son Robert 'bastard', thus impugning her chastity. Cooper argued that Robert Fuller had first called him a 'Pockie nosed knave and his nose was eaten with the French Pox . . .', and that no one had thought of Katherine's chastity when he called Fuller a bastard. Who said what first, and what people really thought, can never be known. But the interrogatories to witnesses show how villagers solved these problems. There were five chief witnesses. Robert Banes, a blacksmith from Shelfanger, aged fifty-six, had been born in Shelfanger and had lived there for the previous sixteen years. He and his son William, a twenty-two-year-old blacksmith who had lived in Shelfanger all his life, testified for Katherine Fuller. They were joined by William Wright, a thirty-year-old yeoman who had lived in Shelfanger for ten years. All three signed their names. Cooper's witnesses included William Paston, a twenty-year-old 'husbandman', or

[53] Hudson con Noble, in DEP/43, f. 248, also ff. 165–7, 222v–7v, 247v–50v, and DEP/44, ff. 13–22 (esp. 14v).

[54] DEP/52, Francis Leach con Obadiah Browne, Cler., 1689: testimony of Elizabeth Prentice, Robert Holmes.

[55] B.L. Egerton Ms. 2714, f. 347, William Rugge to Bassingbourn Gawdy, Kt. September 1603.

farm servant; he had been born in the neighbouring village of Bunwell. He was joined by Robert Neale, a forty-year-old linen weaver. Neither Paston nor Neale signed their names. In this case, literacy, not occupation, allows an initial distinction between witnesses. But there were other differences. Each witness was asked about the reputation of the others. Their responses confirm the ranking suggested by literacy. There was no question that Katherine Fuller's witnesses were respected inhabitants, but the position of Paston and Neale was less clear. William Banes was most emphatic:

> Robert Neale and William Paston were and are poor persons of idle conversations and no credit or estimation to whose sayings little credit is to be given, and for such were and are commonly accounted . . . and the said Neale is a Binn-Bailye and helpeth the producent Cooper in such business.

William Wright was kinder, but said that Paston and Neale were 'poor persons of little estate', and Robert Banes agreed with his son's evaluation. From other sources, we know that Neale had sold most of his patrimony to his father-in-law Robert Gowen, Sr shortly after he inherited it; Gowen placed most of the lands in trust for his daughter and her children so that Neale could not touch the profits. Neale obviously lacked 'credit', in at least the fiscal sense of the word.[56]

Paston and Neale presented different images of each other. Paston had 'never heard but that the said Neale was a man of honest life and one that will swear the truth'. Neale addressed some of the issues raised by Banes: 'William Paston is a young man and liveth in service, but of no great estate, yet well reputed and of good estimation and one to whose swearing he believeth much credit is to be given'.[57] We do not know the grounds on which Neale and Paston made their judgements; they were, after all, trying to establish their credibility as witnesses, so they may have been disingenuous or even dishonest. But it is also possible that the equation of wealth with moral worth assumed by wealthier

[56] DEP/42, Fuller con Cooper, ff. 130–3, 144–5, 207–16, 250v–1, esp. f. 209; for Robert Neale, see Amussen, 'Governors and governed', pp. 92–3, and Shelfanger Court Books Warnes 19.12.68 R 192 D–E, Book 1, court for 1616, and Book 2, courts for 1623 and 1624.

[57] DEP/42, Fuller con Cooper, ff. 212, 213v–14.

inhabitants and implicit in Banes's statement was not accepted by those to whom it applied; certainly the concept of credit is never used by those labelled poor. Like the abilities of women, the character of the poor depended on the angle from which it was viewed.

The concept of credit as it was used in early modern England meant that the poor could be defined and categorized without further effort. The poor did not acquiesce in this, however, and did not label each other as of 'no credit'. Credit was a concept of the governors of early modern England, and it made their job easier; it was not universally accepted. The concept of 'credit' simultaneously masked and facilitated the increasing importance of wealth in the evaluation of social position.

The equating of wealth with moral worth implicit in the use of the term 'credit' created high expectations for local elites in early modern England. In their households and villages they were responsible for governing and caring for their inferiors. The way they used their position was therefore important, and frequently judged by their neighbours. The uses and abuses of power, and the problems of order are revealed by the ways in which authority was exercised.

Possibly the most benign use of power was to petition the justices of the peace to enable a poor but worthy villager to be more self-sufficient. Local notables might ask that regulations for alehouses, midwives or housing be set aside for the benefit of the deserving. Regulation should make it possible to get rid of undesirables, but not harm the worthy. The petitions indicate the extent of local control that was expected. In 1657, for instance, the people of Castle Rising supported a request by Anne, wife of William Bassham, for a licence to draw small beer. She had long done so, 'to the great advantage of the poor of the town', but had stopped when complained of, 'whereby the poor . . . receive much prejudice'. Her brewing was 'necessary and for the good of the greatest part of the town'.[58] Those defended from regulation need not be poor: thirty-five inhabitants of Harleston signed a petition in support of Thomas Benton, Katherine Whytinge and Edmund Greygoose when their brewing was suppressed at the request of

[58] C/S3/43, 1657, Petition of Castle Rising.

George Jackson, a newcomer who had erected a brewhouse. The petition illustrates both the expectations of local control, and of the appropriate behaviour of local notables. Greygoose, Whiting and Benton had lived in the town, paying rates, for at least twenty years; they were 'true and obedient subjects', had held office and their brewing had been to 'the benefit of the commonwealth and great relief of the poor'. Furthermore, they had maintained 'at their own costs and charges divers poor of our said Town', who otherwise would have needed parish relief. In spite of this, they needed the full weight of public opinion behind them when dealing with the justices of the peace.[59]

Petitions against regulation were often aimed at providing a substitute for parochial relief. In 1693 the rector, churchwardens and overseers of the poor of Acle wrote to the Bishop of Norwich about Elizabeth Barber, an elderly widow who was

> very helpful and succesful with women in childbirth. She is so poor that she was never able to purchase a licence. Since her summons to your court she have not been with any. The truth of this her low condition being made known, we hope your charity will not hinder but rather encourage her to do what good she can toward a poor livelihood.[60]

Similarly, in 1600 John Hill wrote to Sir Bassingbourn Gawdy to request an alehouse licence for John Simpson, who had lately moved to Diss. Simpson had kept an alehouse for fourteen years, and Hill had 'not known him attacked but commended of the best sorts. Besides he is fit for nothing else by reason he is so gross a man as he is not able to travail'.[61]

Even gleaning, that characteristic activity of the poor, was regulated to ensure simultaneously that the poor got sufficient grain and that property owners did not suffer unduly. In 1659 there were apparently some difficulties, as the Quarter Sessions at both Swaffham and Fakenham had to set out rules: gleaning was to begin only when all the corn was tithed and collected, and was to last only three days. The permission of the churchwardens and

---

[59] C/S3/13A (c. 1600), Testimonial from Harleston; although George Jackson's identity is unclear, his wealth and connections are obvious.

[60] TES/8, 1693, Letter from Acle re. Elizabeth Barber.

[61] B.L. Egerton 2714, f. 107, John Hill to Sir Bassingbourn Gawdy, 9 January 1601.

minister was necessary to glean, affirming patronage and deference between governors and governed.[62] Parish elites protected the worthy poor, and expected to be supported by justices and others responsible for local regulation.

Not all the poor could have their problems solved by a licence to work. Some needed waivers of the legal requirements for cottages. Thus when Robert Roand was indicted in 1635 for building a cottage without the requisite four acres, his neighbours asked that the cottage be allowed to stand lest he become a charge on the parish. In the same year, John Beckham, Gent., the lord of the manor of Narford, sought permission to build a cottage on the waste for William Lee, 'an impotent very poor man, and hath a wife and ten children, and now want a habitation'.[63] Exceptions could always be made if the request to do so had the proper support.

The paternalistic behaviour of local governors was often matched by that of masters to servants, who showed corresponding deference even after service had formally ended. Such exchanges rarely lacked ulterior motives. In 1710 Oliver LeNeve received a letter from his former servant Hannah Hoskins which began, 'I could never forgive myself should I omit this opportunity of telling my Dear Master that on Tuesday last I pulled up all the courage I had and entered on the hazardous state of matrimony'.[64] The letter was probably an indirect request for a wedding present. More than a century earlier, Edmund Moundford Esq. had invited Sir Bassingbourn Gawdy to the wedding of two of his servants, to 'help towards that charge which marriage bringeth'; Moundford added that he would reciprocate in similar circumstances.[65] Not everyone shared Moundford's attitude. Ten years later, Edmund Doyly only reluctantly acceded to a request from one of his servants that Doyly invite his friends to the servant's wedding to help set him up as a householder. Doyly's grudging invitation to his friends suggests his discomfort with the situation, even though the servant in question had been with him since childhood.[66]

[62] C/S2/2, July 1659, Swaffham and Fakenham Sessions: see above, chapter 3, n. 40.

[63] C/S3/31, 12 Charles I, Northwold Petition on behalf of Robert Roand, labourer, January 1638; C/S3/31, Petition of John Beckham, Gent.

[64] B.L. Egerton 2721, f. 300, Han. Hoskins to O. LeNeve, 29 July [1710?].

[65] B.L. Egerton 2714, f. 220, 18 August 1602, Edmund Moundford, Esq. to Sir Bassingbourn Gawdy.

[66] AYL/16, Edmund Doyly to John Browne and Thomas Bransley in Poringland, 20 May 1612.

In asking, directly or indirectly, for support from their masters and their masters' friends, servants used a broad definition of family. But calling servants family could never change what Edmund Doyly was uncomfortably aware of: servants were employees paid by the year. Especially in the sixteenth century, children from prosperous families sent into service were the social equals of the family they worked for. In such cases, servants may well have been treated as family members, but this was rare. The sense of obligation to servants may have been more extensive in county families like the Moundfords and Gawdys than in less elite families; social distance made paternalism possible. The social gap between the experience of servants and family members widened during the seventeenth century, at least in yeomen's households. In 1723, William Carpenter of Aldeby claimed £60 from his parents' estate for raising his sister Judith, who had been orphaned when eleven years old. The central question was whether or not she had done the work of a servant. As Carpenter's sister, she would have done only what work she wished, but as a servant, she would have earned her keep. One witness, a former servant of Carpenter's, described her work:

> Judith Carpenter ... used to do all manner of work as a servant, as at the time of harvest she used to go every day with the tithe cart to the fields and to rake up after the cart, and at other times used to do all the common business of the house, as looking after the dairy, dressing the fowls for market, and if the business of the house was over, she used to spin, and ... was [never] treated any better or ever fared better or otherwise than as the rest of the servants did and ... Judith Carpenter deserved her board or victuals at least for what service he observed she did about the house.[67]

William Carpenter farmed about 300 acres. In a family such as his a sister or a daughter was not expected to work at all times. The ease with which the distinction between the work of family members and of servants was made indicates its familiarity. This distinction

---

[67] DEP/60, Childerhouse con Carpenter, esp. testimony of William Finch; Chamberlayne, *Angliae Notitia*, pp. 435–6, complains about the practice of gentry fathers apprenticing their sons, and suggests that it continued into the later seventeenth century.

underscores the changing nature of yeomen's family economy that is suggested by their wills.

The ideal community bound together by ties of patronage and deference did exist outside the world of theory, but the power of masters – and of local notables – could easily be abused. When those who were to maintain social order abused their position, the fabric of social relations was torn. There was little tolerance for those notables who failed to perform their duty, or abused their power, and constant efforts were made to maintain elite unity. In 1704 Clement Hyrne wrote 'I have been for sometime and still am concerned for the divisions amongst ourselves, which render us too little with our neighbours and the whole hundred uneasy at our disjointed proceedings'.[68] Only a united – and just – local elite could maintain the authority and effectiveness of local government. It is therefore instructive to examine abuses of class power, and responses to them.

Abuses were common even within families, where the intimacy – and relative privacy – of master–servant relations made servants vulnerable. A master could, for instance, rape or seduce a servant without observation by neighbours. Sexual relations between masters and servants involved a double exercise of power – as a master and a man. The relationship might be established, maintained and kept secret through coercion. Robert Dey, the Rector of Cranwich in the 1590s, seduced two of his servants: one, Elizabeth Purkey alias Bate, he married off when she became pregnant; the other, Agnes Greene, left his service. When Greene left, she began to talk about his behaviour, so he brought a defamation suit against her which he dropped (at the instigation of a local justice of the peace) in return for her promise of silence. Neither Elizabeth Purkey or Agnes Greene had much control over the outcome, and the class power of Dey made it very difficult to speak against him.[69]

Sexual exploitation of servants was the most common abuse of class power within households, but it was not the only one.

---

[68] B.L. Egerton Ms. 2720, f. 81, Clement Hyrne to [?O. LeNeve], 6 July 1704.

[69] DEP/28, Dey con Leonard Poole, Richard Dey, Robert Bate and Elizabeth Purkey alias Bate, Ex. Offic. con Robert Dey, Cler., ff. 3–11v, 25–7, 89–91v, 235–7v, 239–42, 244v–5v, 247–51v, 253–6; Wrightson, 'Puritan reformation', pp. 56–7 for servants made pregnant by masters.

Another form of abuse was neglect, visible only in its extreme form, when it led to death. In 1663 Sara Patrick of Wickmere demanded an inquest when her daughter, Rebecca Russells, who had been a servant of William Hower and his wife, was found dead after being 'hardly kept'.[70] Neglect of servants concerned the whole village. In 1610, William Childerhouse of Saham Toney had gone to the house of John Tennant at the request of William Wright and reported that,

> about Christmas time last past . . . he did see William Wright's daughter being the said Tennant's servant laid in a barn in a little straw covered with flaggs, the said servant being at that time very sick of the Pox, . . . And it seemed to him and to many . . . at that time that the said Wright's daughter was very carelessly looked to and provided for by . . . her said Master.[71]

Standards for the proper treatment of servants were difficult to enforce. Masters lived with servants as family but their power was based on a combination of household government and class power. The double power of masters made their abuse of it simultaneously more possible and more dangerous.

The concerns of villagers are evident in their response to masters who withheld wages or belongings at the end of a servant's employment. The servant would eventually collect the wages, but not without struggle. In 1658, Sarah Gill, a Stow Bardolph widow, refused to pay Thomas Tiffen 2s. wages; by the time the justices of the peace ordered her to pay him, she had to pay an additional 17s. in costs![72] It took several meetings of the quarter sessions to gain a final concord when John Maston, Jr, of Clippesby, gentleman, detained the goods and clothes of his former servant Francis Exham.[73] Servants were paid at the conclusion of service, so such exploitation was simple. Yet those in authority looked askance on

---

[70] AYL/304, 1662/3, Evidence of Sara Patrick: there is no record of an inquest in this case, although there may have been one.

[71] C/S3/17, Information of William Childerhouse against John Tennant of Saham Toney.

[72] C/S3/43, and C/S2/2, Lynn Sessions, January 1659.

[73] C/S2/5: the final concord between Maston and Exham is recorded at the October 1699 Norwich Sessions; cf. AYL/1, 31 March 1662, complaint of Thomas Spurrell, who was never paid for work by Thomas Lubbock, and DEP/47, Mulier con Emperor, ff. 279v–80.

such practices, and helped servants to recover wages. If tolerated, such abuses would diminish respect for masters, and by implication, all in authority.

Law enforcement in early modern England depended on the respect of the governed for those in authority. Not only masters, but all those in authority were expected to exercise power with care. West Winch complained to the justices of the peace about its overseers in 1649: they were giving relief to some who did not need it, using the town stock for their own benefit and had served several inhabitants with warrants for failing to pay a poor rate made without the consent of the parish. There were similar complaints against John Waters, overseer of Terrington in 1629, who had embezzled funds by charging the town more than the market price for grain and coal.[74] In 1615, the fen village of Emneth complained about Edmund Waskott, the parish clerk and vicar's churchwarden, who also farmed the vicarage tithes. As churchwarden he presented people to the church courts for not paying a rate which had never been agreed upon, and was alleged to have presented another villager simply because he was related to 'some of those that he presented'. When he brought suits as a tithe farmer, he delayed explaining the cause so the victims had less time to prepare their defence.[75] Those who represented outside institutions could also wreak havoc. Edward Durrant of Brinton, a diocesan functionary, took excessive fees at visitations; he also suggested to the churchwardens of Saxlingham that they present Nicholas Ringould instead of Sir Henry Sidney for not paying a rate. When Gregory Saslye and the questmen of Sharington refused to follow Durrant into an alehouse, Sasley was summoned 'from court to court, two courts after the year was out, that he was discharged from his office without any authority contrary to law'.[76] Durrant intervened in the affairs of communities, and undermined local discipline.

Officeholders had been given a formal trust by their neighbours; anyone could misuse the legal process to create disorder or conflict in the community. But those who did so were never popular. In 1670 the townsmen of Wymondham complained to the judges of

---

[74] C/S3/40, Petition of West Winch; C/S3/28A, Petition vs. John Waters of Terrington.

[75] C/S3/20, Articles against Edmund Waskott of Emneth.

[76] C/S3/17, 9 James I, Articles vs. Edward Durrant: Saslye was presumably a churchwarden.

assize that Henry Gay sued 'infants' for trespass when they walked on common paths. The law could be an expensive annoyance. A defence had to be offered to legal action, and one can understand the frustration of the inhabitants of West Winch in 1624 with Richard Sheepheard, 'an incorrigible and a desperate tinker', who brought lawsuits without cause, only to drop them when his neighbours had begun their defence.[77] The law could not be effective in parochial discipline if it were seen as a tool for unjust personal gain. Unjust lawsuits, like the abuse of office, would hamper its legitimate use.

The abuse of the economic power of the elite against poorer neighbours was far less worrisome than the abuse of servants, office or the law. Masters, officeholders and the law had institutionalized power that had to be respected, and thus the whole community was involved if they misbehaved. The abuse of class power usually affected only a few individuals, and rarely involved the mechanisms of social order. John Matthew of Gaywood was the only one affected when 'old Mrs Hare' had him presented as lewd, uncivil, a railer against his neighbours, and a disorderly person. He argued that the presentment was a result of her vendetta against him, and her desire to dispossess him of the house he held for life; no one else cared. George Skrynne of Setchy (West Winch) attempted to remove Alice Bacon and her husband William from the village with threats against anyone who gave them shelter or work. Skrynne even threatened the overseer, who was one of his tenants. Thomas Kemp of Toftrees threw Edward Ellis out of his house, even though Ellis had paid the rent; Ellis found it difficult to get redress because Kemp was not only his landlord, but also the town constable.[78] All these complaints were made by the individual victims, not the village; the use of power in these cases did not threaten social order.

Economic power could, however, be used for purposes a community actively supported. When John Lambert, a blacksmith from Wiveton who had been employed by Sir Nathaniel Bacon,

[77] PRO ASSI 16/20/3, August 1670, Articles of Misdemeanor and Common Barratry against Henry Gay of Wymondham; C/S3/26, 3 Charles I, Articles against Richard Sheepheard, late of West Winch and now of Castle Rising, a liberty where he could escape the bailiffs.
[78] C/S3/30, Petition of John Matthew of Gaywood; C/S3/29, Information of Alice, wife of William Hacon; C/S3/27, complaint of Edward Ellis.

was alleged to have fathered an illegitimate child, Bacon questioned and then dismissed him.[79] The class power of employers and landowners normally helped maintain social order, so its use was less controversial than the misuse of law or office. It was almost impossible to use class power against other local notables; but the law or office could be abused against the whole village. The response of the elite to the two situations reflects this difference.

Conflicts over the changing definition of property and property relations often did involve the elite. In 1667 Henry Riches and Thomas Baxter were cutting 'furze stalks and other sticks' in a close belonging to Sir Thomas Pettus, Bt., in Rackheath (near Norwich) when Sir Thomas came riding up to them. Riches testified that Pettus was shouting furiously, 'God damn me yonder is [sic] the Rogues, I will kill them if I can'; Pettus claimed that Baxter 'told him he had as much to do in those grounds as he this examinate had'. They agreed, however, that Pettus hit Baxter on the head, and that he died from the blow.[80] Baxter's words suggest that enclosure in Rackheath, which adjoined the open spaces of Mousehold Heath, had occurred only recently. Heaths were common sources of fuel and pasture; Baxter's death at Pettus's hands is a dramatic example of the tensions created by enclosure.[81]

Other, less spectacular conflicts provide even more explicit evidence about the disturbance of the traditional economy. Violations of rules of communal agriculture were often sources of complaints to the justices; the complaints suggest the strains which accompanied the transition to capitalist agriculture. Matthew Bremen of Grimston kept his cattle in the fields year round, so they damaged his neighbours' crops. When the beasts were impounded, Bremen picked the lock on the pound and let them out; he also laughed when put in the stocks. The open field agriculture of Grimston required the cooperation of all villagers; Bremen was out only for himself. There were complaints about Humphrey Willson; it was said in 1612 'ever since he came to Ashill as a householder' he was a constant troublemaker who

[79] DEP/25, Golde con Heade, ff. 276v–8v (also 158–9).

[80] PRO ASSI 16/14/6: the depositions are silent on some crucial areas, and Riches, who ran from the conflict, may have feared prosecution for trespass. A coroner's jury found Pettus responsible for murder, but the final outcome is unclear: ASSI 16/20/3.

[81] For other such conflicts, see e.g., Sharp, *In Contempt of All Authority*, and Lindley, *Fenland Riots*.

brought frivolous suits against his neighbours. Willson had made an illegal enclosure in Sir Robert Wind's foldcourse, and then attacked those who broke it down.[82] William Hunt of Horningtoft also abused communal expectations. During shack, he removed the fences between his field and the open fields, and then impounded poor men's cattle when they came into his field. He was also suspected of removing the dole stones which marked the boundaries between parcels in the open fields. Like Willson, he abused the law by having neighbours needlessly bound over to keep the peace.[83]

Such tensions were not confined to agriculture. In 1621 Nicholas Swan, a miller from Hilborough, charged excessive tolls and used false measures of corn, for both rich and poor. A miller was central to an economy which produced its own corn, and the miller who cheated his customers had long been a stock character. In 1711–12, the justices recorded the punishment of the miller Nicholas Whisker of Great Cressingham in unusual detail. Whisker had substituted chalk for one-third of the corn he had ground for Mary Norton, a widow from Saham Toney. He was fined £10, and was ordered to be placed in the pillory at Swaffham, Watton and Downham Market on successive market days.[84]

All of these incidents are signs of the tensions created by the growth of the market economy. It is difficult to examine the process of capitalist development systematically in village records; we only hear of it when it aroused the suspicion and anger of neighbours. Henry Kinge, a newcomer to West Rudham in 1636, blocked an ancient path and then cut down Mr Russell's vetches to make a path to his field. Like others who sought to strictly enforce or even extend their property rights, he brought suits against neighbours for minor trespasses: there were more arrests in West Rudham after his coming, it was said, 'than there have

[82] C/S3/24, Articles against Matthew Bremen; C/S3/18, Articles against Humphrey Willson of Ashill, 10 James I, who stayed in Ashill nevertheless: DEP/37 (1617) Mr Richard Huxley, Cler., con Humphrey Willson, who called him a 'shitten priest, a shag ragged knave, and a base slave', f. 130r–v.

[83] C/S3/24, 21 James I, Petition of Horningtoft against William Hunt; cf. C/S3/23, Petition of Great Fransham against Simon Woodrow.

[84] C/S3/23, Articles against Nicholas Swan of Hilborough; for Nicholas Whisker, see C/S2/6, Jan. 1712, and C/S1/11, July 1711, July 1712; Thompson, 'Moral economy', pp. 80–1, 97–8, 103–4.

been there these twenty years before'.[85] Both Kinge and Humphrey Willson of Ashill were recent arrivals; they lacked finesse, but they also lacked authority. Established villagers could usually silence or placate those who suffered. A poem from 'the poor despairing tenants which hold their land of the Church of Emneth', indicates the surprise that greeted the attempt of a member of a local family to usurp traditional rights. The poem, found in 1617, describes a man of decaying wealth who sought to claim ancient church lands and drive tenants out:

> One comfort have you if he doth prevail
> And force you to depart your habitations
> To fare more hardly than heretofore you have . . .
> And all that he shall get will not be worth a louse
> And every man may fitly say he robs the spittle [hospital] house.[86]

Villages in early modern England were insular, and committed to maintaining traditional relations and customs as much as possible. Yet the commitment to tradition was often at odds with the desire for profit, and the result was the gradual erosion of traditional relations. When change was carried out with the support of local notables, it encountered less difficulty than when carried out by one person, but it did not cause less distress.

Both social status and power accrued to the wealthier inhabitants of early modern villages as agriculture became increasingly market-oriented. Because of their role in local government, all members of the local elite sought to ensure that power was used in appropriate ways. They objected not to all uses and abuses of power, but to those which would undermine respect for authority or which caused needless conflict. Local notables knew that they had to discipline their fellows to preserve their own authority. No one, however important, was independent of correction.

Correction and discipline were most often directed not at erring fellow governors, but at the humbler inhabitants of villages. Challenges to the ideal of the village as an orderly, deferential

---

[85] C/S3/31, Articles against Henry Kinge of West Rudham.

[86] C/S3/21: this poem was found dropped on the ground on the path into Emneth Church.

society often stemmed from people's refusal to accept increasingly strict definitions of appropriate behaviour. Local elites were most likely to make formal attempts to perfect their villages before 1640, but they generally abandoned the use of formal mechanisms of control in the second half of the seventeenth century: only three petitions to quarter sessions survive in Norfolk from after 1660 (and none from after 1670) while the church courts never regained the jurisdiction over personal and moral offences that they had before the Civil War.[87]

We have already seen how petitions to quarter sessions illuminate the abuse of power by local notables. The petitions are revealing because they are not standardized, and illustrate their complaints with detailed descriptions, often of multiple offences; they often bear a tone of some desperation.[88] More than one-half (54.8 per cent) of the sixty-two surviving petitions to Norfolk justices focus on the contentiousness of one neighbour against another, both in verbal quarrels and in violence or threats of violence. Next to contentiousness, the most common reason for complaint was drink – being a drunkard, an alehousehaunter or an alehousekeeper (or both); these show up in more than one-third (38.7 per cent) of the petitions. More than a third (33.9 per cent) also refer to economic abuses, such as unfairly impounding beasts, breaking down hedges or blocking rights of way. Those who disrupted the local economy were often among the one-quarter (27.4 per cent) who brought unjust lawsuits, complained of minor trespasses and falsely had people bound over to keep the peace. More than one-quarter (27.4 per cent) of those complained of had abused their superiors, but only seven (11.3 per cent) had taken advantage of their office, and eight (12.9 per cent) had taken advantage of their social position to exploit their neighbours. Finally, more than a fifth (21 per cent) of the petitions complained that the subject had abused family members or neglected family obligations.

[87] Quarter sessions records are more complete after the Restoration, so it is not merely an issue of record survival; it is possible that the ecclesiastical courts were beginning to lose business before 1640, but the records are not adequate to prove such an assertion: see below, n. 122; this pattern seems to be common, as studies of social regulation fade out after the Restoration: Wrightson and Levine, *Poverty and Piety*, is the most notable of these.

[88] The following is based on petitions in the quarter sessions rolls for Norfolk (C/S3), some filed in the assize rolls (PRO ASSI 16) and several which are found in the Raynham collection (RAY).

Quantitative analysis merely outlines the concerns of local notables. The nature of disorder is more effectively illustrated by the petitions themselves. Simon Keeper of Newton next Castle Acre was the subject of petitions in 1615 and 1623. The first complained primarily of his treatment of his family (he beat his mother, locked her in her house and bound his brother-in-law to keep the peace for trying to stop him) but added that he also 'set strife' between his neighbours. The second petition said that Keeper was a talebearer, who encouraged fights between minister and parish, landlord and tenant. He also stirred up trouble so that he could bring lawsuits.[89] Keeper deliberately created disorder, and encouraged the intervention of outsiders in the life of the village.

Order had to be maintained both inside and outside the household. Contention, abuse of power and contempt for authority were regular complaints; so were abuse and disorder in the household. Petitions underline the social and communal implications of family relations and sexuality. Holme Hale, for instance, criticized Henry Eaton, who in 1622 was charged by his servant Marie Hobbert of fathering the child she was then carrying. Eaton sought to have Hobbert accuse others of paternity, and gave her savine as an abortifacient, 'affirming that it was no sin so to do, except the child were already quickened within her, and that it was a common thing in London, for such women, to use such practices in such cases'. After Hobbert had publicly accused him, Eaton threatened to beat her brains out for 'disclosing his lewd practice'.[90] Eaton's abuse of his power threatened household order; the village had to step in.

The mistreatment of servants or wives created disorder through a failure of responsibility; disorder could also be actively encouraged. Hugh Ithell, Gent., it was alleged in 1600, 'doth consort himself with many such bad and lewd persons being his servants and retainers as are ready at his or his wife's request to commit any enormity'.[91] The importance of familial order to the community is particularly clear in the petition brought by Beeston against Thomas Vyollett, Gent., and his servant Elizabeth Hewes. Vyollett severely beat and starved his wife Susan, installed Elizabeth Hewes, a servant, in the house as his mistress and gave her the keys to the cupboards.[92] The people of

---

[89] C/S3/20, 24, Petitions against Simon Keeper of Newton next Castle Acre.

[90] C/S3/23A, Articles of Holme Hale against Henry Eaton.

[91] C/S3/13A, Articles against Hugh Ithell, Gent. and Parnell his wife.

[92] C/S3/27, Articles against Thomas Vyollett, Gent. and his servant Elizabeth Hewes.

Beeston supported Susan Vyollett's separation from her husband. By allowing his servant to give orders to his wife he inverted the social order, and such behaviour, particularly by a gentleman, encouraged social chaos.

Mistreatment of a wife or other family members was often one offence among many. Matthew Loose was 'disobedient to all authority', and 'at continual strife with his wife often beating her and seldom quiet with her'.[93] In 1621, Simon Woodrow of Great Fransham not only threatened his pregnant wife, but also killed his neighbours' cattle and fowls, and left his fences open to the common so that beasts could wander into his land and be impounded. Robert Johnson of Northwold, who 'heinously railed upon his wife' in 1631 was also a common drunkard, had assaulted the constable who warned him not to frequent alehouses, and attacked the parson in the churchyard.[94] Richard Sheepheard, the 'desperate tinker', brought needless lawsuits, failed to accept local authority and refused to pay the rent for his town house. When he was asked to pay the rent he abused and cursed both the churchwardens and other inhabitants, 'then and at other times [he] vomiteth out such fearful blasphemies, oaths, reproaches and threatenings as that divers of the inhabitants near him report they are afraid he will set their houses on fire'. Neighbours feared that he might combine with 'all the most desperate tinkers in the country'. Sheepheard also mistreated his family, coming home drunk and beating 'his wife and her children'.[95] The peace of the town could be disturbed by disorder within the family as much as by disorderly alehouses or unjust lawsuits.

Offences related to drink were common in petitions against disorderly villagers because of several widespread assumptions about popular behaviour. The first was that any popular gathering was a potential source of disorder, particularly if it took place in an alehouse. The second was that alehouses harboured undesirables. One solution was the frequent repetition of rules seeking to limit participation in alehouse sociability. Residents in towns were only to drink in alehouses when attending a market, lodging there, working away from home, when invited by a traveller or on

[93] C/S3/26, Articles against Matthew Loose.
[94] C/S3/23, Articles against Simon Woodrow of Great Fransham; C/S3/28A, Articles against Robert Johnson of Northwold.
[95] C/S3/26, Articles against Richard Sheepheard of West Winch.

'urgent and necessary occasions to be allowed by two justices of the peace'.[96] Bonds were required of licenced alehousekeepers to enforce such rules, but in 1690 the justices at the Norwich sessions still worried that unlicenced alehouses, 'do harbour and entertain all sorts of wandering and travelling rogues, vagabonds and suspicious persons', and were not always effectively suppressed.[97] The links between alehouses and other forms of disorder are clear both in petitions to justices and in presentments to the church courts. In 1578 Margaret Fishe of Catton was alleged to have said, 'there cannot be any alewife thrive without she be an whore or have an whore in her house',[98] while in 1640 Michael Gage of West Walton was reputed to be 'an alehousehaunter, one that neglects wife and children, church and sacrament and lets his fence to the churchyard wall lie open'.[99]

Assumptions about disorder in alehouses, like most common ideas, were exaggerated but not wholly imaginary. Robert Pennell of Islington, it was alleged in 1657, got his poor customers so drunk that they did not know what was happening, and 'then doth make what reckoning he pleaseth'. He also allowed both inhabitants and 'strangers' to tipple in his house on Sundays.[100] When the residents of Harpley sought to restrict alehouses in 1621–2, they said that both Thomas Laskey and Bartholemew Collins allowed servants to drink in their houses; after a drinking bout at Laskey's one of his customers had committed manslaughter, with another servant standing by. In 1642 the townsmen of Colkirk complained about John Barecklow, whose alehouse was disorderly and 'much suspected for naughtiness'.[101] The character of the alehousekeeper was of considerable importance: Edward Myller, a blacksmith from Hockwold cum Wilton was clearly unfit, 'being a notorious

---

[96] NRS 2604 12 B 2, 'Articles touching disorders in inns, alehouses . . .', 1604; cf. Bod. Lib. Ms. Top Norfolk c.2 (30745), 1634, which forbids children or servants of neighbours from tippling, gambling and drunkenness; they also regulate the hours of operation, and demand that if 'any rogues, vagabonds, or masterless men' resort to the house, the constable be informed; Peter Clark, *The English Alehouse: a social history, 1200–1830* (London and New York, 1983), chapter 3.

[97] C/S2/4, Norwich Session, April 1690.

[98] ANW/1/6, 1578/9, Catton: Fishe's husband was later presented for having an unmarried couple in his house, and Margaret was presented for adultery.

[99] ANW/3/2/74, 1640, West Walton presentment of Michael Gage.

[100] C/S3/43, Petition against Robert Pennell of Islington.

[101] C/S3/23, 23A, Harpley petitions against alehouses; C/S3/34, Colkirk petition against John Barecklow.

swearer, a scoffer at religious duties, a choleric hasty moody man'.[102] Furthermore, he had a trade; keeping an alehouse was for those who could do nothing else. John Mayhew of Gaywood was one of those; he confessed in 1635 that 'he draws a small quantity of beer to his neighbours, out of pure want . . . towards the maintenance of his poor wife, and three small children'.[103]

Attitudes toward alehouses were ambivalent; an alehouse was a respectable source of supplementary income for the poor, yet alehouses also threatened both the morals and resources of their customers. In 1716 the townsmen of Diss were concerned about alehouses, especially that of Thomas Bullen and his wife Elizabeth, in an 'obscure corner' of the town. Bullen's house was one,

> whereto the poor labourers that have families and great charges of children do the more privately resort and spend their money which they work for and which ought to go to the support of their wives and families. By means whereof the charges to our poor is very greatly raised increased and the poor farmers thereby greatly burdened.[104]

Because drink was necessary, to sell beer provided the poor with an assured source of income; because drink could be abused, its unregulated consumption, especially in 'obscure corners', could not be tolerated.

The association of the poor with alehouses was linked to their association with disorder. The unruly rich were only sometimes a problem; the poor were unruly by definition. Behaviour which was a natural consequence of the lot of the poor, like vagrancy and begging, was illegal. The mobility of vagrants seemed to offer freedom from parochial discipline – and thus potential disorder. In 1715, the justices of the peace decided that William Holt, a maimed soldier, should no longer receive his pension, 'he being

---

[102] C/S3/34, Hockwold cum Wilton petition against Edward Myller.

[103] C/S3/30, Petition of John Mayhew of Gaywood; Wrightson and Levine, *Poverty and Piety*, pp. 134–5; Wrightson, 'Puritan reformation of manners', chapter 5; Peter Clark, 'The alehouse and the alternative society', in *Puritans and Revolutionaries*, eds D.H. Pennington and K.V. Thomas (Oxford, 1978), pp. 47–72.

[104] PD 100/141, Petition to Justices from Diss, 1716; Diss is a long parish, with the town itself in the south but farms stretching some four or five miles north, which accounts for the obscure corners.

an incorrigible vagrant and one that will not settle anywhere'.[105] Henry Savery of Stow Bardolph was brought before the justices twice on vagrancy charges, in 1630 and 1636. In 1629 he was in service in Denver but left and went to London. There he apprenticed himself to a merchant, took ship, but was put ashore because he was seasick and had swollen legs, and was conveyed back to his mother in Wimbotsham. In July of 1636 he reported that,

> He departed from Stow Bardolph about Midsummer last was twelvemonth and that he had at the same time about six or seven shillings in his purse that he travelled into high Suffolk to the town named Kant's Ashe [Campsea Ashe] where he remained one quarter of a year, and from thence to London where he stayed some two months and so travelled into Yorkshire and so up and down the country until he was taken near Highgate and sent by pass into Norfolk aforesaid.[106]

Savery refused to conform to expectations: he would not settle as a servant to be disciplined by a master. His wanderings remind us that stability was a goal not often accomplished in early modern villages.

Henry Savery's wanderings were unacceptable in early modern England: people who wandered might commit crimes, and therefore all wandering was regarded as criminal. It did not matter that Savery, clearly bitten by wanderlust, always followed work. Those who stayed in one place could also be dangerous when they rejected the values of the community, but as long as they stayed in one place they were subject to correction. In 1592, John Ellison, a Cawston carpenter, had

> neither land nor living to our knowledge, doth live uprightly without labour or trade to get his living, haunteth the alehouse daily and that as well by night or by day, [is] an outrageous fellow with his tongue, such a one as hath moved divers quarrels, walking with a long dagger and a pitchfork in so

[105] C/S2/7, Norwich Sessions, July 1715; Herrup, 'The common peace', finds that outsiders were more likely to be executed than residents in East Sussex: pp. 268–70, 294.

[106] C/S3/27, Examination of Henry Savery of Wimbotsham, 13 March 1630, and C/S3/30, Examination of Henry Savery of Stow Bardolph, 23 July 1636.

much that divers are in fear to meet with him alone or displease him, and to our knowledge hath not done one week's work this twelve month except this last harvest to gather tithe at Cawston.[107]

Ellison insulted his superiors; he failed to complete work for which he had been paid, and then insulted the employer who asked that it be completed. Ellison was not poor – he bought subsidized corn at the highest price in 1597 – but he did little to support himself. He later abandoned his wife, who was buried at the expense of the parish in 1601–2. John Ellison was not unique. In 1606, the people of Outwell complained about the behaviour of Barnard Shipabarrow, who was 'a common alehouse haunter, not having any honest or lawful means to live by'. He played at cards, swore, and blasphemed and was a 'common defamer and detractor of his neighbours'. The complaints continued,

5 He refuseth to work in harvest, and at other times except he have unreasonable wages.
6 He is an ordinary railer and a very foul mouthed person.
7 He liveth very suspiciously, not following any trade, or honest means to live as other men do.
8 And lastly there is not any evil vice usually amongst men that he hath not part thereof.[108]

Shipabarrow's failure to work was, significantly, mentioned twice. It represented his rejection of the role of honest, hard-working, poor labourer. Only work, deference and self-effacement could make the poor respectable.

The exploitation of poverty, unlike that of wealth, was particularly disgraceful. In 1659, John Games of Terrington St Clements, a man of 'lewd life and conversation' who had often 'abused sundry of the inhabitants both by filthy reviling words and by striking and quarrelling', was imprisoned for debt, but freed when the inhabitants paid the debts out of the town stock.

---

[107] NRS 2604, 12 B 2, draft petition against John Ellison; see also lists of poor in NRS Accn. 1.8.63, P 186 D.

[108] C/S3/15, Articles against Barnard Shipabarrow: the place is not given, but several of the names of those who signed are found later in Outwell.

Reformation was not forthcoming, so they wanted him bound to his good behaviour.[109] To those in authority, the honest poor were exceptions; poverty meant potential disorder.

Petitions against disorderly villagers were the last step in a long process of discipline, necessary only for incorrigibles who were not improved by punishment. In 1623 Matthew Bremen and his wife were charged by their neighbours in Grimston with being 'common hedgebreakers', and with several minor thefts. Matthew's attitude was unsettling. He had often been put in the stocks for being drunk on Sunday, but said 'he careth not for it, and after he is let out he raileth on the officers and laugheth at his correction in scorn'.[110] Richard Cutter and his wife Francis, who had been given 'condign' punishment for their faults, failed to express remorse, but instead threatened those who punished them. Their attitude toward authority was so insolent that the villagers of Barningham asked in 1642 that the justices of the peace 'take some sharp course with them for the amending of their evil courses'.[111] Local discipline required an acceptance of the standards and authority of superiors and a susceptibility to shame. Short of the courts, shame was the most powerful weapon, used – in gossip, the stocks and public rebukes – to remind the poor and disorderly of their obligations. Thomas Hadley of Banham, who lived in a town poor house but did not receive relief, was unrepentant when he reported that he had twice been sent to Wymondham Bridewell: he rejected the standards by which he had been judged, and saw no wrong in his behaviour.[112] The governed were expected to honour the values of the governors, even when they were irrelevant to their experience.

The multiple attempts to discipline villagers recounted in the petitions reveal the reluctance of village notables to turn to outside institutions: just as they expected to determine who should or should not have an alehouse licence, so they expected to discipline their own neighbours. The inability to discipline a household

---

[109] C/S3/44, Terrington St Clements against John Games, August 1659; cf. C/S3/26, Complaint of East Beckham against Robert Claxton.

[110] C/S3/24, Articles against Matthew Bremer and his wife of Grimston; C/S3/26, Articles against Matthew Loose.

[111] C/S3/35, Petition of Barningham against Richard Cutter and his wife Francis.

[112] DEP/58, February 1725, Robert Colby con Mr William Leach, testimony of Thomas Hadley; Amussen, 'Féminin/Masculin'.

necessitated communal action; inability to discipline a villager also required outside intervention. In both cases, however, the outside intervention represented a failure of the ideal, and of those in authority. Parish elites sought as much as possible to make their communities self-contained.

These attitudes shaped the behaviour of local notables in all conflicts and disputes. They often tried to resolve disputes outside the courts. Some mediators were self-appointed, others chosen by those involved. When Jasper Taverner brought a defamation suit against Sara Mayhew of Brockley, Suffolk, 'the same was taken up by neighbours and ended'.[113] In 1579 a presentment to the Archdeacon complained that many cases had not been brought before the court but had been resolved by the parson of Morston: effective mediation reduced the fees of court officials, but was favoured by parishioners because it contained conflict within the community. When Anne Caulthropp of Wingfield, Suffolk, alleged that Thomas Owles had attempted her chastity, he denied the charge; the parties were left alone for half an hour, and appeared to have come to a settlement, so Owles was not presented to the Archdeacon. John Suckling, a Norwich alderman, settled the disputes between Peter and Emma Dey and John and Katherine Kempster in Wroxham Broad, and both parties agreed to withdraw all suits, civil and ecclesiastical. Such settlements were preferred to costly litigation.[114]

Mediated settlements depended on the satisfaction of those involved, and their respect for the mediator. Most of our evidence for informal mediation comes from the refusal of one party to live up to the agreement, but the reasons for the refusal are rarely given. The failure of mediation may have reflected the status of the mediators. In 1566 Robert Edgar of Sotterly, Suffolk and John Colefax of Wrentham failed to resolve the dispute caused when John Matthew called Jane Fraunces 'whore' after she called him 'thief'; Matthew was 'willful and stout', and they were unable to impose a settlement. Neither mediator was a native of the area; in

---

[113] DEP/37, Offic. dmni promot. per Dr Welles con Sara Mayhew: this evidence is provided in discussing the 'credit' of a witness.

[114] ANW/6/2, 1578–9, Blakeney per Walker; DEP/17, Anthony Caulthropp and ux. Anne con Thomas Owles, ff. 116–17; DEP/16, Bk. 17a, 1576/7, Emma Dey con Katherine Kempster, ff. 123–4: the suits are both in the ecclesiastical courts and the common law courts. In all these cases we only know of the attempted mediation because it failed.

spite of the elegant signatures which suggest extensive education, they lacked the local standing to enforce a settlement.[115] In other cases, the unstated problem was undoubtedly the intransigence of those involved.

The disorders punished, formally and informally, in early modern England ranged from obvious problems like fighting with neighbours to more minor problems like ringing churchbells or playing unlawful games.[116] The complaints of those who enforced order suggest a desperate struggle to contain events which were rapidly running away from them. To a certain extent these feelings were justified; with the expansion of population, inflation and the increase in poverty and vagrancy, village society was irrevocably altered. Social mobility, both upward and downward, was a fact of life; those who had just attained higher status through the accumulation of property had great difficulty in disciplining their neighbours. The methods of discipline available were appropriate for geographically and socially stable, vertically integrated village communities. None of these conditions existed any longer in early modern England. Geographical stability was undermined by the constant mobility of English women and men – especially before marriage. Social stability was threatened by inflation and social mobility. Vertical integration and local loyalty was threatened by those who most sought to restore order; in the process of imposing order they separated themselves from their neighbours, and often allied themselves with those of similar position – as well as perhaps religious persuasion – in nearby villages.

This struggle to contain disorder explains why many studies of local elites have suggested that they were often attracted to Puritanism. Both the doctrine of election and the social doctrine developed by Calvinist preachers offered comfort to those in authority. 'Election' explained their differences from their neighbours; the social doctrine justified their imposition of discipline. For Puritans like George Sawer, a godly, disciplined life was a

---

[115] DEP/10, Bk. 11a, 1566, Jane Fraunces con John Matthew, ff. 205v–6.

[116] E.g., ANW/2/48 (1605–7), Edward Bretts of Cawston, who rang churchbells at night; ANW/2/42, Robert Booth and others of Cawston for campball (campball was the East Anglian form of soccer); ANW/2/58, 1614, prosecution of Calthorpe campball game; ANW/2/58, 1615, a stoolball game in Castle Acre; C/S3/12, 38 Elizabeth I, Indictment of John Beales and Robert Gartle of Saham Toney for playing stoolball on a Sunday; for dancing, see presentments of Great Witchingham in ANW/2/66, 1627, and Beetley in ANW/2/27; cf. Underdown, *Revel, Riot and Rebellion*, chapter 3 passim.

possible sign of election; discipline of both self and others – even the reprobate – was a duty to an all-powerful and merciful God. The campaigns against alehouses, dancing and other communal recreations, like that against scolds, did not necessarily mean that there was more drinking or dancing. Such activities took on a symbolic role for Puritan village governors. The stricter definition of order which became prevalent in the early seventeenth century was the result of a variety of religious and social changes, but was frequently justified by Puritan social thought. The stereotype of the Puritan killjoy does not do justice to the problems faced by village governors, or to the religious basis of their opposition to popular recreations. It is impossible to disentangle the theological and social dimensions of Puritan attitudes. The concern for the souls of the ungodly joined with concern for the consequences of disorder for the godly – most often higher poor rates.[117] Puritan theology made the struggle against disorder part of a cosmic struggle against sin, and so gave it meaning.

A changing class hierarchy, challenges to the symbolic and actual social order, and disorder all undermined the ideal hierarchy of early modern England. But the challenges changed over the period we are considering, and some examination of this change is necessary. Some types of popular disorder fade from our view after 1660 when they were less often subjects of litigation. In particular, the refusals of deference to social superiors changed in character. After 1660, there is extensive evidence of straightforward sedition and insults, but claims to social equality disappear. Attacks against those in authority were more likely to take the form of protests against taxation, not assertions of status. Richard Duffield refused to pay a constable's rate in 1682; he alleged that there was 'no law in England to recover a constable's rate'.[118] In a similar case, William Salter, a deputy searcher for the Excise, was assaulted in the course of an inspection in 1662.[119] The social heirarchy was

[117] E.g. Wrightson and Levine, *Poverty and Piety*, esp. chapter 6; Hill, *Society and Puritanism*; William Hunt, *The Puritan Moment: the coming of revolution in an English county* (Cambridge, Massachusetts, 1983), chapter 6, esp. pp. 140–4; Puritanism is not, of course, unique to village governors, and some of the radical varieties which flourished during the Civil War rejected the culture of discipline: Hill, *The World Turned Upside Down*.

[118] C/S3/54A, Complaint against Richard Duffield of Burrough St Margaret.

[119] C/S3/45, Information re. attack on William Salter; C/S3/54A, Complaint against Richard Duffield of Burrough St Margaret.

accepted, but government interference was not. Villagers were, however, now more politicized, and sedition and criticism of the Catholic sympathies of the Court remind us that they were not isolated from the political world.[120]

At first this development seems paradoxical. One would have expected the Civil War and Revolution to lead to increased familiarity with doctrines of social equality, not acceptance of social inequality. Opposition to the social hierarchy was muted or channelled in new ways after the Restoration. Several factors contributed to this change. First, the pressure of population, and with it some of the problems of poverty, eased after the mid-seventeenth century. At the same time, the land market was less active, village elites more stable and social mobility less frequent. The tensions which arose from rapid changes in the distribution of wealth diminished.[121]

At the same time, the elite responded to challenges more effectively after the trauma of the Civil War and Revolution. Any comparison of events before and after the Civil War is hampered by the gradual changes in the judicial and administrative methods used for dealing with disorderly villagers that followed the Restoration. The ecclesiastical courts never regained the role they had in Norfolk before the Civil War. Their level of activity fell slowly from the 1660s, and more abruptly after about 1680, and was increasingly confined to the issues over which the church courts had exclusive jurisdiction – matrimonial, testamentary and tithe cases. Defamation became less prominent as a cause of litigation. Quarter sessions also changed after the Restoration. In 1640, 565 people were bound to respond or keep the peace by the justices of the peace; the numbers declined to 398 in 1664 and 369 in 1684, and to 147 by 1711. Gone are the detailed petitions against unruly neighbours. It is possible that such cases may now have been handled in petty sessions, whose records do not survive, although they were active by the end of Elizabeth's reign. But it is

---

[120] In addition to the cases cited in n. 33 above, see PRO ASSI 16/38/3, Information against Dr Samuel Jessop of East Braddenham (1679); ASSI 16/47/4, Information against Robert Bottulph of Shipdham and his wife Alice; and C/S3/56, Information of John Fuller of Massingham.

[121] Wrigley and Schofield, *Population History of England*, pp. 532–3; Wrigley, 'London's importance'; J.H. Plumb, *The Growth of Political Stability in England, 1675–1725* (London, 1967, 1969), pp. 16–23.

also possible that disputes were more effectively handled informally, or mediated locally.[122]

Resort to formal procedures, as we have seen, had always been a last rather than a first resort, so when local notables were able to enforce their authority, disorder need not come before the courts. This is what changed in Norfolk during the seventeenth century. If accepted at face value, the decline in court activity would suggest that Norfolk suddenly became a paragon of order, but the rapidity of the drop suggests that the way in which conflicts were resolved by village notables had undergone a transformation. By the end of the century, most conflicts and disturbances were not dealt with in the courts. Thus the decline in claims of equality represents a twofold change: a decline in social tension as a result of slight improvements in the material condition of poorer villagers, and a social stability which strengthened the informal control of conflict and no longer required the formal mechanisms of control.

The enforcement of the social order was a continuous process; order was affirmed in church, by the kindly intervention of local notables in disputes, by the protection of the deserving and the prosecution of the undeserving. The methods varied with the situations; formal proceedings were expected to sharpen the offenders' sense of remorse – hence the importance of penance – while informal proceedings enhanced the authority of those who acted in them. In the more stable world of Restoration England, the elite may have tolerated a wider range of behaviour than their grandfathers had done, but they were also more successful in asserting their own position and authority. They gave up attempts to create a perfect world in order to sustain their position. While they no longer faced grave confrontations over the nature of order, the 1640s and 1650s were always remembered. The local elites of early modern England, having given up the dream of a heaven on earth, settled for a respectful and outwardly deferential people.

---

[122] Cf. Norma Landau, *The Justices of the Peace, 1679–1760* (Berkeley and Los Angeles, 1984), pp. 8–10; Hassell Smith, *County and Court*, pp. 103–5; the Consistory Court of Norwich heard ninety-two cases in 1600 (DEP/31, ff. 1–165), ninety-five in 1635 (DEP/42) but only thirty-three in 1665 (DEP/47, ff. 174–323v) and twenty-seven in 1675 (DEP/49, ms. for 1675). Quarter sessional statistics are based on the entries in minute books, C/S1/6, January 1640–October 1640; C/S1/8, January 1664–October 1664; C/S1/10, January 1684–October 1684, and C/S1/11, January 1711–October 1711.

Everyone should at least act as if they knew their place, and there were ways to ensure they did – notably the settlement laws and the Poor Law. The problems implicit in the relations between labourers and farmers, landlords and tenants, did not openly re-appear until the early nineteenth century. The silence of the intervening century and a half reflects not the absence of the problems, but their containment by a careful local elite.

6

Conclusion:
Gender, Class and Society

The analogy between family and state has forced us to examine both families and villages as economic and political entities. In 1560, most families and most villages had corporate economic roles: the family was usually the locus of production, and at least in arable villages, the open fields sustained a collective economy. The organic conception of society which was commonplace made both the family and village important political institutions – places where society was ordered and disciplined. By 1725, all this had changed. In villages throughout England, enclosure and agricultural improvement had undermined communal agriculture. The polarization of wealth, the disappearance of the medium-sized holdings and the emergence of large capitalist farms meant that an increasing number of families did not work together, but as wage labourers. These families still had a collective role in consumption, but not in production.

If the economic role of both families and villages underwent a transformation between the sixteenth and early eighteenth centuries, so too did their political role. Families were still expected to be orderly, but villagers felt less need to interfere directly in their affairs; disorder in families no longer warranted recourse to the courts. Disorderly women fade from our view. If the father of the family was still expected to govern well and carefully, collective concern about how he did so had diminished. Villages retained their role in local government, and it became more important in the eighteenth century, as more and more labourers were dependent on poor relief. The parish notables' use of power, however, centred on administration, not moral reform. The political roles of both families and villages became less visible – not because they were less important, but because the rules were less contested. The full significance of these changes can only be seen if they are integrated.

The organic conception and structuring of society meant that
changes in one area necessarily affected the others. The nature and
conception of authority in early modern England are revealed by
these changes.

The power of the analogy between family and state is most
evident before 1640. The intensive regulation of behaviour in both
families and villages illustrates the importance placed on order
both within families and in villages. But why so much regulation,
so much anxiety? Why did village notables feel so nervous about
the gender and class order of society? Part of the answer can be
found if we turn to the demographic and economic developments
of the late sixteenth and early seventeenth centuries. No discussion
of legal continuities can mask the dramatic transformation of the
countryside in this period. As a consequence of the population
explosion and rapid inflation, legal continuity remained in form
but its content changed. Some sense of the problems posed by
these developments can be gained by looking at the rest of Europe.
Economic depression and contraction are the dominant characteristics of international trade after 1620; in the second half of the
century, the population of many parts of Europe fell. The
demographic stagnation of England was an achievement, thanks to
the flexibility of English property systems, which allowed
agriculture to increase its productive capacity. The methods by
which that productive capacity grew – up and down husbandry,
enclosure, in short the agricultural revolution – were disruptive
changes for communities. They effected profound transformations
of local social and economic relations.[1]

These social and economic changes – and their consequences –
were for the most part complete by the middle of the seventeenth
century, but until then, many English men – particularly those
with the responsibility for governing – felt that the world was out
of control. Their behaviour in trying to limit disorder, as Margaret
Spufford has pointed out, resembles that of village elites some 300
years earlier as they struggled with a similar period of population

[1] For France see, Pierre Goubert, *Cent Mille Provinciaux au XVIIe Siècle: Beauvais et les
Beauvaisis de 1600 à 1730* (abridged ed., Paris, 1968); Emmanuel Le Roy Ladurie, *The
Peasants of Languedoc*, tr. John Day (Urbana, 1974), part IV; Niels Steensgaard, 'The
seventeenth century crisis' and Ruggiero Romano, 'Between the sixteenth and seventeenth
centuries: the economic crisis of 1619–22', in *The General Crisis of the Seventeenth Century*,
ed. Geoffrey Parker and Lesley Smith (London, 1978), pp. 26–56, 165–225.

growth. Thirteenth- and fourteenth-century local governors lacked the rhetoric of Puritanism, but had the same fear of disorder. The comparison with the period preceding the famines and plagues of the fourteenth century also emphasizes the severity of the problems faced in the early seventeenth century.[2] The panic resulting from rapid social and demographic changes is reflected in the ecclesiastical court records of the period between 1560 and 1640. The attempts to control unruly villagers so common in this period suggests a growing inability to control disorder within the normal local channels. Here the analogy between family and state was particularly useful. As we have seen, although the gender order was challenged, that challenge was never explicit or direct. Women did not ask to govern, claim equality with their husbands or declare the family an irrelevant institution. Challenges to the class order were far more direct. People asserted their social and moral equality with 'superiors', they criticized and insulted the local governors and they refused to accept existing hierarchies. Because of the ideological relationship between family and state, the control of gender disorder symbolically affirmed all social order. It may have been impossible to make all poor villagers accept the authority of their neighbours of 'credit and estimation', but the affirmation and insistence on the father's role asserted the position of those local governors. The nature of challenges to the gender order made such an affirmation relatively simple.

The concern with proper gender order was demonstrated in many ways. There are two that bear mentioning, in addition to those already discussed. First, the period between 1560 and 1640 was the great age of witchcraft persecution in England. Whatever the explanation of the witch hunts, witches were mostly women; they were also generally widows who were outside patriarchal control, and by their cursing they rejected their meek and submissive role.[3] Second, the early seventeenth century saw a great debate on the nature of women: were they good or bad,

[2] Spufford, 'Puritanism and social control'.

[3] For witchcraft generally, see Keith Thomas, *Religion and the Decline of Magic* (New York, 1971), chapters 14–18; Alan Macfarlane, *Witchcraft in Tudor and Stuart England: a regional and comparative study* (London, 1970); Clive Holmes, 'Popular culture? Witches, magistrates, and divines in early modern England', in *Understanding Popular Culture: Europe from the Middle Ages to the nineteenth century*, ed. Steven L. Kaplan (Berlin, 1984), pp. 85–111 notes that gender was unnecessary for the theological definition of witchcraft, but was a 'perdurable component of popular belief' (p. 95).

orderly or disorderly? The contributions to this debate range from the profound to the obscene, but the existence of the debate is itself evidence of concern about the gender order. Such pamphlets sold well – people were interested in the role of women. William Gouge may well have been referring to this debate when he defended himself from the charge of being 'a hater of women'.[4]

Parallels between the family and state were effective because in spite of the analogy, the two were quite different. The family was held together by emotional and sexual bonds quite different from the local loyalties which united villages. Families were never perfect, and that very fact posed a threat to order. But the problems faced by families were caused most obviously by human failures, not the social and economic changes of the period. The impact of the social transformations of the period on families is therefore difficult to discern. Among the wealthier villagers, it led eventually to the withdrawal of women from productive labour, but even that development took a century or more; among poorer villagers, the organization of work in families changed, but not the work itself. Even those who had lost land still had to work. Families did not become egalitarian. Families are essentially conservative institutions, which adapt slowly to social change, and their ideology is even more conservative: change is absorbed only slowly into the family's conception of itself. The American or British family of the 1980s is undoubtedly different from that of the 1950s, though the dominant rhetoric of family has changed very little. The English family in 1725 was certainly different from that of 1560, at least in its relation to work, but the changes are difficult to identify.

Changes in families were subtle, slow and perhaps unacknowledged, so they were far less fraught with anxiety for villagers. The changes in villages were not always gradual; over a period of just a few years, the distribution of land and wealth in many English villages changed dramatically. As one husbandman accumulated land, so his neighbour lost it. It was the rapidity and seeming capriciousness of the changes which undermined social order and

---

[4] For recent discussions of the debate on women see Henderson and McManus, *Half Humankind*; Linda Woodbridge, *Women and the English Renaissance: literature and the nature of woman* (Urbana, 1984).

often led to explicit criticism of local elites, struggles within elites over status, and challenges to their authority.

Demographic and economic changes are the most dramatic and measurable sources of tension in English villages before 1640. But village notables and their gentry neighbours were affected and worried by many other issues. Their behaviour was shaped as much by their political and religious concerns as by their economic interests – although all these concerns are undoubtedly connected. Local control of government was threatened, particularly under Charles I, by increased monarchical centralization: a steady stream of orders from the privy council sought to direct local policy. At the same time, the traditional approval of Parliament for taxation was by-passed by the financial expedients of Charles's personal rule. Constitutional innovation joined to intervention in local affairs led to general opposition to royal policy in 1640. Though the conception of opposition varied, and the unanimity of 1640 rapidly dissipated in 1641, its significance should not be underestimated. The political conflicts of the early seventeenth century exacerbated the anxiety of local governors, whose position was under attack from two sides; if there was little they could do against royal centralization, they could insist (even if with little affect) on the obedience of the governed in their communities.[5]

Religion provides another link between the high politics of the period and social order in the localities. While 'the country' was alienated from the court of James I by reports of its prevailing immorality, it was alienated from that of Charles I because of the prominence of Catholics, and the superficial resemblance between Arminianism and Catholicism. There is no evidence, in Norfolk or elsewhere, of popular support of Arminianism; the religious conflict in the countryside was between Puritan Anglicans – the 'godly' – who drew themselves apart and sought to reform their communities, and those who saw in Anglican liturgy and theology an expression of a united Protestant community. Arminianism challenged all other Anglicans, Puritan and non-Puritan alike. By moving the Communion table to the east end of the church and railing it in, Arminians symbolically placed the priest at the centre of the community. Such a re-ordering was resented by many of the

---

[5] The most recent treatment of these themes is Anthony Fletcher, *Reform in the Provinces: the government of Stuart England* (New Haven and London, 1986).

laity; anti-clericalism was widespread. The doctrinal and liturgical conflicts brought out by Arminianism were fuelled at least for Puritans by the immorality condoned by the Book of Sports. Parochial discipline was a matter of social, and for many village notables, theological importance; now it was undermined by a royal policy that disrupted local discipline. Once again, local concerns were linked to national ones.

This is not to say that the English Revolution and Civil War were *caused* by the events in villages; such an argument, ignoring the issues of law, the constitution and factional conflict, would plainly be absurd. However, one important result of an organic conception of society is that connections between its parts are constantly being made. The response of local governors – justices, local gentry and yeoman – to the political and religious conflicts which developed in the early seventeenth century were ineluctably shaped by their roles in local government, and the challenges and problems seen there. In the face of threatened chaos, they sought to preserve their own position – from challenges from below, from encroachments from London and from religious agendas not their own. The nature of authority and the social order were being challenged or re-defined from above and below, and this undoubtedly shaped responses to the political crisis.

If the analogy between family and state, the social transformation of English society, and political and religious tension all contributed to the regulation of behaviour in the period before 1640, what explains the decline of regulation after the Restoration? Did disorder cease to exist? Do village governors cease to care? The answer to the first question is a resounding no; to the second, only in part. Any explanation of social regulation in Stuart England which assumes that all disorder disappeared would be true to the extant sources, but unrealistic. Disorder continued, though not always as a major problem, but those in authority moved from moral reformation to administrative regulation. Village governors ceased to worry about some forms of disorder: the attempt to reform manners and to create a godly commonwealth was abandoned after 1660. The character of the poor elicited different reactions: in 1749 the Rev. Henry Loftus admitted to Lady Andover that 'the Norfolk common people in general are very loose and ill-principled', but the solution he advocated was the re-building of the church in his parish of

Castle Rising.[6] Similarly, the great expression of Puritan sensibility in the Restoration is the internalized spiritual journey taken by Christian in John Bunyan's *Pilgrim's Progress*: he leaves the City of Destruction, rather than trying to reform it, when no one listens to him.

Parish discipline was more subtle after 1660. The great strains of the earlier period had disappeared, and the authority of village notables was less explicitly challenged. In the more favourable demographic climate of the late seventeenth century, vagrants and beggars were a less serious problem, and most of the poor had already lost their land. Local governors were still concerned to maintain their authority – as is shown by their response to insults – but those insults challenged the character, not the authority, of the elite. The whole structure was no longer under attack. Local notables could bring defamation suits against the poor, but no longer needed to prosecute them for gaming on Sundays in order to assert their own importance. And on many occasions, village notables had sufficient stature to enforce mediated settlements, or to impose an appropriate resolution to conflicts within the village. The threats of unemployment, or perhaps the withdrawal of poor relief, were sufficient.

Because the social order of Restoration England was not explicitly under threat, the family became less important to social order. Order no longer depended on the reiteration of an ideal of the family as the only apparently unchanging institution, as it had in the early seventeenth century. Both before 1640 and after 1660 the family played its role as the educational and political core of English society. But in the later period, village governors were sufficiently secure that they no longer needed to worry about it. Locke could argue that the family was not a political institution because it was no longer the only effective and unchallenged institution for maintaining order.

Everyone, even today, remains part of the hierarchies of gender and class. Together, their interactions shape many different patterns of experience. Although the meaning of gender has changed over time, one's place in the gender hierarchy is determined by birth. This is not so for the class hierarchy, whose organization is more fluid, and certainly less obvious. But because

[6] HOW 666, 329x1, Rev. Henry Loftus to Lady Andover, 17 April 1749.

each individual participates in both, the concepts of hierarchy and authority in one are transferred to the other. The developments in both are generally parallel. In early modern England, the hierarchies of class and gender became increasingly polarized, as the experience of women and men, and rich and poor, became ever more distinct. The experience of women and men diverged: in wealthy families, women were less economically active; in poor families, the wage labour of women was different from that of men. And as the family became a less important part of local government and discipline, women's role in family government lost its public significance. The insults of women were taken ever more seriously by other women, and less seriously by men. At the same time, the polarization of landholding widened social divisions in the class hierarchy. The divisions, which originated with economic changes, were reinforced by differences in education and culture. The relative absence of conflict about both class and gender after the Restoration rested on this increasing distance between women and men, rich and poor; distance simultaneously made the elite more secure and deprived those they ruled of the proximity – social and economic – necessary for effective challenges.

Authority is socially constructed. The authority of particular individuals or groups rests on the conception of society developed in a particular period. It is also a product of social relations – hierarchies, distances and power – rooted in both the material and the ideological worlds. Authority carries with it social and political consequences. Any change in one of the components of authority will have consequences for the others; the equation must be balanced.

In early modern England, several aspects of this equation were changing or being challenged: the economy was transformed by demographic growth and inflation; the political order was explicitly challenged by the gentry who tried to regain control of royal policy and prevent the establishment of what they sometimes perceived as absolutism; the family was changing as women in wealthy families gradually withdrew from work, and as poorer families became increasingly dependent on wages; the social order of villages was challenged by those who sought to introduce new agricultural practices, by those who challenged church seating and by those who rejected the power of local notables. We have seen the tensions and problems posed by such changes, and the emergence, after the Restoration, of a more secure elite, whose authority was based more on income than on status. Members of this elite used their power to maintain order and the status quo; their more limited goals allowed them to abandon close regulation of familial behaviour.

A society with an organic social and political theory will naturally believe that everything is connected. That this conception was commonplace in early modern England is unquestionable. Its practical consequences are readily visible, for instance in the importance of reputation, and the contribution of sexual behaviour to its definition. The organic conception of society survived on a popular level even after it disappeared from theory, but it was productive of less tension when the pace of social and economic change had slowed. Rather than compartmentalizing their world, early modern villagers tried to hold it together. But the gradual erosion of the organic conception reduced the anxiety about individual 'personal' behaviour. The family did not become private immediately, but some people began to think it was.

We are most comfortable in a world where families are 'private' institutions, 'havens in a heartless world'. This conception undoubtedly owes much to the Industrial Revolution, but it is rooted in the theoretical discussions and communal practice of late seventeenth-century England. It is only then that a discussion of the family separate from other social institutions became possible, and then only because people could ignore the construction of its privacy. As families were turned in on themselves, villagers found that they could govern through fear as effectively as through massive regulation and court-sponsored discipline. To speak of the family as a private institution in the eighteenth century would be a misrepresentation, just as the image of a deferential, quiescent eighteenth century has recently been cracked open to show the conflict and coercion which underlay it.[7] The construction of the eighteenth-century world can best be seen in its contrast with the late sixteenth and early seventeenth centuries, and in the ways in

[7] Thompson, *Whigs and Hunters*; Hay, 'Property, authority and the criminal law'; cf. John Langbein, '*Albion's* Fatal Flaws', *Past and Present*, 98 (1983), pp. 96–120; my disagreements with Langbein's position are spelled out in Susan D. Amussen, 'Paysans et la loi en angleterre de l'époque moderne', in *Études Rurales* (1987).

which the discipline of families and villages was used to impose a modicum of order on society. In the eighteenth century the links between family and state had not disappeared, but the problems faced in each had changed, and so too had the social forms taken by authority and order. The privacy of the family in the eighteenth century was constructed through the success of seventeenth-century parish notables in securing control over the behaviour of the poor and disorderly. And once social inferiors had learned 'their own particular duties', families were no longer needed as 'seminaries . . . to Church and Commonwealth'.[8]

[8] Gouge, *Domesticall Duties*, f. 2v.

Selected Bibliography

This bibliography includes all printed sources cited more than once in footnotes, as well as important books relevant to the study.

Printed Primary Sources

Bayley, Lewis J. *The Practise of Piety*, 3rd edn, London 1613.

Brathwait, Richard, Esq. *The English Gentleman*, London, 1630.

Chamberlayne, Edward *Angliae Notitia; or, the Present State of England: Together with Divers Reflections upon the Antient State thereof*, 2nd edn, London, 1669.

Digges, Dudley *The Unlawfulnesse of Subjects taking up Armes against their Soveraigne, in what case soever, Together with an Answer to all Objections scattered in their severall Books*, Oxford, 1643. T.T. E. 29 (1).

Dod, John and Clever, Robert *A Godly Forme of Household Government: for the ordering of private families, according to the direction of God's Word*, London, 1612.

Filmer, Robert *Patriarcha and Other Political Works*, ed. Peter Laslett. Oxford, 1949.

Fitzherbert, [John] *Booke of Husbandrie*, London, 1598.

Gataker, Thomas *Marriage Duties Briefely Couched Togither*, London, 1620.

Gouge, William *Of Domesticall Duties: Eight Treatises*, 3rd edn, London, 1634.

Gough, Richard *The History of Myddle*, New York and Harmondsworth, Middlesex, 1981.

Griffith, Matthew *Bethel; or a forme for families*, London, 1633.

Hood, Christobel M. (ed.) *The Chorography of Norfolk*, Norwich, 1938.

Leigh, Dorothy *The Mother's Blessing*, London, 1616.

Locke, John *Two Treatises of Civil Government*, ed. Peter Laslett. Cambridge, 1960.

[Mocket, Richard] *God and the King: or a Dialogue shewing that our soveraigne Lord King Iames, being immediate under God within his Dominions, Doth rightfully claime whatsoever is required by the Oath of Allegiance*, London, 1615.

Parker, Henry *Jus Populi, Or A Discourse wherein clear satisfaction is given, as well concerning the Right of Subjects, as the Right of Princes. Shewing how both are consistent, and where they border one upon the other*, London, 1644. TT E. 12 (25).

Platter, Thomas *Thomas Platter's Travels in England, 1599*, Tr. Clare Williams. London, 1937.

Poole, Elizabeth *An Alarum of War, Given to the Army and to their High Court of Justice (so called) revealed by the will of God in a vision to E. Poole*, London, 1649. TT E. 555 (23).

Smith, Thomas *De Republica Anglorum: a discourse on the Commonwealth of England*, ed. L. Alston. Cambridge, 1906.

Swan, John *Redde Debitum, or, a Discourse in defense of three chiefe Fatherhoods . . .*, London, 1640.

Tilney, Edmund *A Brief and Pleasant Discourse of Duties in Marriage, called the Flower of Friendshippe*, London, 1571.

Woodhouse, A.S.P. (ed.) *Puritanism and Liberty, Being the Army Debates (1647–9) from the Clarke Manuscripts*, London, 1951.

Secondary Sources

Allison, K.J. 'The Norfolk worsted industry in the sixteenth and seventeenth centuries', *Yorkshire Bulletin of Economic and Social Research*, 12 (1960), pp. 73–83.

—— 'The sheep–corn husbandry of Norfolk in the sixteenth and seventeenth centuries', *Agricultural History Review*, 5 (1957), pp. 12–30.

Amussen, Susan Dwyer 'Féminin/Masculin: le genre dans L'Angleterre de l'époque moderne', *Annales: Économies, Sociétés, Civilisations*, 40 (1985), pp. 269–87.

—— 'Gender, family, and the social order, 1560–1725', in *Order and Disorder in Early Modern England*, ed. Anthony Fletcher and John Stevenson. Cambridge, 1985, pp. 196–217.

—— 'A Norfolk village: Cawston, 1595–1605', *History Today*, 36 (April, 1986), pp. 15–20.

Appleby, Andrew *Famine in Tudor and Stuart England*, Stanford, 1978.

Blomefield, Francis and Parkyn, Charles *An Essay Towards a Topographical History of the County of Norfolk* (11 vols), London, 1805–10.

Brewer, John and Styles, John (eds) *An Ungovernable People: the English and their law in the seventeenth and eighteenth centuries*, New Brunswick, New Jersey, 1980.

Chaytor, Miranda 'Household and kinship: Ryton in the late 16th and early 17th centuries', *History Workshop Journal*, 10 (1980), pp. 25–60.

Clark, Alice *Working Life of Women in the Seventeenth Century*, London, 1919, reprinted with an introduction by Miranda Chaytor and Jane Lewis, 1982.

Cockburn, J.S. (ed.) *Crime in England, 1550–1800*, Princeton, 1977.

Cressy, David *Literacy and the Social Order: reading and writing in Tudor and Stuart England*, Cambridge, 1980.

Daly, James *Sir Robert Filmer and English Political Thought*, Toronto, 1979.

Evans, Nesta *The East Anglian Linen Industry: rural industry and the local economy*. Pasold Studies in Textile History, 5. Aldershot, Hants, 1985.

Finberg, H.P.R. *The Agrarian History of England and Wales*, vol. IV: *1500–1640*, ed. Joan Thirsk. Cambridge, 1967.

Fletcher, Anthony and Stevenson, John (eds) *Order and Disorder in Early Modern England*, Cambridge, 1985.

Fressingfield Workers Education Association *Looking Back at Fressingfield*, Fressingfield, 1979.

Gillis, John R. *For Better, For Worse: British marriages, 1600 to the present*, New York and Oxford, 1985.

Goody, Jack, Thirsk, Joan and Thompson, E.P. (eds) *Family and Inheritance: rural society in Western Europe, 1200–1800*, Cambridge, 1976.

Hay, Douglas 'Property, authority, and the criminal law', *Albion's Fatal Tree: crime and society in eighteenth century England*, ed. Douglas Hay et al. New York, 1975, pp. 17–63.

Henderson, Katherine Usher and McManus, Barbara F. *Half-humankind: contexts and texts of the controversy about women in England, 1540–1640*, Urbana and Chicago, Illinois, 1985.

Hill, Christopher *Economic Problems of the Church from Archbishop Whitgift to the Long Parliament*, Oxford, 1956.

—— *Society and Puritanism in Pre-revolutionary England*, New York, 1964.

—— *The World Turned Upside Down: radical ideas during the English Revolution*, New York, 1972.

Hoffer, Peter C. and Hull, N.E.H. *Murdering Mothers: infanticide in England and New England*, New York, 1981.

Holmes, Clive 'Drainers and fenmen: the problem of popular political consciousness in the seventeenth century', *Order and Disorder in Early Modern England,* ed. Anthony Fletcher and John Stevenson. Cambridge, 1985, pp. 166–95.

Howard, George Elliot *A History of Matrimonial Institutions, Chiefly in England and the United States* (3 vols), Chicago and London, 1904.

Hunt, William H. *The Puritan Moment: the coming of revolution in an English county,* Cambridge, Massachusetts, 1983.

Ingram, Martin 'The reform of popular culture? Sex and marriage in early modern England', *Popular Culture in Seventeenth Century England,* ed. Barry Reay. New York, 1985, pp. 129–65.

Kelly-Gadol, Joan 'The social relations of the sexes: methodological implications of women's history', *Signs* 1(1976), pp. 809–24.

Kussmaul, Ann *Servants in Husbandry in Early Modern England,* Cambridge, 1981.

Laslett, Peter 'Mean household size in England since the sixteenth century', *Household and Family in Past Time,* ed. Peter Laslett with Richard Wall. Cambridge, 1972, pp. 125–58.

—— 'Long-term trends in bastardy in England', *Family Life and Illicit Love in Earlier Generations,* Cambridge and New York, 1977, pp. 102–55.

Leites, Edmund *The Puritan Conscience and Modern Sexuality,* New Haven, Connecticut, 1986.

Leonard, E.M. *The Early History of English Poor Relief,* Cambridge, 1900.

Macfarlane, Alan *The Family Life of Ralph Josselin: an essay in historical anthropology,* Cambridge, 1970, reprinted New York, 1977.

—— *Marriage and Love in England: modes of reproduction, 1300–1840,* Oxford and New York, 1986.

—— *The Origins of English Individualism,* New York, 1979.

Obelkevich, James *Religion in Rural Society: South Lindsey, 1825–1875,* Oxford, 1976.

Powell, Chilton Latham *English Domestic Relations, 1487–1653,* New York, 1917.

Prior, Mary (ed.) *Women in English Society, 1500–1800,* London and New York, 1985.

Quaife, G.R. *Wanton Wenches and Wayward Wives: peasants and illicit sex in early seventeenth century England,* New Brunswick, New Jersey, 1979.

Ravensdale, J.R. *Liable to Floods: village landscape on the edge of the Fens, AD 450–1850,* London and New York, 1974.

Rye, Walter *An Account of the Church and Parish of Cawston in the County of Norfolk,* Norwich, 1898.

Schochet, G.J. *Patriarchalism in Political Thought: the authoritarian family and political speculation and attitudes especially in seventeenth century England*, New York, 1975.

Scott, Joan W. 'Gender: a useful category of historical analysis', *American Historical Review*, 91 (1986), pp. 1053–75.

Seaver, Paul S. *Wallington's World: a Puritan artisan in seventeenth century London*, Stanford, California, 1985.

Shanley, Mary 'Marriage contract and social contract in seventeenth century English political thought', *Western Political Quarterly*, 32 (1979), pp. 79–91.

Sharp, Buchanan *In Contempt of All Authority: rural artisans and riot in the west of England, 1586–1660*, Berkeley and Los Angeles, 1980.

Sharpe, J.A. *Defamation and Sexual Slander in Early Modern England: the church courts at York*, Borthwick Papers No. 58, York, 1980.

Skipp, V.H.T. *Crisis and Development: an ecological case study of the Forest of Arden, 1570–1674*, Cambridge, 1978.

Smith, A. Hassell *County and Court: government and politics in Norfolk, 1558–1603*, Oxford, 1974.

Somerville, J.P. *Politics and Ideology in England, 1603–1640*, London, 1986.

Spufford, Margaret *Contrasting Communities: English villagers in the sixteenth and seventeenth centuries*, Cambridge, 1974.

—— 'Peasant inheritance customs and land distribution in Cambridgeshire from the sixteenth to the eighteenth centuries', *Family and Inheritance: rural society in Western Europe, 1200–1800*, ed. Jack Goody et al. Cambridge, 1976, pp. 156–76.

—— 'Puritanism and social control?', *Order and Disorder in Early Modern England*, ed. Anthony Fletcher and John Stevenson. Cambridge, 1985, pp. 41–57.

Stone, Lawrence *The Family, Sex, and Marriage in England, 1500–1800*, New York, 1977.

—— 'Social mobility in England, 1500–1700', *Past and Present*, 33 (1966), pp. 16–55.

Thirsk, Joan 'The farming regions of England', *The Agrarian History of England and Wales*, ed. H.P.R. Finberg, vol. IV: *1500–1640*, ed. Joan Thirsk. Cambridge, 1967, pp. 1–112.

Thomas, Keith *Religion and the Decline of Magic*, New York, 1971.

Thompson, E.P. 'The grid of inheritance: a comment', *Family and Inheritance: rural society in Western Europe, 1500–1800*, ed. Jack Goody et al. Cambridge, 1976, pp. 328–60.

—— 'The moral economy of the English crowd in the eighteenth century', *Past and Present*, 50 (1972), pp. 76–136.

—— *Whigs and Hunters: the origins of the Black Act*, New York, 1975.

Underdown, David E. *Revel, Riot and Rebellion: popular politics and culture in England, 1603–1660*, Oxford, 1985.

—— 'The taming of the scold: the enforcement of patriarchal authority in early modern England', *Order and Disorder in Early Modern England*, ed. Anthony Fletcher and John Stevenson. Cambridge, 1985, pp. 116–36.

Wales, Tim 'Poverty, poor relief, and the life-cycle: some evidence from seventeenth century Norfolk', *Land, Kinship, and Life-cycle*, ed. Richard Smith. London, 1984, pp. 351–404.

Walter, John 'Grain riots and popular attitudes to the law: Maldon and the crisis of 1629', *An Ungovernable People*, ed. John Brewer and John Styles. New Brunswick, New Jersey, 1980, pp. 47–84.

Walzer, Michael *The Revolution of the Saints: a study in the origins of radical politics*, Cambridge, Massachusetts, 1965, reprinted New York, 1976.

Wrightson, Keith *English Society, 1580–1680*, London, 1982.

—— 'Two concepts of order: justices, constables and jurymen in seventeenth century England', *An Ungovernable People*, ed. John Brewer and John Styles. New Brunswick, New Jersey, 1980, pp. 21–46.

Wrightson, Keith and Levine, David *Poverty and Piety in an English Village: Terling, 1525–1700*, New York and London, 1979.

Wrigley, E.A. 'A simple model of London's importance in changing English society and economy, 1650–1750', *Past and Present*, 37 (1967), pp. 44–70.

Wrigley, E.A. and Schofield, R.S. *The Population History of England, 1541–1871*, Cambridge, Massachusetts, 1981.

Unpublished Theses and Papers

Amussen, Susan Dwyer 'Governors and governed: class and gender relations in English villages, 1590–1725', Brown University Ph.D., 1982.

Evans, Nesta 'The community of the South Elmhams (Suffolk) in the sixteenth and seventeenth centuries', University of East Anglia M.Phil., 1978.

Herrup, Cynthia Brilliant 'The common peace: legal structure and legal substance in East Sussex, 1594–1640', Northwestern University Ph.D., 1982.

Ingram, Martin J. 'Ecclesiastical justice in Wiltshire, 1600–1640, with special reference to cases concerning sex and marriage', Oxford University D.Phil., 1976.

Patten, John H.C. 'The urban structure of East Anglia in the sixteenth and seventeenth centuries', Cambridge University Ph.D., 1972.

Souden, David 'Pre-industrial English local migration fields', Cambridge University Ph.D., 1981.

Wales, T.C. 'Poverty and parish relief', unpublished paper, 1983.

Wrightson, Keith Edwin 'The Puritan reformation of manners with special reference to the counties of Lancashire and Essex, 1640–1660', Cambridge University Ph.D., 1973.

Index

Unless otherwise noted, all places are in Norfolk based on seventeenth-century boundaries.